Unbearable Lightness

Unbearable Lightness

A STORY OF LOSS AND GAIN

PORTIA DE ROSSI

ATRIA BOOKS

NEW YORK   LONDON   TORONTO   SYDNEY

ATRIA BOOKS

A Division of Simon & Schuster, Inc.
1230 Avenue of the Americas
New York, NY 10020

First Atria hardcover edition November 2010

ATRIA BOOKS and colophon are trademarks of Simon & Schuster, Inc.

Photograph credits: pp. 265 and 267 © Davis Factor/D R Photo Management; p. 269 © Albert Sanchez/CORBIS OUTLINE; p. 271 © Lisa Rose/jpistudios.com.

For information about special discounts for bulk purchases, please contact Simon & Schuster Special Sales at 1-866-506-1949 or business@simonandschuster.com

The Simon & Schuster Speakers Bureau can bring authors to your live event. For more information or to book an event contact the Simon & Schuster Speakers Bureau at 1-866-248-3049 or visit our website at www.simonspeakers.com.

Designed by Dana Sloan

Manufactured in the United States of America

10 9 8 7 6 5 4 3 2 1

Library of Congress Cataloging-in-Publication Data is available upon request.

ISBN 978-1-4391-7778-5
ISBN 978-1-4391-7780-8 (ebook)

To Ellen, for showing me what beauty is

Unbearable Lightness

PROLOGUE

E DOESN'T WAIT until I'm awake. He comes into my unconscious to find me, to pull me out. He seizes my logical mind and disables it with fear. I awake already panic-stricken, afraid I won't answer the voice correctly, the loud, clear voice that reverberates in my head like an alarm that can't be turned off.

What did you eat last night?

Since we first met when I was twelve he's been with me, at me, barking orders. A drill sergeant of a voice that is pushing me forward, marching ahead, keeping time. When the voice isn't giving orders, it's counting. Like a metronome, it is predictable. I can hear the tick of another missed beat and in the silence between beats I anxiously await the next tick; like the constant noise of an intermittently dripping faucet, it keeps counting in the silences when I want to be still. It tells me to never miss a beat. It tells me that I will get fat again if I do.

The voice and the ticks are always very loud in the darkness of the early morning. The silences that I can't fill with answers are even louder. God, what did I eat? Why can't I remember?

I breathe deeply in an attempt to calm my heartbeat back to its resting pulse. As I do, my nostrils are filled with stale cigarette smoke that hung around from the night before like a party guest who'd passed out on the living room sofa after everybody else went home. The digital clock reads 4:06, nine minutes before my alarm was set to wake me. I need to use the restroom, but I can't get out of bed until I can remember what I ate.

3

My pupils dilate to adjust to the darkness as if searching for an answer in my bedroom. It's not coming. The fact that it's not coming makes me afraid. As I search for the answer, I perform my routine check. Breasts, ribs, stomach, hip bones. I grab roughly at these parts of my body to make sure everything is as I left it, a defensive measure, readying myself for the possible attack from my panic-addled brain. At least I slept. The last few nights I've been too empty and restless, too flighty—like I need to be weighted to my bed and held down before I can surrender to sleep. I've been told that sleep is good for weight loss. It recalibrates your metabolism and shrinks your fat cells. But why it would be better than moving my legs all night as if I were swimming breaststroke I don't really know. Actually, now that I think about it, it must be bullshit. Swimming like someone is chasing me would have to burn more calories than lying motionless like a fat, lazy person. I wonder how long I've been that way. Motionless. I wonder if that will affect my weight loss today.

I feel my heartbeat, one, two, three—it's quickening. I start breathing deeply to stop from panicking, IN one two, OUT three four . . .

Start counting
60
30
10 =
100

I start over. I need to factor in the calories burned. Yesterday I got out of bed and walked directly to the treadmill and ran at 7.0 for 60 minutes for a total of negative 600 calories. I ate 60 calories of oatmeal with Splenda and butter spray and black coffee with one vanilla-flavored tablet. I didn't eat anything at all at work. And at lunch I walked on the treadmill in my dressing room for the hour. Shit. I had only walked. The fan I had rigged on the treadmill to blow air directly into my face so my makeup wouldn't be ruined had broken. That's not true, actually. Because I'm so lazy and disorganized, I'd allowed the battery to run down so the plastic blades spun at the speed of a seaside Ferris wheel. I need that fan because my makeup artist is holding me on virtual probation at work. While I am able to calm down the flyaway hairs that spring up on my head after a rigorous workout, the mascara residue that deposits under my eyes tells the story of my activities during my lunch break. She had asked me to stop working out at lunch. I like Sarah and I don't want to make her job more difficult, but quitting my lunchtime workout isn't an option. So I bought a fan and some rope and put together a rig that, when powered by fully charged batteries, simulates a head-on gale-force wind and keeps me out of trouble.

As I sit up in bed staring into the darkness, my feet making small circles to start my daily calorie burn, I feel depressed and defeated. I know what I ate last night. I know what I did. All of my hard work has been undone. And I'm the one who undid it. I start moving my fingers and thumbs to relieve the anxiety of not beginning my morning workout because I'm stuck here again having to answer the voice in my head.

It's time to face last night. It was yogurt night, when I get my yogurt ready for the week. It's a dangerous night because there's always a chance of disaster when I allow myself to handle a lot of food at one time. But I had no indication that I was going to be in danger. I had eaten my 60-calorie portion of tuna normally, using chopsticks and allowing each bite of canned fish to be only the height and width of the tips of the chopsticks themselves. After dinner, I smoked cigarettes to allow myself the time I needed to digest the tuna properly and to feel the sensation of fullness. I went to the kitchen feeling no anxiety as I took out the tools I needed to perform the weekly operation: the kitchen scale, eight small plastic containers, one blue mixing bowl, Splenda, my measuring spoon, and my fork. I took the plain yogurt out of the fridge and, using the kitchen scale, divided it among the plastic containers adding one half teaspoon of Splenda to each portion. When I was satisfied that each portion weighed exactly two ounces, I then strategically hid the containers in the top section of the freezer behind ice-crusted plastic bags of old frozen vegetables so the yogurt wouldn't be the first thing I saw when I opened the freezer door.

Nothing abnormal so far.

With that, I went back to the sofa and allowed some time to pass. I knew that the thirty minutes it takes for the yogurt to reach the perfect consistency of a Dairy Queen wasn't up, and that checking in on it was an abnormality, but that's exactly what I did. I walked into the kitchen, I opened the freezer, and I looked at it. And I didn't just look at the portion I was supposed to eat. I looked at all of it.

I slammed the freezer door shut and went back to the living room. I sat on the dark green vinyl sofa facing the kitchen and smoked four cigarettes in a row to try to take away the urge for that icy-cold sweetness, because only when I stopped wanting it would I allow myself to have it. I didn't take my eyes off the freezer the whole time I sat smoking, just in case my mind had tricked me into thinking I was smoking when I was actually at that freezer bingeing. Staring at the door was the only way I could be certain that I wasn't opening it. By now the thirty minutes had definitely passed and it was time to eat my portion. I knew the best thing for me in that moment would be to abstain altogether, because eating one portion was the equivalent of an alcoholic being challenged to have one drink. But my overriding fear was that the pendulum would swing to the other extreme if I skipped a night. I've learned that overindulging the next day to make up for the 100 calories in the "minus" column from the day before is a certainty.

I took out my one allotted portion at 8:05 and mashed it with a fork until it reached the perfect consistency. But instead of sitting on the sofa savoring every taste in my white bowl with green flowers, using the fork to bring it to my mouth, I ate the yogurt from the plastic container over the kitchen sink with a teaspoon. I ate it fast. The deviation from the routine, the substitution of the tools, the speediness with which I ate silenced the drill sergeant and created an opening that invited in the thoughts I'm most afraid of—thoughts created by an evil force disguising itself as logic, poised to manipulate me with common sense. *Reward yourself. You ate nothing at lunch. Normal people eat four times this amount and still lose weight. It's only yogurt. Do it. You deserve it.*

Before I knew it, I was on the kitchen floor cradling the plastic Tupperware containing Tuesday's portion in the palm of my left hand, my right hand thumb and index finger stabbing into the icy crust. I ran my numb, yogurt-covered fingers across my lips and sucked them clean before diving into the container for more. As my fingers traveled back and forth from the container to my mouth, I didn't have a thought in my head. The repetition of the action lulled the relentless chatter into quiet meditation. I didn't want this trancelike state to end, and so when the first container was done, I got up off the floor and grabbed Wednesday's yogurt before my brain could process that it was still only Monday. By the time I came back to my senses, I had eaten six ounces of yogurt.

The alarm on my bedside table starts beeping. It's 4:15 a.m. It's time for my morning workout. I have exactly one hour to run and do sit-ups and leg lifts before I get in the car to drive forty-five minutes to the set for my 6:00 a.m. makeup call. I don't have any dialogue today. I just need to stand around with the supercilious smirk of a slick, high-powered attorney while Ally McBeal runs around me in circles, working herself into a lather of nerves. But even if I'd had actual acting to think about, my only goal today is to be comfortable in my wardrobe. God, I feel like shit. No matter how hard I run this morning, nothing can take away the damage done. As I slip out of bed and do deep lunges across the floor to the bathroom, I promise myself to cut my calorie intake in half to 150 for the day and to take twenty laxatives. That should do something to help. But it's not the weight gain from the six ounces of yogurt that worries me. It's the loss of self-control. It's the fear that maybe I've lost it for good. I start sobbing now as I lunge my way across the floor and I wonder how many calories I'm burning by sobbing. Sobbing and lunging—it's got to be at least 30 calories. It crosses my mind to vocalize my thoughts of self-loathing, because speaking the thoughts that fuel the sobs would have to burn more calories than just thinking the thoughts and so I say, "You're nothing. You're average. You're an ordinary, average, fat piece of shit. You have no self-control. You're a stupid, fat, disgusting dyke. You ugly, stupid, bitch!" As I reach the bathroom and wipe away the last of my tears, I'm alarmed by the silence; the voice has stopped.

When it's quiet in my head like this, that's when the voice doesn't need to tell me how pathetic I am. I know it in the deepest part of me. When it's quiet like this, that's when I truly hate myself.

PART ONE

1

M Y HUSBAND left me.

Two months ago, he just left. He had gathered evidence during the trial known as couples' therapy (it was revealed to me during those sessions that not every woman's idea of a fun night out was making out with another woman on a dance floor; I was shocked), judged me an unfit partner, and handed down to me the sentence of complete sexual confusion to be served in isolation. I watched breathlessly as he reversed out of our driveway in his old VW van packed with souvenirs of our life together: the van that had taken me camping along the California coastline, that had driven me to Stockton to get my Maltese puppy, Bean, and that had waited patiently for me outside casting offices in LA. As he cranked the gearshift into first and took off sputtering down the street, I ran after him with childlike desperation, panicked that my secret, true nature had driven him away. And with it, the comfort and ease of a normal life.

In a way, I loved him. But I loved the roles that we both played a lot more. I had assigned him the role of my protector. He was the shield that protected me from the harsh film industry and the shield the prevented me from having to face my real desires. Standing by his side in the role of his wife, I could run away from myself. But as his van drove away from our California bungalow with its white picket fence, it became clearer with the increasing distance between me and the back of that van that I was, for the first time in my life, free to explore those real desires. The shield had been ripped from me, and standing in the middle of a suburban street in Santa Monica with new skin and gasping for air, I realized that as his van turned the corner, so would I. It was time to face the fact that I was gay.

I had met my husband Mel on the set of my first American movie, *The Woman in the Moon,* three years earlier. During the arduous filming schedule of the lackluster indie movie, which had brought me from Australia to the Arizona desert, I entertained myself by creating a contest between him and a girl grip whose name I forget now, mentally listing the pros and cons of each of the two contestants to determine who was going to be my sexual partner. The unwitting contestants both had soft lips and were interesting choices for me. Mel was my onscreen lover and his rival was part of the camera crew that captured our passion on film. Of these two people I had met and made out with, Mel was the winner. The fact that I chose him over the girl grip was surprising to me because, although I didn't show up to the movie a full-fledged lesbian, I was definitely heading in that direction. During my one year of law school prior to this movie, I'd had an entanglement with a very disturbed but brilliant girl that I guess you could call "romantic" if it hadn't been so clumsy. By this point, I knew that the thought of being with a woman was exciting and liberating, and the thought of being with a man was depressing and stifling. In my mind, being with a woman was like being with your best friend, forever young, whereas being with a man felt like I would be trapped in adolescence with acne and a bad attitude. So it was surprising to me when I felt a rush of sexual attraction to Mel. (It was surprising to him, too, when I showed my attraction by breaking into his Holiday Inn hotel room, pummeling his chest and face and stomach while yelling "I'm gay," and then having sex with him.) And not only was I attracted to him, I could actually imagine living with him and his black Lab, Shadow, in LA. The mere thought that maybe I was capable of living a "normal" life with a man made me so excited that at the airport lounge waiting for my connector flight that would take me to Sydney, Australia, via Los Angeles, I drew up another list of pros and cons, this time for getting off the plane in LA.

Pros: 1. Acting. 2. Mel.
Cons:

Almost immediately after arriving in LA, however, the rush of sexual attraction evaporated into the thin air of my wishful thinking. By the end of our first year together, despite my desire to be attracted to him, my latent fear of my real sexuality was simmering and about to boil. I was almost positive I was gay. So I married him. The fact that I got shingles the minute we returned from city hall didn't deter me from my quest to appear normal, and so my husband and I attempted a happily married life in an apartment complex in Santa Monica that had closely resembled the television show *Melrose Place*.

There was a girl who lived next door. She introduced herself to me as Kali, "K-A-L-I but pronounced Collie, like the dog. She was the goddess of the destruction of illusion." Kali. A quick-witted artist with elegant tattoos and a killer vocab that made you feel like carrying a notepad so you could impress your less cool friends with what you'd learned. Every night she'd be sprawled on the floor of her studio apartment sketching voluptuous figures in charcoal, her thick burgundy hair spilling onto the paper. Every night I'd excuse myself from watching TV with my husband to go outside to smoke. I'd find myself positioning the plastic lawn chair to line up with the one-inch crack where her window treatments didn't quite stretch all the way to the wooden frame so I could watch her. I would smoke and fantasize about being in there with her, but due to my being married and the fact she was straight and only flirted with me for sport, all we ever had together was a Vita and Virginia–type romance—a conservative exploration of hypothetical love in handwritten notes. She would often draw sketches of me and slide them underneath our door. Kali's drawings were so precious to me that I locked them away in the heart-shaped box my husband had given me one Valentine's Day. This was a contentious issue between Mel and me, which culminated in him demanding that I throw them away in the kitchen trash can while he watched. A seemingly endless succession of thick, wet tears dripped into my lap as potato peels slowly covered ink renditions of my face, my arms, my legs.

During my evening ritual of smoking outside and watching her, I was in heaven. Until invariably I was dragged back to earth forty minutes later by a loud, deep voice asking, "Are you smoking another cigarette?" Mel and Kali. Melancholy.

Strangely enough, none of this seemed strange to me. In fact, playing the role of heterosexual while fantasizing about being a homosexual had been my reality since I was a child. At age eight I would invite my school friends over on the weekends and convince them to play a game I called "husband and wife." It was a simple game that went like this: I, in the role of husband, would come home from a grueling day at the office and my wife would greet me at the door with a martini and slippers. She would cook dinner on the bedside table. I would mime reading the paper. Occasionally, if I had the energy to remove my clothes from the closet, I'd make her remove hers to stand inside the closet's long-hanging section to take a make-believe shower. The game didn't have much of a sexual component to it; we were married, so the sex was insinuated. But I carried the role-play right up until the end where I judged my friend on her skills as a wife by timing her as she single-handedly cleaned up the mess we'd made playing the game in my room. Although I was aware of that manipulation (I could never believe they fell for that!), I think my intentions behind the game were quite innocent. I wanted to playact a grown-up relationship just like other kids would playact being a doctor.

It was the beginning of a recurring theme until the day my husband left me: I was pretending to be in a heterosexual relationship while exploring a gay one. My husband leaving put an end to the flirtation between Kali and me, as I realized I was no longer playacting. I couldn't pretend to be in love with my next-door neighbor anymore, I had to find a relationship with someone who could simultaneously make me grow up and keep me forever young. I continued therapy, painted the kitchen walls, and fantasized about my future life: I would bring water lilies home to her every day in summer, I would wrap my arms around her waist as she chopped vegetables, I would fall asleep holding her hand . . .

2

OOD NEWS!" It was early to be calling my mother. It was 2:00 p.m. in Los Angeles, which would be only 7:00 a.m. in Australia, but I couldn't wait a second longer.

"Hang on a minute, darling. I'll just get my robe on and go to the other phone." I stood breathlessly next to my car in the parking lot of Fox Studios, my cell phone plastered to my ear. I was too excited to get in my car and drive.

"Okay, darl. What's going on? Did you get a job?"

"Ma. I'm going to be on *Ally McBeal*! I'm their new cast member!" I waited for the enormity of what I was saying to compute, but as the show hadn't yet reached Australia, I was forced to say this: "Ma, I'm going to be famous!" Both of us fell into an awe-filled silence. I was excited, wondering what my brand-new life would be like, but with the excitement came a little fear. I was gay. I knew that being openly gay wasn't an option, but what if they—the press, the public, my employers—found out? As the silence grew I couldn't help but wonder how I was going to pull this off. I could sense by the length of the silence that my mother was thinking the same thing, since the subject of my being gay had featured heavily in all of our recent conversations since my breakup with Mel six months prior. Although I had come out to my mother at age sixteen after she found *The Joy of Lesbian Sex* under my bed, I had thwarted my own attempts to convince my mother that

17

I was a lesbian by being with Mel, despite the fact that my dalliance with heterosexuality was actually the "phase" she referred to when talking about my lesbianism. However, after months of hour-long phone conversations, she finally accepted that I'd married Mel to try to bury my homosexual tendencies, and she was forced to take my sexuality seriously. Her feelings about it were a source of conflict to her and of confusion to me. She would be supportive to the point where she would talk to me about dating girls, but still she encouraged me to be secretive with everyone else, especially people who had the power to advance my career. She told me not to tell anyone, that it was "nobody's business," including close family members. She convinced me that because they were from another generation and from small towns, "They just wouldn't understand." So I didn't talk to anyone about it. I didn't want to upset anybody. I had upset myself enough as it was. And at least I could talk to her.

After several moments of processing and a few exclamations of pride, my mother gently said, "You'd better be careful, darling."

"Don't be crazy, Ma! I'm not even dating anyone. No one will ever know."

And with that, my excitement about my impending fame dropped substantially. Well and truly enough to allow me to drive. I got in the car but instead of going straight home, I drove down Santa Monica Boulevard to a popular lesbian coffee shop called Little Frieda's. I sat outside and savored every sip of coffee and every moment of being at a lesbian coffee shop, because after this, I knew I would never allow myself to go there again. The feeling that came with getting *the* job, the feeling that I had been chosen, was better than limply sitting outside at a lesbian coffee shop too afraid to glance at the other patrons much less approach them. I was not ready live my life as a gay woman. I had a career to establish. Being a regular cast member on a hit TV show was what I had been working toward. Famous actresses were special people. At last I had a chance to be special.

• • •

My quest to be special had begun in childhood. My aunt and uncle had lifelong family friends, the Goffs, and the Goffs had three daughters. The eldest, Linda, was a lawyer. The middle one, Amanda, was a physiotherapist. And the youngest, Allison, was a model. Despite the obvious accomplishments of her sisters, Allison received the lion's share of my family's interest, admiration, and praise. There wasn't a week that went by that my mother didn't point out "pretty Allison" in a catalogue that would be left in our mailbox to announce a spring sale or a winter bargain. Although I was quite a smart kid and received A grades, I needed something that would be exciting to people. I needed to be the girl my mother pointed to in a catalogue. So I decided to become a model.

I wasn't that pretty, nor was I particularly tall. I was okay looking, but I certainly wasn't good-looking enough to have one of those annoying stories that supermodels tell on talk shows about how the boys teased them at school and called them "horse face" and "chicken legs" because they were so skinny and "plain." When I was eight, Anthony Nankervis used to call me "Lizzie," which was short for "Lizard Eyes" because, as he brought to my attention daily in a singsongy chant, my eyes turned into slits when I smiled. Instead of deflecting the insult like any other eight-year-old would have done with a retort about his body odor, I took him to a mirror in the playground to explain to me what he meant. To the soundtrack of bouncing balls and playground squeals, I alternately smiled and frowned and to my horror, I discovered he was right. When I smiled, my eyes disappeared behind two fatty mounds of flesh. The memory of Anthony and me standing in front of that mirror, both of us horrified by my fatty, slitty eyes, is still quite painful. Being called a lizard is not something that ages into a compliment, not like having the legs of chicken.

If her parents had allowed her to pursue modeling, my friend Charlotte Duke would've been that girl with the annoying talk show story. Not only was she teased for being tall and skinny, her nickname was MX Missiles because she had unusually large breasts for her age. She had short, sandy hair, and freckles covered her face, and when she got head-hunted for an editorial modeling job (which her mother wouldn't allow her to take), I couldn't have been more shocked. She was so ordinary in my opinion. She never wore makeup or put hot rollers in her hair. She didn't care about fashion or models or magazines. At twelve, what I thought was beautiful was the cast of *Dynasty* and anyone who guest starred on *The Love Boat*, and I looked more like any of them than Charlotte Duke did. With Breck Girl hair and my face covered in makeup, I thought I could pass as pretty. What I lacked in looks and physique I made up for in determination. I took a series of Polaroid pictures of myself in various outfits, including an Indian-style headdress, in the front yard of our suburban house, and sent them to the modeling agencies in the big city, an hour from where we lived.

But I wouldn't just hit the Melbourne modeling scene unprepared. I'd already been to deportment school, as my mother thought having ladylike manners and learning about makeup was part of a well-rounded education. For me, it was one step closer to becoming a model. I finished first in the class at a runway show/graduation ceremony that took place in the daytime in a dinner-only restaurant, but with the win came my first flush of insecurity. There was a girl called Michelle who was a very close runner-up. We were locked in a dead heat and received the exact same scores for Correct Posture, Makeup Application, Photographic Modeling, and Social Etiquette, but due to my ability to walk better in high heels, I took the Catwalk Modeling category and took center stage to receive my trophy. (Actually, I stood on the carpet between two tables already set for dinner and received a sheet of paper.) But the fact that another girl had been close to taking my crown made my mother and me equally nervous and had a huge impact on both of us. I know this is true for me because I can still remember every physical detail of that girl, and for my mother because whenever my child-hood accomplishments are discussed she says, "Do you remember that girl in deportment school who nearly beat you?"

Two weeks after sending the photos off to various modeling agencies, I received a call from the Modeling World. A new agency by the name of Team Models had seen me in my Indian headdress and were impressed enough to request a meeting. This was slightly problematic because after my father's death three years earlier, my mother had taken a full-time job at a doctor's office and she couldn't just take time off to drive me to appointments. Although she enjoyed the idea of me modeling almost as much as I did, she told me that I had school and to be realistic. So I did what any twelve-year-old would do. I screamed and cried and told her that she was ruining my life. I threw a tantrum so violent and relentless that my mother was forced to take a sick day and chauffeur me to the meeting. As it was my foray into the working world, I felt I had to appear independent and in control, so I instructed my mother to wait in the car while I went in to "wow" them. I'd rehearsed just how I was going to do this several times in the two weeks since I'd sent the photos and waited for the call. My plan was this: I would walk through the lobby and would pause in the doorway of the agency, my hands on either side of the frame, and once I got the bookers' attention, I would simply announce my name, "Amanda Rogers." They would show me to a chair, tell me that I was the face they were looking for, and welcome me to the Team Modeling family. And honestly, that's not too far off from what actually happened. Except for "the face" line. And, thank God, no one saw me posing like a fool in a doorway. But even then I knew that it wasn't my looks that got me a place in the agency, it was my gift of gab. I talked them into it. I told them that I would be the youngest model on their books and that I would make them the most money. I told them that my look was both commercial and editorial. I told them that I was dedicated to modeling and would be professional and always available. They were no doubt amused by the bravado of this twelve-year-old, and because of that they decided to give me a shot. I collected my empty gray and pink Team portfolio and walked like a model back to the car where my mother was patiently waiting. "Good news," I told her when I got into the passenger seat. "I'm going to be a model." And from that day on, "good news" was the phrase I would use to tell my mother when I booked a modeling job, a TV show, or a feature. And "good news" remains the phrase that my mother is always the happiest to hear.

3

URING THE week before I started work on *Ally McBeal*, my excitement about my new job continued to be overshadowed by my fear of public scrutiny. Perhaps it was because I was so judgmental of other actors when they were less than brilliant on talk shows or when their answers to red carpet questions didn't convey the information in a succinct, perfectly witty quip designed to politely yet definitively wrap up the probing interviewer. I've always had a gut-wrenching feeling of embarrassment for people when they say stupid things. And now I was going to be held up to the same scrutiny. Would I be smart enough? Would I have the perfect comeback to Letterman's subtle jab? Would I be able to convey intelligence and yet be fun and flirty with Leno? And how was I going to answer anybody's questions when my answers couldn't be truthful? Truthful answers to any of those red carpet questions would kill my career in an instant. "I'm not a fan of *Ally McBeal*. I've only seen one episode and I didn't really like it." Or "I actually don't follow fashion and I prefer engineer's boots to Jimmy Choos" wouldn't be a friendly introduction to the world, and I'm sure Joan Rivers wouldn't have appreciated it either.

The more I thought about it, the more I realized that David Kelley had made a mistake by casting me as the new hot lawyer on a show about hot lawyers and their romantic entanglements. When I met Mr. Kelley to discuss a possible role on *The Practice*, a show I had watched and liked, something I did—like flicking my hair off my shoulder or the way I crossed my legs—made him say, "I see you more for *Ally.*" And with that I was Photoshopped into a poster of the cast, squeezed into the show's trademark unisex bathroom. He had made a mistake for sure. Apart from not being that fun and flirty leading-lady type that I knew the character had to be, I just wasn't good-looking enough for the role. I was okay at certain angles, but my profile was ugly (I knew this from years of modeling), and my face was very large and round. Plus the character itself was a stretch. Playing a commanding, intimidating professional brimming with self-confidence was going to be a challenge. While I would eagerly accept such an acting challenge for a movie, the thought that I had to play this powerful woman who was so vastly different from myself year after year on a television show was daunting. How was I going to stop my head from tilting in deference to the person I was talking to like I did in real life? How was I going to always remember to stand with my weight evenly balanced on two high-heeled legs when I usually slouch over my left hip in boots? Because I would need to fight every natural instinct to act out the character, I decided it would be immensely helpful if I could change my natural instincts. I would teach myself to stand straight and listen with my head straight. I would practice sounding self-assured and confident. I would stop sounding Australian and always sound like an American when I spoke. It was too late to get out of it, so I had to change myself significantly in order to get into it.

I needed to shed my old self and step into this new role. And not only did I have to become the role of Nelle Porter, I also had to play the role of a celebrity. But what did celebrities do? Did they go to parties, get spray-tanned, become philanthropic? Did they get their hair and makeup done when they went to the supermarket? Did they go to the supermarket at all? Becoming a celebrity felt like a promotion to me. The problem with thinking that being a famous actress was an upgrade from being just an actress was that I wasn't given a new job description. As an actress, I learned my lines, interpreted and performed them. But there was no actual profession that went along with being a celebrity. After observing Elizabeth Hurley's meteoric rise from actress to celebrity, I knew, however, that becoming a celebrity had a lot to do with clothes. As I didn't read fashion magazines or care which celebrity wore the same gown more elegantly than her counterpart, how was I going become the fashionable celebrity that the new cast member on *Ally McBeal* was expected to be? I was given this promotion but then left alone to guess how to do the job.

Either that or I could ask an expert.

When Kali wasn't painting, she was absorbing fashion. I say "absorbing" because watching her hunched over a *Vogue* magazine, her arms protectively wrapped around it, her body still and focus intent as she traced the outline of clothing with her eyes, you'd swear she was recharging her life source. You couldn't talk to Kali when she began to read the new issue of *W* or even talk to anyone else within her earshot. One summer, a houseguest of Mel and mine saw a plastic-wrapped *Vogue* on the stoop next door, unwrapped it, and was discovered by Kali reading it in the courtyard. After finding out that this thief who had robbed her of the great pleasure of being the first and only one to handle her subscriber's copy was a friend from my modeling days in Australia, Kali stood in our living room in a state of shock quietly repeating, "Who would do something like that?" Mel and I were forced to take sides: My husband, who leapt at the chance to argue with Kali, told her she was overreacting and took the model-friend's side. This argument was one of many that created the state of melancholy in which I lived, as there was a lot of tension between Mel and Kali. Naturally, I took Kali's side. Since she was a creative genius, whatever inspired her was obviously important. It didn't matter that I didn't care for fashion magazines.

With only one week before I had to begin work, I called Kali in a panic. Kali told me not to worry about buying new clothes and becoming someone else. She told me that they hired me for my uniqueness. She told me to be myself.

"A lesbian?"

Kali agreed to meet me at Banana Republic that afternoon.

Dressed in a vintage Iggy Pop T-shirt, faded black denim jeans, and a pair of perfectly worn black leather engineers' boots, I walked across the outdoor mall in the heat of a Pasadena summer toward Kali, who was waiting for me in the store. She was going to help me put together a new, casual, everyday look that I could wear to work. I chose Banana Republic, because I figured that I could find clothes there that would help me smooth out the sharp edges and make me look more like an acceptable member of society. Or at least less like an outcast.

I saw Kali among the racks of white and beige dressed in a uniquely cool vintage dress that made her stand out in the store designed to help you blend in. My face must have conveyed the anxiety in my head because Kali just skipped the "hello"s and hugged me, wrapping her arms around my waist, each hand clasping shirts on hangers that dug into my back.

"Thanks for doing this, Kals."

"It'll be fun. I don't know if you need me, though, Pickle. You have a great sense of style."

"Yeah, well, I don't see too many photos of leading ladies in ripped black jeans and engineers' boots."

I became self-conscious of my black clothing. No one else in the store was wearing heavy black boots or a black T-shirt. They were wearing summer prints and skirts.

"You could use some lighter colors for summer. Do you need skirts?" Kali was looking me up and down like I was more of a project than a friend.

"I guess so. I don't know. Do I?"

She smiled at me sweetly and handed me the two shirts she was holding.

"Why don't you start with these and I'll find you some pants. Do you like Capri pants?"

As I wasn't certain that I knew what they were, I shrugged my shoulders and took the shirts. I found a dressing room with a full-length mirror and tried on the shirts. I tried the white one and then I tried the other white one.

As I waited in the dressing room for Kali to bring Capri pants in a color palette that would make me more palatable, I looked at my body. I looked at my big thighs, the fat around my knees. I looked at my hips and how they formed a triangle where my butt hit the top of my legs. It wasn't the first time I was critical of my body. I'd spent my life trying to change it, but I was overcome with the feeling that it would continue to beat me—that I could never win the game of successfully changing its shape. I thought about the time when I was eighteen and got stoned and stared at my reflection in a sliding glass door, sobbing, "I will always look like this." Or when I met the voice when I was twelve and a modeling client asked me to turn around so she could see my butt. She asked me to take down my pants, turn around, and face the wall so she could see my ass. I faced the wall with my pants around my ankles for what seemed like a long time before she asked me to turn back around to face her. "I'm surprised your butt is so saggy for such a young girl," she said in a friendly, inquisitive tone. "Do you work out?"

You need to work out. That was the first thing the voice said to me. It was a very deep, male voice that was so loud and clear I wondered if the other rejected models in the elevator with me could hear it. It continued to ring like a shock wave long after it had delivered the message. And standing in front of the mirror in Banana Republic, I was ashamed to think that at twenty-four, it had to keep giving me the same message.

"What size are you?" Kali's innocent question sent me into a mild panic. Not because I thought I was fat other than the parts that needed reshaping, I just didn't know how sizes ran in the States. In Australia, the perfect size to be was a size 10. But in the States, what was the equivalent to a 10? I'd only ever shopped at thrift stores or at Urban Outfitters with their "one size fits all" clothing since coming to the States, or I wore the same old jeans and T-shirts I'd always had.

"What size should I be?"

"What do you mean?" She looked at me with an inviting smile on her face, like we were about to play a game. She had no idea that her answer to my question was going to change my life.

"What size are models?"

"Well, a sample size is usually a six." Kali knew a lot of things like this.

"Then I'm a six." As it turned out, I actually was a 6. Mostly. The Capri pants that were a size 6 were too tight, but I bought them anyway as incentive to lose a few pounds. It didn't occur to me to go up to the next, more comfortable size because as far as I was concerned, a size 8 didn't exist.

As I left the store with my new buttoned-down wardrobe I felt immobilized with anxiety. I sat down with Kali on a concrete bench in the outdoor shopping mall, bags strewn around my feet, feeling overwhelmed. I had a few days' worth of acceptable clothes, but what would happen after that? I would have to keep shopping for this new personality or else people would figure out who I really was, and if that happened, I would lose my career. Nobody would hire a lesbian to play a leading role. Ellen DeGeneres's TV show had just been unceremoniously canceled after her decision to come out, and there had never been any openly lesbian "leading lady" actresses—ever. In the three years I'd lived in LA, I'd realized that in Hollywood, there were really only two kinds of actresses: leading ladies and character actresses. The character actresses wait around all day in a toilet-sized trailer for their one scene, and they get to eat from the craft service table for free, while the leading ladies get the story lines, the pop-out trailers, and dinners with studio executives at The Ivy. Oh, and the money. No one I could think of in the history of acting had ever been a leading lady and a known homosexual, and being revealed as such a person would mean sudden career death. Of that I had no doubt whatsoever. After I explained this to Kali in order to convince her how stupid her suggestion to "just be myself" was, I was able to collect my new things and head to the shoe store for some high heels—something to wear with my size 6 clothes. As I walked across the mall wondering if the way I walked made me look obviously lesbian, my mind switched to thinking about how much weight I'd have to lose to fit comfortably into those Capri pants. And so I gave myself a goal. I would wear those pants on my first day of work.

The diet was a very simple one. It was the same diet that I had gone on six to eight times a year since I did it to get ready for my first fashion show. Instead of eating 1,000 calories a day, which seemed to be the recommended weight-loss calorie consumption for women, I ate 1,000 kilojoules. I was Australian, after all, and turning it metric was only right. It was a pun with numbers that I thought was funny. As 1,000 kilojoules was approximately 300 calories, I embarked on my 300-calorie diet with the goal of a one-pound weight loss per day and I would do it for seven days. I knew how it would work because I'd done it so many times before. The first three days I'd lose a pound each day, and then days four and five I'd see no movement on the scale, then day six I would lose a satisfying three pounds, and the last day I'd round it off with a one-pound weight loss to total seven pounds. It was a no-fail diet, and losing weight just before starting my new job seemed like the professional thing to do. Not only would it make me look fit and healthy, but because being thinner always made me feel more attractive, psychologically it would help me to feel confident and ready for whatever acting challenge I'd be given. And then of course, there was the imminent wardrobe fitting. If I could lose weight it would make the costume designer's job easier, since she could pick up any sample size for me and know that I'd fit into it. Losing weight was the silent agreement I'd made with the producers, and I was ready to keep up my end of the deal.

4

AS I pulled into my parking space out front of a sound stage on Kelley Land, aka Manhattan Beach Studios, I was dizzy with excitement and nerves. It was my first day at work on the set of *Ally McBeal*. I got out of the car, smoothed out the wrinkles in my comfortably fitting Capri pants, and looked around. It was a very austere and sterile lot. It had been built recently and accommodated David Kelley's production company, and it appeared that the final touches that would make it look habitable still needed to be done. The studio lots I had worked on in Hollywood and in Burbank were bustling with people walking in and out of a café or from a newsstand manned by a colorful employee who knew every actor and producer who went there for *Variety* or the *LA Times*. But there were no people at Manhattan Beach Studios, only cars. There was no commissary, no park where you could read a novel at lunch under a tree. In fact there were no plants or trees. The buildings were huge, monolithic peach rectangles with no overhangs for shade, so the sun bounced off the clean white pavement and onto the windowless structures making the whole lot look like every corner was lit by a spotlight. In Kelley Land there wasn't a shadow in which to hide. It looked like headquarters for a research and development company where scientific tests were conducted under the intense scrutiny of plant managers, unseen by the outside world. Either that or a minimum-security prison.

I walked out of the late-morning summer heat and into the hallway of the air-conditioned building looking for the dressing room with my name on the door. The first door read Peter MacNicol, next was Greg Germann, and then there it was: Portia de Rossi. I had arrived. It was the nicest dressing room I'd ever had. There was a deep green sofa and matching chair, a desk with a desk chair, and a bathroom with a shower. Everything was squeaky clean and new. No actor had ever been here before, it was a sterile environment, and that was comforting and yet also somehow disquieting. No actor had rehearsed her dialogue, paced the room in anticipation of a scene, or smoked cigarettes out of boredom or nerves in this dressing room. There were no memories or stale cigarette smoke trapped in these walls. It was just going to be an alternately anxious and bored Portia de Rossi wanting to smoke but unable to smoke, looking at her flawed reflection in the full-length closet door mirrors.

I threw my bag on the sofa and checked my watch. It was 10:30. I was early. At 11:00 I had a wardrobe fitting and then at 12:00 I would begin makeup and hair. The reason for wanting to be early was less about first-day jitters than it was about my appearance. Despite being told as a child model to show up to shoots with a clean face and clean hair, I have never turned up to a job with a freshly scrubbed face or just-hopped-out-of-the-shower hair. I just got better at concealing it. I loved concealer. The magic oily stick of beige makeup was as essential to me as oxygen. I could have half my face covered with the stuff and still look like I was clean and naturally flawless. Of course, this careful application of concealer was painstaking and time consuming (trying to cover up shameful secrets always is), and it was for this reason I arrived a full half hour early. Naturally, before leaving home, I'd made the first pass over my red, blotchy skin, dark circles, blemishes, and scars of blemishes, but the drive across town was a long one, and I had anticipated that I would need to patch the areas where the heat had melted away my artistry. After I was satisfied that I'd done all I could to be the attractive, new actress that the wardrobe girls were no doubt expecting

to meet, I headed over to the wardrobe room. It was in another building quite far from my dressing room and I roamed around in search
of it for what seemed like an eternity. Finally, I was intercepted by a
production assistant and escorted the rest of the way.

The PA wore shorts and sneakers. She looked flustered and told me
that she'd been frantically looking for me. She told me that she was
scheduled to be waiting for me at my parking space at 10:45. The more
she talked (who feels confident enough about their legs to show them
off without the help of high heels?) the more stupid I felt for arriving
so early and for leaving my dressing room before a PA came to get me.
*Damn it. All I had to do on my first day was appear to be professional, to know
what I'm doing, and I have already given myself away.* By the time I got to
the wardrobe rooms, I had a knot in my gut. I was dying for a cigarette.
What was a lesbian doing here on this show playing an ice-cold attorney in the courtroom who would, no doubt, be hot in the bedroom in
an upcoming episode? Would I fit into a size 6 suit?

I hovered at the doorway of the costume designer's office, waiting
for her to acknowledge me as she sat at her desk. When she turned to
find me standing at the door, I could see that she was on the phone.

"Come in," she mouthed, gesturing for me to enter. I walked across
the threshold and into the rooms that would be the main stage for
the drama my life was about to become—a drama in which I wrote, directed, produced, and played all parts: my very own one-woman show.
I stood in the middle of the room since racks of clothing flanked the
walls and took up most of the space, leaving only a small, carpeted
square in the center like a tiny stage, but instead of facing an audience,
it faced a large, full-length mirror.

"Hi. I'm Portia." I extended my hand and smiled at her as she hung
up the phone and walked toward me from her desk.

"It's nice to meet you in person. I'm Vera. Welcome to the show."

Vera and I had met over the phone when she asked for my measurements.

"Thirty-four, twenty-four, thirty-five."

That sounded better than the truth, which started at around 32 and probably ended up around 38. I stopped measuring after my first interview with my modeling agents at age twelve when they told me to call them with my bust, waist, and hip measurements when I got home.

"Thirty-two, twenty-seven, thirty-seven," I had told the Team Modeling booker.

"Are you sure?" A long silence followed, then my next instruction. "Well, just tell people you're thirty-four, twenty-four, thirty-five, ok? We'll put those measurements on your card."

Now I stood center-stage in the *Ally McBeal* fitting room in front of the mirror, dressed in a pinstriped suit with a nipped-in waist and a large, rounded lapel. All the suits I had tried so far had fit. I was relieved. After all my anxiety preceding the fitting, I felt relaxed. I admired my reflection in the mirror. The suit I was wearing was my favorite for no other reason than it was a size 4. I was almost giddy with excitement. For my first episode of *Ally McBeal*, I would wear a size 4.

"Ugh. Take that off. That's horrible."

As I began to reluctantly take off the size 4 suit, Vera walked to her desk and picked up a large folder. I could see that the script inside had colored tabs and notes all down the margins.

"I think your character would only wear monochromatic suits. Conservative. Do you think there would be a hint of sexiness to her—like, say, a slit in the leg of a pencil skirt?"

"Umm. Sure." I thought Nelle should have some sexiness and I guessed a pencil skirt was really the only way to make a business suit sexy. I was worried, though, that my hips looked big in pencil skirts.

"What do you think she'd wear on weekends?"

I attempted to sound like I had given the character's costumes a great deal of thought, but it was immediately obvious to me that Vera's exploration of my character was far more extensive than my own. To my surprise, her preparedness was the only unnerving part of the whole fitting. I was so busy trying to fit into the size 6 suit, to be the perfect-looking addition to TV's hottest legal show, I'd forgotten to think about the clothes as an expression of the character I was about to portray, potentially for years. She closed her folder and walked back to her desk.

"Well, we've got a pretty good start. Let's just go with what we have for this week and we'll figure the rest out later."

I put my Capri pants back on, thanked Vera, and headed out. I left the fitting and was escorted by the PA to the makeup trailer in a state of mild shock. I was amazed that I could ever walk out of a fitting feeling ashamed for something other than my imperfect body. Still, I had passed my first big test of fitting in, and in the case of clothes, fitting into a sample size, and I was on to my second. My body had passed the test, next was my face.

As I shook the hand of the makeup artist, Sarah, and looked her in the eyes, I registered her pupils dilating to begin their scan across my face. Could she see imperfections? Discoloration? Makeup?

"Are you wearing makeup?" The question was straightforward, but her tone was slightly incredulous. Enough to make me feel very embarrassed.

"No." When attacked, defend by lying.

"Sit down. Let's get started. Is there anything I should know before I start?"

"No. You're the expert. I'm sure it'll be great."

The truth was, I wasn't so sure. Practically every time I sat in a makeup chair, I'd look worse at the end than I did before we started. But I had never really learned what it was that made me look bad, plus even if I had, I didn't feel it was my place to tell a makeup artist how to do her job, much less the head of the makeup department for *Ally McBeal*. As I was shuffled back and forth between the two chairs due to the hair and makeup artists alternately being needed on set (God, what was going on in there in the scene before mine? What was I about to face?), I applied a similar philosophy of trusting the experts in the hair department to do their job. After we collectively decided that Nelle Porter should wear her hair in a bun, how my hair was pulled back and all other decisions were my hairstylist's business. After all, I was the new girl. I didn't want to make a scene or stand out, I just wanted to fit in. I wanted everyone I met to think of me as quiet and professional. I wanted the headline to be "how the new character melted seamlessly into the ensemble cast." And now that I'd left Portia on the floors of the hair, makeup, and wardrobe rooms, it was time for Nelle Porter to meet the cast.

5

CAGE

Everyone. I'd like to introduce the newest member of Cage and Fish. Please welcome Nelle Porter.

ELAINE

(to Ally and Georgia)

Just so we're clear, we hate her, right?

ALLY AND GEORGIA

(nodding in agreement)

Uh huh.

"Cut. Back to one."

I stood on the stairs of the law office set staring out into the crowd. There they were. Ally, Billy, Georgia, Elaine, Fish—assembled on the floor of the office foyer, looking up at me standing midway down the staircase preparing to deliver a speech about how I was going to breathe new life into the firm and shake things up around the place. I hadn't even met them yet. I just stood on the staircase smiling awkwardly at each cast member as they tentatively smiled and waved, sizing me up just as their characters were directed to do in the script. I was meeting the lawyers as Nelle Porter for the first time, and I was meeting the cast as Portia de Rossi in the same way, from the same step, and we were all carefully and awkwardly smiling and waving. How ironic that my character was supposed to be intimidating to these people, and yet I was too scared to hold a script to check my lines because I knew the shaking piece of paper would give me away—the trembling hands that were supposed to encase nerves of steel, the hands that belonged to "Sub-zero Nelle," the self-assured woman whose only purpose in the show was to be the antithesis to insecure Ally. I worried about meeting them. I worried that I would say something that would show them that I wasn't going to be the outstanding addition to the cast that they'd been told by the show's producers I would be. What if they could immediately see that I wasn't exceptional and special, that I was merely an average girl?

I knew I was average. I had learned this fact on my first day of Geelong Grammar School. In Grovedale, the suburb of Geelong where I grew up, we had the biggest and most beautiful house in the neighborhood—a brand-new two-story AV Jennings home with a swimming pool. My father was a well-respected community organizer, the founder of the Grovedale Rotary Club, and there was talk of him running for mayor. But on my first day at my new school, when I saw one kid being dropped off in a helicopter and others arriving in BMWs and Jaguars, it became obvious to me that I was not like them. They owned things my family couldn't afford. And while I had felt jealousy before, seeing that boy get out of a helicopter elicited a brand-new, uncomfortable feeling. Jealousy for me had been rooted in the belief that what I was jealous of was attainable, but this was different. I felt intimidated. I felt less than, not equal, and on a completely different, un-relatable level. Throughout the day I heard stories from the students of summer vacations spent yachting around the Caribbean while I had spent my summer pretending to be an Olympic gymnast in the cul-de-sac. I was embarrassed to think that I had been strutting around town like a spoiled little rich girl when I wasn't rich at all.

"Why didn't you tell me we were poor?" I fired at my mother with uncharacteristic anger when I got into the car. (I have since learned that anger is my first response to embarrassment.) My mother was clearly hurt by my question, and as we drove home in her Mazda 626, she stared at the road between her hands clenched at 10 and 2 on the steering wheel, and explained to me with tears in her eyes that she'd tried very hard to make sure our lives continued as if dad were still alive.

"But we've always been poor!" She couldn't possibly know how poor we were. She probably didn't even know what a yacht was.

When I saw my brother later that night, I attacked him. I was especially angry with my brother, since he had attended the school for two years prior to my arrival. Surely he could've told me the truth.

"We're not poor, stupid. We're average."

Average. It was the worst, most disgusting word in the English language. Nothing meaningful or worthwhile ever came from that word. In my twelve-year-old mind, there was no point in living if you were average. An average person doesn't cure cancer, win Olympic medals, or become a movie star. What kind of a boring, uninspired life was I going to live if I was thought of as "average" in any category? My brother could not have levied a greater insult than calling me average with the exception of "normal," "ordinary," and "mediocre." These were words that I hated just as much as the word "average," and I knew they were lined up right around the corner ready to attach themselves to me like a name badge unless I did something exceptional and gave myself a better label, starting with my unexceptional, common-sounding name. My name was average. I knew this because I wasn't the only one who had it. When I was eight, I was a track and field star. My race was the 200 meters. At the regional track and field meet, there was a girl in my heat with the same name—Amanda Rogers—who was my only real competition. I simply couldn't see the point of running the race. Where's the glory in beating the girl with the same name? Why make a name for myself when somebody else already had it? Amanda Rogers in first, followed by Amanda Rogers in second?

I needed to give myself a better label. Model. Law student. Actress. No one was average at my new school. They were rich. I needed to be exceptional just to fit in.

The thought of being in the middle of the pack had always worried me. From my first awareness of competition—that someone could win and another person could lose—the pressure to excel in everything I attempted was immense. I had to win, get an A, and take home the prize. Even when I took first prize, topped the class, won the race, I never really won anything. I was merely avoiding the embarrassment of losing. When ability is matched by expectations, then anything less that an exceptional result was laziness. And laziness in my opinion was shameful.

But I wasn't naturally inclined to excel in all the tasks I was given as a child. For example, I was never good at math. Even basic addition eluded me. I learned my multiplication table at school because we used to have "heads up" competitions in front of the class. The teacher would invite two students to come to the blackboard and would then proceed to ask them various multiplication questions such as "six times seven" or "five times three." I drilled the answers into my brain. All day long this little eight-year-old would be silently playing the game of teacher and student; the teacher firing questions with machine-gun rapidity, the student, armed with preparation, deftly deflecting every bullet. I made it through the third grade undefeated. But I wasn't a math champion for long. By age fourteen I was bawling over my physics homework.

Devastation was my usual reaction to things I couldn't comprehend. It would start with mild anxiety if the answer wasn't at the ready, and would progress to full-blown terror, physically manifesting in sweating, yelling, crying, hitting myself on the head, and chanting, "I don't understand" until I was exhausted and on the verge of collapse. In order to prepare myself for a less than perfect result, I would occasionally give myself the opposite of a pep talk by writing hundreds of times in a journal, "I will not get honors," as I awaited the results of a ballet exam, for example. I'm not sure if this ritual actually helped me to accept the less than perfect grade I was preparing myself for, because I always did get honors. Dancing six days a week for two hours a day, plus hours of practice at home will get anyone honors, much less a nine-year-old whose only competition had just learned to point her toe. The ballet school I attended was a small side business of a onetime professional dancer who rented out a church hall to teach young kids the basics of dance in a suburb of a mid-sized town. Nobody took it seriously. I treated it like it was the Australian Ballet.

I don't know where this pressure came from. I can't blame my parents because it has always felt internal. Like any other parent, my mother celebrated the A grades and the less-than-A grades she felt there was no need tell anybody about. But not acknowledging the effort that ended in a less than perfect result impacted me as a child. If I didn't win, then we wouldn't tell anyone that I had even competed to save us the embarrassment of acknowledging that someone else was better. Keeping the secret made me think that losing was something to be ashamed of, and that unless I was sure I was going to be the champion, there was no point in trying. And there was certainly no point to just having fun.

FISH

Can I have your attention please? Everybody. I really have splendid news. I would like to introduce to you all, Nelle Porter. As of today she'll be joining us as a new attorney. She is going to be an outstanding addition, and I trust that you'll all help make her feel as welcome as I know she is. Nelle Porter.

NELLE

Thank you. Thank you. It's a tough decision to change jobs, but I'm excited. I'm grateful to Richard and to Paul for the offer and also Ally . . . my brief chat with her . . . well, I knew coming here it would be fun.

6

COULDN'T LIGHT a cigarette fast enough. In fact, even though I was scared that someone would catch me, I greedily inhaled a lungful of smoke before my car had driven off the lot. My first day had definitely been challenging, and not having a hiding place in which to smoke made it even worse. I hadn't eaten all day either. But my need for food wasn't from hunger as much as it was the need to fill a hole in my gut. Since I didn't have to go to work the next couple of days, my brother Michael and I decided to meet at our favorite restaurant to celebrate my first day. When my husband left me, my brother moved in to my place. I loved that he lived with me. The living arrangement was to keep both of us company after my husband ran off with his wife. My husband ran off with his wife, so we kept each other company and we liked to go out for margaritas and Mexican food to commiserate. Or to celebrate. And after the day I'd had, I wasn't sure which of those things I would be doing tonight. Naturally, he'd think we were celebrating and I wouldn't let him think otherwise. He already thought I was a bit of a drama queen as it was.

"How did it go, Sissy?" He called me Sissy when he was happy to see me and the feeling was reciprocated. If I'd had a cute way of turning "brother" into something to express my love, I would've done it then, too. I just called him "brother." Since moving to LA, he'd had to deal with a lot. He had married his longtime girlfriend, Renee, just before leaving Australia and the two newlyweds moved into an apartment in the same *Melrose Place*-style complex that was home to me and Mel. In the evenings, the four of us were inseparable, but during the day, when my brother and I were at work, Renee and Mel formed partnerships. They were professional partners in my husband's cappuccino business and in his carpentry business. The fact that Renee would wear skimpy, lacy underwear clearly visible underneath her oversized, gaping overalls should have indicated to my brother and me that a personal partnership was also forming, but when Mel left me and Renee suddenly sabotaged her marriage to my brother to be with Mel, Brother and I were left idiotically scratching our heads in disbelief.

My brother's first year in Los Angeles was tough. Apart from his wife falling in love with my husband, he had a great deal of drama in his new job as a manager of a biomedical engineering company. We had both come to the United States to pursue our dreams of a bigger, more challenging life. Either that or we were both really influenced by our father's love of America after he came back from a business trip with stories of wide freeways and snowy mountains, fancy cars and Disneyland. In any case, the fact we both ended up here together was a blessing.

"It was great, Brother. The scene went well, the place is great, and the people are really nice."

"That's great. Table for two on the patio, please."

"Certainly, sir, right this way."

The Mexican restaurant was a dark, seedy place with greasy food and an outdoor patio where I could smoke. I started smoking when I was fourteen for two very good reasons: to win over the cool girl at school with the shaved head and to suppress my appetite—a tip taught to me by my modeling colleagues. While I never really became friends with the cool girl, I did learn that the more I smoked, the less I'd eat, which is particularly important when you sit down to dinner at a Mexican restaurant. So despite its average food, the fact that this restaurant was the closest one to our house with an outdoor patio made it my favorite.

As I smoked and talked and allowed the tension of my day to melt into my margarita, I made the decision to eat nachos. The blend of cheese and sour cream with the crispiness of the corn chips and creaminess of guacamole will always turn a sour mood into a happy one. A peace came over me when I ate food like that. Like life had no other purpose than pure enjoyment. I had nowhere to go and nothing to accomplish. For that moment, I could put life on hold and believe I was perfect the way I was. I was focused in the present—in the moment—and the moment was bliss on a corn chip.

I hadn't eaten any bad food since the day at Banana Republic when I decided to get professional, and I really felt like I needed to reward myself for all the hard work that went into getting into that size 6 suit. Besides, I'd made too much of a big deal out of it, anyway. The suits were very conservative and would easily hide a pound or two. I didn't need to be rail thin to wear them. So I didn't feel bad when I ordered an additional meal of enchiladas. I simply wouldn't eat the following day.

"So that idiot in lab went over my head today and told Chris . . ." As he talked about his lab geeks and his psychotic boss, I wondered how he'd take the news that I was gay. I hadn't told him yet because it was too soon after my marriage to Mel and I was afraid he wouldn't believe me. Of the few people I'd told, most didn't believe me for some reason. Some thought it was a phase, some thought I was just saying it to be different, to get attention. It's a particularly bad reaction because sharing that deep secret with someone takes a lot of courage, and disbelief feels like ridicule. Like two little girls together is something silly not to be taken seriously. I simply couldn't risk my brother reacting that way. He was all I had.

I kept ordering margaritas and eating enchiladas, and when I was done with mine, I got to work on his. After the main course was over, I went back to the appetizers we'd been served at the beginning of the evening and ate the last of the corn chips with the puddle of salsa that was left in the stone bowl. I was amused at the thought that an appetizer was supposed to stimulate appetite and I silently congratulated ours for doing its job.

As my brother and I finished up our conversation, our watered-down drinks, the last drag of a cigarette, I knew I'd done some damage. There was a dull ache in my gut and a layer of fat on the roof of my mouth that proved it. It's a weird sensation knowing that you've just altered your course. In a fleeting moment of arrogance, in one self-congratulatory thought, I decided I was good enough, that I could stop right there. My quest for perfection, for discipline, for greatness, was over. I'd reached my goal. I had nothing more to do. I'd completed one day of work, worn the suit with the character in it, and done a good job, and that was enough. As I got up from the table, I looked down at the wreckage. I saw the ugly plastic checkered tablecloth and the flimsy utensils for the first time that night. I saw the cigarette ash on the table, pools of water dripped from the glasses that were cloudy with greasy fingers, lipstick-tipped butts in an overflowing ashtray that wasn't clean to begin with. And then there was the food. Food looks so ugly when it's half-eaten and torn apart. The refried beans smeared on the plate looked like feces, and the browning guacamole and clumps of rice looked like vomit. What disgusted me the most in this grotesque tableau was that the cheese from the enchiladas had a wide greasy ring around it that separated it from the plate. Like a beach separated land from the ocean. I had ingested a beach of grease. I grabbed my keys from underneath a few grains of rice that had spilled over the edge of my plate during this mindless, repetitious act of filling my mouth with food and headed out to the car.

There's a big difference between eating and what I had just done. What I'd done was an act of defiance.

I pulled away from the curb and lined up behind my brother's car that was barely visible through the curtain of exhaust smoke that separated us. The bright red stoplight reflected off the black road and as I sat there on the cold leather seat, I wondered who I was being defiant toward. *You're only hurting yourself,* was the phrase I kept thinking, and while I knew that was true, why did my bingeing feel like someone else was going to be pissed off and hurting, too? Was anyone else really invested in my weight and how I treated my body? All I thought about when I continued to eat after the initial rush of the food wore off, after the taste became familiar, and after my stomach was full was *HA HA! You can't stop me!* But who was I saying that to? As I drove down the road toward home, now separated from my brother by several cars and a lane or two, I wondered if my little act of rebellion was over for now or if it would continue with a stop at 7-Eleven.

I stopped at 7-Eleven on the way home for food. I barely felt any anxiety as I pulled into the parking lot because I think I'd subconsciously planned this stop from my first bite of nachos. As I'd already blown the diet, I figured I might as well keep going—I might as well eat all the things I'd denied myself for the last few weeks. And I had to get it all done in one sitting because if I allowed myself to do this again—to eat all this food—I'd get fat. If this reckless eating continued into the following day, I'd get fat and I'd end up in TV purgatory, kept on the show due to an unbreakable contract, yet disappearing, making only the occasional background cross as my character's life with all the promise of great story lines faded into the blank page from whence it came. Of course, I'd have to throw up after, but that was okay. I would've had to throw up anyway just from the Mexican food. I didn't have work for the next two days so I had time to get rid of the dots above my eyes that were caused by my blood vessels bursting from all the pressure and strain of purging. With that much pressure, something had to burst.

I could either force myself to throw up the food or gain weight from it. Of the two options, I figured that it was better concealing a few red dots on my eyelids than showing up to my second day of work two pounds heavier with my skirt stretching across my thighs. And if I had to throw up anyway, I might as well eat all I could. I might as well eat everything.

Throwing up was something I had taught myself as a child. I learned from the more experienced models I worked with that it was something you could do if you had to eat in front of people, including the clients that book you. Apparently, it was more desirable to look as though your body was naturally stick thin than trying hard to get it that way, so models ate pizza before a fashion show, then threw it up quietly before showtime. That would take a lot of practice, since you'd have to be neat and clean about it. No matter how much I practiced, I was never good at it. Apart from the red dots above my eyes, my eyes and nose watered badly from the heaving efforts. Plus I was so loud. The gagging sounded like really loud coughing and would serve as an alarm to let everyone in the public restroom know what I was doing.

Unlike the other girls, I didn't throw up because I had to eat to impress the client but because I wanted to eat. Nothing was better after a modeling job than food. It was the only thing that took all the bad feelings away. Like an eraser, it allowed me start over, to forget the feelings of insecurity and awkwardness I'd experienced that day. But the comforting ritual of rewarding myself with food started to back-fire as the jobs started being booked back to back. Instead of having a week of starving to counteract the weight gained from eating fries, ice cream, and candy, I was given a day or two to get back on track, to be the 34–24–35 model that they'd booked off my card. The client was expecting an image of me that wasn't who I really was. They wanted a self-confident young woman who was naturally thin, beautiful, com-fortable in her skin. Who I really was, was an average-looking child staving off puberty with its acne and weight gain just waiting to expose me for the phony I was. So I'd throw up.

After my first day of *Ally*, I needed to start over. I needed to forget the insecurity and awkwardness I felt standing on that staircase, pre-tending to be the fabulous Nelle Porter. Just hearing the words "outstanding addition" gave me a hole in my stomach that no amount of food seemed to fill.

Go on, eat it, you fat piece of shit. You're pathetic. You can't even handle one day of work without bingeing. You have no self-control. You don't deserve this job.

Driving home from 7-Eleven with a bag full of food, I hated that my brother lived with me. Now I had to eat in the car a block from my house and throw up in the street so he wouldn't know what I was doing. And I had to do it fast because he'd wonder where I was. I started by eating a large bag of Cheetos. The bright orange color would serve as a marker during the purge. It would be a map, almost, telling me how far I'd come and how much further I needed to go. When I saw orange vomit cascading from my mouth and flowing in chunks between the two rigid fingers jammed against my gag reflex, I'd know I'd passed 7-Eleven and then I'd make my way back to the restaurant and back through each course beginning with the corn chips, the enchiladas, and ending with the nachos. As I shoved the jelly doughnut into my mouth, I came up with my lie. Mom called and my cell service was beginning to drop out so I had to pull over to complete the call. That would do. I barely swallowed my last item, the Snickers bar, before I began regurgitating it. I shoved my fingers down my throat and threw up in the plastic bag five times before I was satisfied that I'd gotten most of the food out. I took off my T-shirt from underneath my sweater and wiped my face and hands on it. I found a trash can. I drove home.

As I walked in the front door, I saw my brother on the couch with the phone to his ear.

"Where the hell have you been? Mom's on the phone."

He handed the phone to me.

"Hi, darl! How did it go?" My mother was more excited than I'd ever heard her. I knew that she'd been thinking about me the whole day, just waiting to hear news of the cast, the set, and my new life as a star of a hit TV show.

I took a deep breath. I mentally selected the appropriate pitch to my voice.

"It was really great, Ma. I had the greatest day."

It was a lie, but it should've been the truth. It would've been the truth if not for my debilitating insecurity, and I was certain that insecurity would fade with time once I had proven to myself that I deserved the job. In time, I was sure that I would be happy. After all, anyone else would've been. Most people would kill to have the opportunity that was given to me. How could I possibly complain to anyone that I didn't like it, that loads of money and fame, the most desired things in society, made me feel uncomfortable? While I waited for my genuine enjoyment of it to set in, I would simply lie about how much fun I was having. Complaining to my mom would have just been immature and embarrassing. In fact, anything short of perpetual joy seemed pathetic.

I'd pretended to enjoy modeling also, so I'd had practice in pretending. It was my goal to be known as a model because I wanted to be the envy of my seventh-grade peers and be thought of as beautiful and worldly. But being called a model and actually having to model were two different things entirely and caused me to experience very different feelings. At the very beginning of my modeling career, I needed test shots by a well-known photographer whom my new agents had chosen for me, and filling a modeling portfolio cost money that we didn't really have. I was told that I was lucky that I had caught the photographer's eye and should jump at the chance to have my pictures taken by him. His fee was a whopping $1,400 for three different looks. Prints would cost extra. So I struck a deal with my mother. If she bankrolled my test shots and drove me to Melbourne, I'd pay her back all the start-up money with my earnings from my first few jobs. She agreed, and my modeling career began.

In preparation for the test shots, my mother had rolled my hair in rag curls the night before, and the lumpy twisted rags felt like steel rods between the pillow and my head and made it impossible to sleep. This method of curling the hair was really unpredictable because often one section refused to curl at all and so the "naturally curly, I can't help it, I just woke up this way" look became the "I hate my straight, limp hair and so does my mother, who spent all night curling it in rags" look. On top of that, the rags had stray threads of cotton that would snag in my hair, and prying them out gave other sections an Afro-like frizz. I knew I had done the wrong thing by curling my hair the minute I walked in the door. The hairstylist grabbed my hairsprayed ringlets and proceeded to lecture me on how I should go to every job with clean, unstyled hair. As a twelve-year-old it never occurred to me I may have insulted him by doing my own hair. I was just avoiding what I thought would be an instant cancelation of the shoot if the photographer saw that I had just ordinary, limp, straight hair and, as a consequence, wasn't worthy of his time. I felt like I'd bullshitted my way into making the modeling agency take me in the first place and that my hair was going to expose me for the fake I really was. Luckily, my hair and makeup were done before the photographer arrived, so my real identity, with my ugly hair and my red, blotchy skin, remained undiscovered.

The photographer was a sluggish, heavy-set man whose droopy eyes accidentally registered me as he was glancing around the studio looking for something of interest—like a light or an assistant. After several hours of ordering and eating lunch, tweaking lights, and touching up my makeup, I began the actual modeling part of the photo shoot tired and wilted, and spent several more hours in that sweltering hot studio shooting the three different looks. For $1,400 I got a close-up wearing a jean jacket and a beret, a ridiculous jumping-up-and-down photo on a mini trampoline wearing a Mickey Mouse T-shirt, and a more grown-up look in a skintight black dress with a black plastic trash bag on my head scrunched into an abstract shape. The latter, I was told, was high-fashion, avant-garde.

Although the photos turned out to be something that I showed anyone who cared to look at them, the experience of taking them was horrible. No matter which pose I struck for him, he had a correction, each more embarrassing to me than the last. "Don't jut your hip out like that, stand normally. Chin down, relax your mouth, open your eyes." He yelled his orders at me all day, demanding that I change what I was doing, chipping away at my joy and confidence with each command. By the end of the shoot, I had stopped attempting to inject my personality into the pictures. Instead I was like a scared puppy that sees its master and automatically rolls over because it knows that's the one thing it can do to avoid a beating. I left the shoot feeling tired, anxious, and insecure, but because my mother had paid for it and taken another day off work to act as my chauffeur/chaperone, I felt I couldn't tell her the truth of how the photo shoot made me feel. So I lied and told her that I was excited about my new career.

On the way back to Geelong from the big city, we stopped at McDonald's. I held her hand as we stood in the "order here" line among other twelve-year-olds and their mothers. I stuffed myself with cheeseburgers, French fries, and a vanilla milk shake. And for the first time since the start of my career as a model, I was happy. Stopping at McDonald's became a ritual for my mother and me after a go-see or a modeling job. It was a midway point between the big city and the smaller bay city where I lived, and it became the midway point between the person I was and the person I was pretending to be. I sat down to eat as a child, but talked about my exciting day at work like an adult. For that one moment, I let it all go and my mother watched me without judgment or concern. I'd passed the test, and food was my reward. I'd pretended to be an adult, and going back to who I really was, a child excited to be at McDonald's, was my prize for being such a good pretender.

The only problem was that I couldn't stop rewarding myself. Returning to regular school life, I started to gain a little weight. I don't know why exactly, but I just couldn't stop eating. After my first photo shoot, eating seemed to be a huge comfort to me, and so every day after school, my friend Fiona and I would walk to the local supermarket to buy potato chips and candy. I knew I shouldn't be doing it, I knew I should be working out and trying to stay skinny for a potential modeling job that could happen at any moment, but eating just felt so good. My friend was a year older than me, and she told me that when I got to thirteen, my body would start changing, that I would hit puberty and get my period and get fat. Because she was older and knew more than I did, and because she had definitely gotten fatter since turning thirteen, I had no reason to doubt her, and so the inevitability of my weight gain made me think depriving myself of eating candy was futile. If it was going to happen anyway, I might as well make myself feel less anxious about it by soothing my nerves with a bag of potato chips. But I knew it was wrong. I knew my mother couldn't see me doing it. She'd just lent me thousands of dollars to get my modeling portfolio with the proviso that I would model my way out of debt. No one would hire me in this condition. I weighed 120 pounds!

After four long weeks, I received a call from the Modeling World. My agency was hosting a runway show in Melbourne with a local designer so they both could show off their wares to the fashion industry. They asked me to walk in the show, which would take place in a nightclub, and the event was only five days away. I felt no excitement, just panic. I dreaded the fashion show and I hated myself for getting so fat. I was nervous about being on a catwalk in front of the fashion industry anyway, much less modeling clothes that might show them all the reasons not to hire me—my big hips, my bulky calves, my fat stomach. To be perfectly honest, after my experience with the test shots, I would've been happy if I'd never gotten hired to model. I had the glamorous pictures to prove that I was pretty, and a story to tell of what it was like to be a model while never having to admit how terribly insecure modeling made me feel. Proving that I could do it if I wanted to but not actually having to keep proving it over and over again would've been perfect.

The only thing between me and this plan was my ego with its inflexible stance on failure. The embarrassment of failure was too much for me to bear. I'd already told everyone that I was a model, I'd convinced an agency that I had what it took to be a success, and, of course, I couldn't disappoint my mother. The only thing standing in the way of devastating embarrassment and success and admiration was a Cadbury Caramello Bar. There was no other option but to starve myself for the five days and hope that I could at least lose the five additional pounds I'd gained in the last two weeks.

Not eating is pretty easy when you have a gun to your head. I just needed those five pounds off for the fashion show, and then after that I'd eat salads and I'd never again eat junk food. After this stupid, extreme diet, I was going to work out every day and never have to starve myself again to get ready for a job. It was all about being ready, being prepared. As I had discovered, 90 percent of my nerves and feelings of insecurity came from being underprepared—whether I hadn't studied enough for a test or trained enough for ballet exam—most of my feelings of terror would go away when I felt I knew the answer to every conceivable question. Modeling would be no different. If the question was, "Will you look good in this tiny bathing suit at any angle?" then my answer would be, "Yes." It was that simple.

My mother, a dieter from way back, approved of this quick-fix plan not only to get me ready for the show but also to shut me up. Unfortunately, when I was nervous, I'd cry a lot. I'd wail and howl and stomp around the house moaning about how stupid I was and how I was doomed for a life of failure and mediocrity. My plan to starve myself, although not the healthiest plan, was a one-time Band-Aid that was better than the wailing, and so she reluctantly taught me a couple of her dieting tricks. Mostly they consisted of caffeinated beverages without milk, Ryvita crackers with beets and steamed vegetables. Oil, butter, dressings—everything that made food taste good—were out. Dry was in.

And so I embarked on my first diet, wanting desperately to succeed as a good dieter and to get this situation behind me.

Over the next five days, I consumed a total of 2,000 calories and had lost the five pounds. Thanks to my self-discipline and determination, I was a success. I felt like I could accomplish anything. I was proud of myself, and my mother was proud of me, too. We drove up to Melbourne for the fashion show with confidence and maybe even a little excitement. I was ready. I was twelve years old and about to start my career.

I arrived to pandemonium. Due to our hitting some traffic in the hour-long journey from Geelong and the fact that we were left alone to find our way to the backstage area, I was slightly late for the show.

"The girl that just walked in hasn't been through makeup and hair," yelled a man with a clipboard. I was yanked by the forearm from my mother and guided over to an empty stool. From that point on, I was a product on an assembly line. My head was doused with cold water and blown dry, the round brushes tearing at the knots in my hair while I was simultaneously poked in the face with a coarse brush that at certain angles felt like hundreds of fine dressmaking pins. Bright, ugly, unflattering colors were slapped on my face with the brushstrokes a house painter would use to apply primer. I sat in silence looking at my reflection as it became uglier, unable to even introduce myself because of the guilt I felt that my lateness had caused this panic. Nobody had asked me for my name anyway. There were models to the left and right of me in varying stages of completion, none of whom even glanced my way until the makeup artist exclaimed in a shrill voice, "What am I supposed to do with these eyebrows?" And that made the model next to me turn to look at them.

"Whoa. They're some crazy eyebrows!" the male model said to me in a big, stupid way that made me angry rather than ashamed.

"They're exactly like my father's eyebrows and he's dead." That shut him up. I started thinking about my dad and wondered how he would feel about me modeling. Although I felt really bad about using him to justify having big, bushy eyebrows, it wouldn't be the last time I did it to stop people from talking about them. Until I realized you could pluck them. Other than that one interaction with the model, I didn't actually talk to any of the other Team models until after the show when we were directed by the bookers to mingle with the crowd. As I was awkwardly standing alone at a high-top table trying to look sophisticated by sipping sparkling water, I overheard one of the girls say, "Apparently there's a girl here who's only twelve," and I blurted out in excitement, "That's me! I'm twelve!" as only a twelve-year-old could. After that, word spread and other models talked to me in the condescending way adults talk to children. I was hardly a child and they were only a few years older than me, so I didn't appreciate it. But the most upsetting thing about meeting them was that I realized how beautiful all of them were. Stripped of their crazy fashion show makeup I could see their big eyes, set far apart and cradled by their perfect cheekbones that the rest of their face hung from in perfect proportion. Their hair, thrown up messily yet beautifully in a hair tie, and their loose, easy clothes spoke of their attitude toward their beauty—it was effortless and unconscious. It didn't require their critical eye reflected in a mirror to craft it; it just was there. They were so much more beautiful than me that I was in awe of them. I felt so ashamed of the dress and heels I'd bought for the occasion, and so stupid to have reapplied makeup after removing the show makeup. But the thing that gave me the pit in my stomach was the fact that I knew I needed it. Underneath the caked-on foundation was red blotchy skin, and if I didn't wear eyeliner, my eyes looked too small for the roundness of my face. I was different from all those girls, and I had to be careful not to let anyone see it.

The show itself was pretty uneventful. I had to model only one unrevealing outfit—culottes and a T-shirt with built-in shoulder pads. I was sent down the runway with a male model who strutted around like he was line dancing, holding me by the wrist and twirling me around like I was a prize he'd won at the state fair. I felt stupid that I'd made such a big deal about the show. After I'd stood around practically in silence for over an hour, overhearing conversations that intimidated me because I couldn't understand what anyone was talking about, I was finally allowed to go home. I felt relieved that the night was over. I got into my mother's car, took my heels off, and curled my cold feet underneath me. I sat facing her as she drove, talking to her all the way like she was my best friend. I ate a whole bag of mint candies that my mother had put in the car for me as a reward for getting through my first fashion show and for successfully losing all that weight. I ate them greedily and steadily until there were none left. As we pulled into our driveway an hour later at midnight, exhausted and full of sugar, it crossed my mind that eating all those candies might have caused me to gain a pound. As I walked barefoot to the back door, my belly distended in my skintight dress, I devised a plan to stop the sugar from turning into fat. Tomorrow was sports practice at school, and I made a promise to run ten extra laps around the hockey field to make up for it. And that wasn't the only promise I made that night that I didn't keep. I promised myself I wouldn't binge again.

7

EY, PORTIA. How were your days off?" I walked into the wardrobe fitting room passing Jane Krakowski as she was leaving.

"Great, thanks." I was aware as I spoke that I hadn't talked in awhile. It felt unnatural and my voice sounded raspy and constricted with phlegm, the telltale sounds of a chain-smoker. I cleared my throat, embarrassed.

"See you in there." She said it in a way that sounded like we were both in trouble, like we were about to walk into a detention room at school. I couldn't help but smile when I saw Jane. Her facial expressions were infectious, like she was keeping a naughty secret that could crack her up at any moment. Apart from Jane, I hadn't really gotten a sense of the cast yet. They all seemed pretty quiet and professional, more like corporate businesspeople than the actors I had known in the past. The cast of my first movie, *Sirens*, interacted with each other in a much more playful manner than I'd observed with the cast of *Ally*. During *Sirens*, we'd eat lunch together and listen to Hugh Grant's hilarious stories or Sam Neil's dry explanation of what it was like to be a supporting actor to a dinosaur in *Jurassic Park*. But maybe I would eat lunch with them today and hear their stories. Maybe I'd even tell them some of Hugh's stories. They were much funnier than mine.

As I said my hellos to the folks in the fitting rooms, it occurred to me that in a great ironic twist, I could possibly be perceived by the cast as a threat. Any new cast member threatens to take away airtime from the ensemble cast members, their story lines and attention. No television actor really embraces the idea of a new cast member, with perhaps the exception of the overworked titular character. I didn't feel as though the cast was threatened by me, however. I felt that they were threatened by the change that my presence signified, that it prompted them to ask themselves, "If this could happen, then what's next?" While everyone was very pleasant to me, I got the sense that they were all just wondering why I was there. They were celebrities on a hit television show, and I'd only had small parts in three movies and two very short-lived sitcoms to my credit. I guess we were all wondering why I was there.

I was in the wardrobe rooms to check-fit my outfit for Day Two. I was nervous to try on the size 6 suit the tailor had taken in after my first fitting three days prior. After bingeing and purging I feared that I'd gained weight. I always tended to gain a pound after a binge and purge even if it was just bloat. I struggled to zip up the skirt in front of the costume designer, her assistant, and the tailor, who all witnessed the effort.

"It fits," I said to the crowd, as I stood straight with my legs pressed together, careful not to show them that it would likely bunch up at the slightest movement. Even though I had to wear the skirt for the last scene that day, I was too ashamed to admit that it was too tight.

"Is it comfortable?" the costume designer, Vera, asked, squinting as if seeing better would help her sense my discomfort.

"Yeah. It should be fine."

"I think I take in too much," the tailor told Vera in a thick, unrecognizable accent. "I take out a little."

I didn't say anything. I just took off the skirt and handed it to the tailor, allowing her to believe that it was her fault that the skirt didn't fit. I slipped into my new beige Banana Republic pants, walked outside, and headed into makeup, all the while fighting the desperate urge for a cigarette.

. . .

"Hi, Portia. How were your days off?" Peter MacNicol was sitting in the makeup chair next to the empty chair that was waiting for me. He looked tired and I could tell that he was slightly envious that I'd had days off when he was working twelve-hour days all week.

"Great, thanks." It occurred to me that the more important the character, the fewer the days off. I hoped I would never be asked that question again.

I stared into the mirror at the red dots on my eyelids. Despite my efforts to conceal them, they were so pronounced I could see them clearly in the mirror from several feet away. To my amazement, my makeup artist didn't comment. It was almost worse that she didn't, as it suggested to me that maybe she knew how I got them and didn't need to ask. She began my makeup by thickly applying foundation with a wide, flat brush. After several minutes of silence, Peter got up from the chair next to mine.

"See you in there."

The makeup trailer wobbled as he walked down the steps.

"Yeah. See you in there."

"Cut!" the director yelled loudly to the cameraman and the actors, which was then echoed by several ADs stationed all over the set. I heard the word *cut* about ten times after each take to release the background or let the people who were at craft service go back to making noise as they fixed themselves coffee or a snack. We were all waiting this time, however, for the first AD to ask the cameraman to check the gate, which meant that the cast and crew could break for lunch. The scene was a "walk and talk" that took place in the hallway next to the courtroom. It was a short scene where I met up with Ally and asked her to have drinks with me at bar at the end of the day, explaining, "I would like to talk to a woman's woman" before making a decision to join the law firm of Cage and Fish. I did well, even though it made me nervous as it reminded me of a scene I did in the movie *Scream 2*, in which my character, a nasty sorority girl, walked up to the entire assembly of the movie's stars, and for some reason, had to say, "In a six degrees of Kevin Bacon sort of way." I kept screwing it up. Take after take I would wrongly say, "In a six degrees of separation sort of way." I was panic-stricken before each take and the panic made my head spin with fear and my mind go blank. I literally saw white light as I incorrectly repeated the same line over and over again. In this scene where I bullied Ally into meeting me for a drink, despite my urge to say, "I'd like to talk to a woman first," I got the line out without any cause for panic. I was very nervous, though, as I was lauding it over Ally, intimidating her. In between takes I felt just as nervous, feeling as though I should fill in the silence with small talk, even though no one was really doing much talking. I, like the crew, was breathlessly waiting to be released for lunch, only I didn't need to eat. I just needed to be released from the stress of being looked at, being judged. Was I good enough?

"Check the gate."

The cameraman shone a penlight into the camera to check for dust on the film. "Clear."

"Gate's good. That's lunch. One hour."

I walked from the set to the dressing rooms with Calista and Peter.

"Where do you guys normally eat lunch?" The minute I said it, I felt stupid, and like a nerdy schoolgirl who was attempting to force an invitation to be part of the cool kids' group. There was a slight gap between my asking and their answering that reinforced my feeling of stupidity.

"I tend to nap during lunch." Peter spoke sweetly but in a way that informed me that there would never be an exception to this routine.

"I have a phone interview." Calista made a slight face that suggested that in another time before she became the poster child for America's changing views on skirt length and feminism, she would've gladly swapped stories over lunch with another actor. The face she made was enough to make me think she really did wish things were different. I knew in that second that I liked her. But I also knew that I would never really get to know her.

"How are you liking it so far?" She looked directly into my eyes.

I inhaled and nodded my head up and down a few times. I wanted to tell her that it felt strange, that I felt out of place, that I was scared of not delivering. I wanted to tell her that I felt pressure to look good, to be fashionable, to be someone other than who I was. I wanted to say that I felt isolated and that maybe I kind of hated the show. But I didn't. In the four years of working on that show I never did say any of that to her.

"I love it."

"Great! See you back in there."

As I walked through the door with my name on it and into my dressing room, I heard my name being called from the hallway. It was Courtney Thorne-Smith in sweatpants walking toward the makeup trailer.

"You break for lunch?"

"Yeah. What are you up to?" Maybe I could have lunch with Courtney. I hadn't had any real scenes with her yet and I wanted to get to know her. I used to watch *Melrose Place*.

"That's weird. They just called me into makeup. Everyone's at lunch?"

"Yeah. You wanna grab lunch with me?"

She looked at me in a way that suggested that she felt sorry for me. I guess you could call it condescending, but there was a glint in her eye that told me that she too thought what she was about to tell me was strange.

"We don't really eat lunch together here."

"Oh. Cool. Okay." I stared down at the carpet, embarrassed, as I began to close the dressing room door. "See you later, then."

I looked at my bag that was sitting on the new green chair opposite the full-length mirror. I had an hour. I grabbed my cigarettes, stuffed them underneath my shirt, and started walking out of the building. I walked away from the windowless monolithic peach rectangles that housed the stages and away from the offices, stacked one on top of the other, David Kelley's office sitting on top of them all. In the far corner of Manhattan Beach Studios, out of sight of anyone and in between the chain-link fence and the loading docks, I embarked on what would become my lunchtime ritual. I hid from the people who made me feel awkward, stupid, or like a schoolgirl. I hid from producers, directors, and people who evaluated me. I hid from the voice that became very loud in front of that full-length mirror in the dressing room that was supposed to make me feel comfortable. And I chain-smoked.

8

FELT NERVOUS. As I walked through the house with wet hair to make myself tea I heard the television broadcasting my thoughts. "What will she be wearing? Who will win for best comedy?" The Emmys was a thing that I'd only seen on TV; I'd never actually helped provide the content that made it a show. *Ally McBeal* was nominated, Calista and Jane were nominated, and I was a debutante about to be introduced for the first time to the public who could potentially love me or hate me. My brother, thinking he was being supportive, had turned on all the TVs in the house for the preshow. I knew at some point my nerves would get the better of me and I'd lose my nonchalant attitude toward it and would tell him to shut it off. But I was trying on a different personality, one that was excited to walk the red carpet and show people who I was because I thought I was perfectly fabulous. This personality was not a bit worried or nervous that I'd say something stupid or be wearing the wrong thing. As I made my tea and listened to what was left of the segment after the kettle had sputtered, boiled, and whistled, I was completely unaffected by the shrill voices of the entertainment news reporters and the judgment of fashion commentators. I liked this new personality. It was calming, mature, balanced. I wondered how long I could keep it.

I found that if I sat still for too long, my insecurity seized the opportunity to take control of my mind. Especially if the chair I was sitting on was positioned in front of a mirror. It's not that I hated the way I looked, it's just that I worried that I wouldn't look good enough. That I wouldn't be transformed from the girl who often forgot to shave her legs and rarely got a facial into Portia de Rossi, Hollywood actress and new cast member of the hottest show on television. In an attempt to avoid looking at my face as my hair was blown-dry, I looked down at the notes in my hands. My hands; my big, ugly, red hands that had only recently seen a manicure because that was what my cast mates did on weekends to ready themselves for the week ahead. I did whatever they did because they knew things I didn't. Although I hated going to a nail salon, I wasn't going to ignore the people around me who were more successful than me and who had figured all this out. I really hated my hands. My hands were manly. They belonged to a working-class boy who helped his dad around the farm. In my ugly hands were the pieces of paper that would act as my safety net, my little bit of reas-surance, proof that if I studied them, I could ace the ensuing exam on that bright red carpet. On sheets of lined, reinforced paper I'd written:

How did you get the role on *Ally McBeal*?

I met with David Kelley for a role on The Practice, *but he saw me more for* Ally, *and within a couple of weeks, I was sent a script that featured my character, and that became the first episode of the new season.*

Describe your character.

Nelle Porter is a very driven, ambitious woman who has sacrificed her private life for her career. She's seemingly ruthless and insensitive, but deep down she wants love and happiness like everyone else. She's so cold her nickname is "Sub-zero."

Were you a fan of the show?

Yes. I love the show and I'm so proud to be a part of it. It's like a dream come true.

What is everyone on the show like? Have they welcomed you to the cast?

The whole cast is great. Everyone is lovely and has been really friendly and welcoming toward me. I feel very lucky to be working with such a talented and nice group of people.

What is in store for Nelle Porter this season?

Well, you'll have to watch and see . . .

As I memorized my scripted responses to hypothetical questions in the kitchen chair that could barely fit in the bathroom of my one-bathroom house, I wondered if anyone else out there sitting in hair and makeup was doing this. Did any other actor rehearse "off the cuff" responses to red carpet questions? Did they rehearse their talk show stories as they sat in foils at the hairdresser's? When you're under spotlights and nervous, it has to help to have a script to fall back on. The fact that my character always knows what to say is one of the reasons I love acting. If I could be given a script to answer the hard questions seamlessly, I wouldn't be so nervous that I might say the wrong thing. Sitting in front of the mirror and learning my answers, a feeling of self-hatred and shame came over me as I remembered a conversation with Greg Germann a couple of weeks earlier. On set and in between takes, in an attempt to be friendly, Greg had asked me what he no doubt thought was a simple question, but it was a question that silenced me with fear.

"Do you have a boyfriend?"

When I froze and was unable to answer this seemingly easy question, Greg raised his eyebrows and in a joking, incredulous tone asked, "Are you gay?"

The question took me off guard. I wasn't prepared. If only I'd had a script of perfect witty responses, I could've flicked through the brilliantly written pages in my brain and found the right one. But without the script, all I could think to say was, "I don't know."

I hated seeing him at work after that. I worried about that conversation every day.

I arrived at the Shrine Auditorium alone after getting into the car an hour earlier and chain-smoking the entire way. The last twenty minutes had been spent circling the venue, waiting in line as the celebrities, in order of importance, were given the drop-off spots closest to the red carpet. My driver told me all of this as we were waiting, which suggested to me that despite my silver dress and diamonds dripping from my neck and ears, he instinctively knew I was a nobody, even though my clothes suggested otherwise.

When I eventually got out of the car at the mouth of the red carpet, I felt assaulted by the heat. For the first time, it occurred to me that it was the middle of the day, the hottest part of the day, and all these people were in gowns and diamonds pretending it was evening. It looked ridiculous to see a sea of sequins and tulle and satin at 3:30 in the afternoon on a hot summer day. Of course, it was just another costume, and these were actors. The red carpet was full of people. There were hundreds of people all jammed on a carpet, some trying to hurry through to the entrance of the Shrine, some lingering, trying to be noticed by photographers. And then there were the publicists, the people in drab black "stagehand" outfits swimming upstream to grab a client by the hand and hurl him or her in front of the firing squad, the section at the beginning of the carpet with photographers, all screaming and sweating, in rows ten deep. The noise coming from this section was aggressive, and it came in surges depending on who walked near them. The photographers yelled the name of the actor to get her attention and then a few minutes later the fans in the bleachers did the same. There was definitely a lot of yelling and sweating, posing and cheering for such a glamorous and important event. I didn't know why, but it seemed different on TV. It seemed like the actors simply walked to the entrance and happened to be shot by photographers, quietly and respectfully as they breezed past. The fans, in my fantasy, would fall silent as the celebrities passed by, awed by their proximity to these precious creatures, like people do at the railing of a zoo enclosure. This seemed more like a sports event.

The Fox publicist found me patiently waiting at the start of the carpet after beads of sweat had formed all over my face and body. This was my introduction. This was my turning point. After today, everyone would know who I was and have an opinion about everything I did. And with my hair in ringlets and my individual eyelashes glued onto the corners of my eyes, scripted answers and a silver Calvin Klein dress, I was ready to face the firing squad. She took me to the start of the photographers' section of the carpet. As I'd just watched several women get their picture taken, I wasn't terribly nervous. I knew I'd stand in four different spots as the photographers yelled out my name and jostled for the best picture. I approached the line of fire as the publicist stated my name and place of business. "Portia de Rossi—*Ally McBeal.*" As I stood there, smiling, hip jutting out in a casual but elegant pose, I was alarmed by the silence. Not one of these people with machines for faces had called my name or asked me to spin around. No one was asking me who I was wearing. I instantly felt like this unenthusiastic response was my fault, like I should do something to make the picture better, more interesting. I felt sorry for these people whose bosses expected something more than just a girl in a silver dress. They expected a star with personality. They wanted to see the reason for adding a cast member to an already successful show. At the end of the stills photography section I saw a news crew whose reporter was handing out plastic fans. In a desperate attempt to justify the photographers' time, the jewelry designer's generosity, the publicist's uphill battle to get me noticed after swimming upstream to come fetch me, and to not make David Kelley look like he made a mistake by casting an ordinary girl with no personality, I grabbed a fan and dramatically posed with it high in the air—like Marilyn Monroe with her dress blowing up, but different. The photographers liked it. They were taking pictures. Some of them were even yelling, "Over here!" so I'd turn more toward them while holding the pose.

I was officially a hypocrite. I wanted to blend in and disappear yet be noticed doing it.

Before I knew it, I was answering questions into a microphone.

"What is the one beauty item you can't live without?"

Shit. I didn't know the answer to that one. I mean, "concealer" was the truthful answer, but what was the right answer?

"Lip gloss."

I hate lip gloss. I hate anything on my lips, but it sounded right. It sounded pretty and feminine and like something boys would find attractive; big, goopy lips, moist and inviting. Next . . .

"What is your must-have fashion item for the season?"

Shit. I didn't know fashion at all. I didn't read magazines and I wasn't really interested. I wished Kali were there; she would've known the answer to that question. In fact, a few months ago she'd wanted Chanel ballet flats . . .

"Chanel ballet flats."

My answer took a little long in coming, and the interviewer could sense it wasn't going to get any easier, so I was dismissed from the interview with a "Thanks for stopping to talk to us." I was surprised by the questions I was asked. Most of the interviewers didn't care about my character or the show. All anyone wanted to know was who I was wearing and what my beauty tips were and how I stayed in shape. As I walked away from the news crews, I heard the last reporter ask my publicist, "What's her name?" The reporter didn't discreetly whisper the question to my publicist in an attempt to save me from having hurt feelings, she yelled it. She had just been interviewing me like I was important enough to tell the public my thoughts about the increasing number of actresses who wore their hair down to the Emmys and yet she had no idea who I was. The answer came over raucous screams

announcing Lara Flynn Boyle's arrival so she asked again as if she wondered if she'd heard correctly. "*What's* her name?"

I was embarrassed and a little afraid. I was often embarrassed to
tell people my name because I had made it up. I had a deep fear of
someone discovering the truth, that this exotic name wasn't mine—that
I'd borrowed it like I had borrowed the dress and the diamonds, that it
was a little too fabulous for me to own and at some point I was going
to have to give it back. Portia de Rossi. A fabulous name. A name that
belonged to a celebrity.

I made it up when I was fifteen. I was illegally in a nightclub when
the club's manager took me into his VIP room to award me with a
coveted all-access, never-wait-in-line medallion. I knew I couldn't give
him my real identity for fear that he would discover my age and never
again allow me back in the club. I was flustered coming up with a name
on the spot, but I knew I had to do it. Not only was he offering me
a key chain medallion to flaunt, a sliver tag announcing to the world
that I was in with the "in-crowd," he was offering me a job. I could be a
hostess for the club, and all I had to do was show up twice a week. All
that—if I could come up with a name other than Amanda Rogers, the
name that belonged to the fifteen-year-old kid that stood before them.
I could be a VIP if I could come up with the right name.

I hated my birth name. Amanda Rogers. It was so ordinary, so perfectly average. It had "a man" in it, which annoyed me because every
time I'd hear someone refer to a man, I would turn my head, waiting
for the "duh." I'd toyed with changing it the way most kids do. When I
became a model, my modeling agents suggested I change it, as reinvent-
ing oneself was pretty common practice in the modeling world in the
eighties. Sophie became Tobsha, and Angelique became Rochelle. What
Amanda could become was something I was still fantasizing about until
I heard one manager in the VIP lair say to another, "What's her name?"
as he hovered over a book of entries with a black fountain pen.

"Portia . . . de . . . Rossi." The words came out slowly but with certainty. I really wanted that medallion.

"How do you spell that?"

I wrote the name in the air with my index finger behind my back to see whether a small *d* or a big *D* would look better. I got Portia from *The Merchant of Venice,* and de Rossi from watching the credits of a movie. The last name stuck in my mind among a million names that flew by. In a sea of a million unimportant names, I saw de Rossi. I put it all together in that room, got my medallion, a job, and walked out in shock. I had changed my identity. Just like that.

As I walked into the Shrine Auditorium where the Emmys were about to take place, I freaked out about how caught off-guard I'd been, how unprepared I was for the biggest test of my life—the test that required me to show them all why I was special and chosen. I made a mental note to buy fashion magazines and start caring about beauty items and perfume and exercising. I needed to find answers to these questions if I were going to feel confident next time. It was time Portia de Rossi earned her name.

9

A S I drove to work, my thoughts kept returning to my wardrobe. For Day One of the scripted days in this episode, I wore the black pencil skirt and long jacket. That would be okay because the waistband on the skirt was a little roomy, unlike the jeans I was currently wearing, which were cutting into my flesh and making my stomach fold over the top of them. I took my right hand off the steering wheel and grabbed my stomach fat—first just under the belly button and then I worked my way over the sides in repetitive grabbing motions. For fun I did it in time with the music. In a way it felt like a workout or a kind of dance of self-hatred. The fat extended all the way around to my back—not enough for a handful, but enough to take a firm hold of between my thumb and forefinger. As I looked down at my cavernous belly button I couldn't help but wonder if I was getting away with it. Did I still look like the girl they had hired? Did people notice? Obviously, my costume designer was aware of my weight gain over my first month on the show as she watched the weekly struggle of trying to pull up a skirt over my hips or straining to clasp the waistband. If pretending not to notice is the kind thing to do, then she was very kind to me. She always blamed the zipper for getting stuck because it was cheap or not properly sewn into the item of clothing even if she had to call her assistant in to hold the top of the zip as she put some muscle into trying to move it.

Did people look at me and think, "She's let herself go?" Did my actress rivals look at me and smirk, satisfied that my weight gain rendered me powerless to steal roles, scenes, or lines? As I pulled into my parking space, I couldn't help but wonder if maybe it was not just increasing familiarity but my nonthreatening physique that was the reason everyone had seemed a lot more comfortable around me lately. My presence no longer prompted them to ask themselves, "If this happened, then what's next?" as another actress, Lucy Liu, had joined the cast and answered that question. I was no longer the new girl, and I had proven to them that I wasn't a threat to their status on the show. With the weight gain, I wasn't exactly the hot blond bombshell that Cage and Fish talked about almost daily in their dialogue to each other. I cringed to read their lines and how they would talk about my character as being "hot" and "untouchable." While I wanted to be considered attractive, it made me uncomfortable to be thought of as being sexually desirable to men. But mainly the dialogue made me uncomfortable because I knew that reality didn't match up to the character David Kelley had written.

"Hey, Porshe. Haven't seen you in awhile. How were your days off?" Jane passed me in the hall on her way to set.

"Great, thanks."

"See you out there."

I walked into my dressing room and threw my bag down on the sofa.

There was a sharp knock on my dressing room door.

"Good morning, Portia. Makeup is ready for you."

"Be right there."

I walked around the desk to look in the mirror. The fat that I'd felt on my way there didn't really show under my sweater. At least not when I was standing. I lifted my sweater so I could see my bare stomach and the fat that I remembered feeling. But I didn't see fat. My stomach was flat. I stared into the eyes reflected in the mirror. They were smiling at me as if to say, "Oh, Porshe, what the hell are you worried about?"

For a brief moment, I felt relief. But it didn't last long. As I opened the wardrobe and looked at its contents, a wave of panic passed through my body; a hot, rolling rush of panic beginning in my stomach and ending at my head. Hanging on the bar were ten, maybe fifteen, sets of bras and panties. They were the kind of bras and panties that are intended to be seen, not the plainer flesh-toned kind that I was used to finding on the rack. Attached to the first pair was a note:

"For next episode. Please try on at your convenience. Thanks, V."

Shit. Shit! The next episode was eight days away. There was a knock at the door. I jumped out of my skin.

"Portia. Can you go to makeup, please? We're going to get to your scene in less than an hour."

"Alright! I'm coming!" As usual, the people who deserved it the least get the brunt of my anger. The person who deserved my anger the most was my fat, lazy, self. I had been in complete denial. I'd decided that rather than get off my fat, lazy ass and accept responsibility for my job, rather than seizing this amazing opportunity and using every scene as a showcase for my talent, I'd just sit around drinking beer and eating Mexican food. I stormed out of my dressing room and walked toward the makeup trailer, the voice in my head berating me.

You can't eat again until that scene. You need to work out. You're such an idiot for thinking you could get away with bingeing on Mexican food and not working out when this kind of thing could've happened at any time.

For a brief moment, I was aware that Peter MacNicol had passed me in the hallway. I'm sure he said hello, but it was too late to reply. The underwear scene probably had something to do with him. Our romance had been heating up and I bet there was some kind of love scene in the next episode. Maybe that's all it was. Maybe it would be a shot of me lying down on a bed in my underwear, or a waist-high shot of me unbuttoning a shirt to expose the top part of one of those pretty, lacy brassieres hanging in my closet.

"Hey!" My makeup artist gave me a hug and with a guttural laugh she said, "Did you read the next episode? You're doing a striptease, girl!"

I pulled the script from her hands and with a cold, emotionless expression I looked at what she'd been reading. I didn't want to give her any more enjoyment at my discomfort than she was already having. Of course, I didn't know if enjoyment was what she was experiencing for sure, but given the way we talked about our weight struggles almost every day, I couldn't imagine that she wasn't enjoying my discomfort a little, if just in that way that people are grateful they aren't dealt the same fate. The "better you than me" comment that is always delivered with a weird laugh makes it seem like they're ready to pull up a ringside seat for the ensuing spectacle. The script read: Nelle waits in her office for Cage. Cage enters. Nelle begins to remove her clothing. Cage is flustered. Nelle, in underwear, walks toward him. He runs out of the office and down the hall. At that moment, I would've done anything to run out of the makeup trailer, to my car, and out of this ugly studio with its square buildings and its one-way windows. I would go home and pack my suitcases and take my car to the airport, get on a plane, go back to Melbourne, Australia, and just start the whole damn thing over. Start my whole damn life over. I'd go to law school, a studious, serious girl who wasn't bopping around from photo shoots to lectures, having earned a place there after attending the local high school where I was the richest and smartest girl in the class. I would never have modeled, and so I'd think I was attractive just as I was, and I'd live in this blissful ignorance with my mother and father, because maybe for some reason he'd still be alive, too, and he wouldn't need me to go out and prove I was pretty and special, because he'd know that I was pretty and special, and he'd tell me that anyone who thought I wasn't the prettiest and smartest girl they'd ever known was stupid. Or jealous. Or both.

"Wow. That's really exciting. That's great for my character." When attacked, defend by lying.

I sat in the makeup chair staring at my reflected image as it was transformed from a hopeful twenty-four-year-old to a beaten down, emotionally bankrupt forty-year-old; the thick foundation covered my pores, suffocating my skin, the heavy eye shadow creating a big, deep crease in my eyelids, the red lipstick drawing the eye to my thin, pursed lips. Until now, it had looked to me like the mask of a character. No matter how scared or insecure I was, there was always a glint in my eyes underneath the thick eyeliner that reminded me that this was just a character, that I was young and exciting and had a life away from this world where there were no trees and no one to talk to. But sitting in the makeup chair at that moment, watching the transformation, the lines were blurred. It seemed like less work to create the defensive, cold character. It seemed like we were just putting some makeup onto my face. We were just defining my eye, giving color to my pale lips, covering up my imperfections. The fat was back, too. The fat that I'd felt in the car, spilling over the waistband of my jeans, was visible through my sweater, and I knew that everyone in the trailer was looking at it, wondering how I was going to get it off in eight days. But no one was wondering more than me.

I joined a gym. It was close to the studio, so if I had a break during the day I could just hop in the car and onto a treadmill. That was part of how I got the weight off. The other part was just not eating, which is a highly underrated strategy as zero meals a day works just as well for weight loss as six small ones. The only problem was I was so hungry and weak I limped to the finish line, no longer caring how I was going to stand in my underwear, or which angle would most flatter my body. I stopped caring to the extent that after the rehearsal, my hunger wrestled with my common sense and like a diva I demanded that a PA go to a Starbucks and bring me back a bran muffin. But if that kind of behavior is ever justified, it was at that moment when the script called for an extreme situation and I was just expected to comply. There was no question in David Kelley's mind as to whether I would do that scene. He demanded that I do it, and so I made my demands in retaliation. "Let's see the new blonde in her underwear!" Well then, I said, "Get me a muffin!" Actually, *demanded* is the wrong word. I asked. But it was so unusual for me to ask for anything, it replays in my mind as being a little harsher than it was. It was very common for actors to ask PAs to get them food or to mail a package or to put gas in their cars, but I always felt quite disgusted by it. I always felt that actors were just testing the limits of what someone would do for them just to see if they'd do it. I hate entitlement. But more than that, I hate that someone else in the same position as me feels entitled when I just feel lucky as hell.

I ate it before I shot the scene. I ate that muffin with its salt and calories and wheat and butter and all of the other bloating ingredients.

I hated everything about the underwear scene. I hated that in just a few episodes, I'd gone from playing a high-powered attorney to a woman desperately trying to get her boss to sleep with her. I hated that I'd have to play a love-interest character from now on, and I especially hated what I wore. I chose black lingerie with tiny red and pink hearts sewn onto it. It was ridiculously uncharacteristic for Nelle, who would have worn a more conservative style, perhaps something in navy blue—small, lacy, and revealing yet dignified, and worn with an air of supreme confidence in the goods the underwear displayed. The lingerie I chose was trashy with a stripper vibe. If ever I was to take care of my own needs before worrying about acting, it was in choosing the most flattering underwear. Here was my thinking: I would wear the largest, fullest cut with the most distracting colors to deemphasize my hips and thighs as much as possible. I would pad up my bra to offset the roundness of my stomach and look more proportional from head to toe. I chose a dress that I could remove in one easy motion so I wouldn't have to bend over and risk rolls of fat creasing on top of each other as I removed a tight skirt or a difficult blouse. I chose the highest of heels, because we all know that the taller you are, the more weight you can carry, and I wore my hair down, shaken all around, in an effort to lift the viewer's eye north of my abdomen and away from my thighs.

I shot the scene and awaited the verdict. I didn't have to wait long as it aired within a few weeks. Of course, when shooting a scene like that, some of the feedback is immediate. The energy of the crew changes, and no matter how professional you are, you still feel exposed, cheapened, paid to show your body. Or at least that's how I felt. And in that scene I was no longer a brilliant attorney who could make the firm more money than it had ever seen. I was stripped of that ability and the respect that comes with it when I stripped down to my heart-covered bra and panties. I was just another blond actress playing a vulnerable woman who has sex with her boss, in the costume of an efficient, crafty attorney. I was just an actress playing a lawyer, which, after dropping out of law school, was the only kind of lawyer I'd ever be. I don't know why I thought I'd be any more respected for simply pretending to be that which I didn't have the stamina to become.

By the time the episode aired, my life had changed. For many reasons, I'd decided to move out of the place in Santa Monica that I shared with my brother; the place that I'd shared with my husband. I moved away from the life I'd known since coming to Los Angeles and into an apartment in Hancock Park. I was on my own. Kali had moved back to Pasadena anyway, and my other friend, Ann, a girl who made difficult, emotional conversations easy, had moved to New York. Ann is the friend that everyone wishes they could have. She pries the truth out of you in a nurturing way and then stays around to clean up the tears. Ann's departure was one of the reasons I moved. But mainly I moved away because of paparazzi. Granted, there was only one photographer who had found my house, but the pictures of me sitting on my front steps, hair in curlers and smoking a cigarette, made me feel ambushed, watched, hunted almost. That one photographer made me feel like any of my private moments could be captured at any given time—unseen, unknown. I felt like I had a peeping Tom and every time I did something that I wouldn't want anyone else to see, my thoughts escalated into paranoid panic—not only over the present moment, but over those that predated the smoking picture. Retroactive paranoia.

There was nothing fun about seeing my picture in the *Star.* It served as a warning that I'd better watch myself or I could embarrass my family. I'd better watch myself or I could ruin my career. The photo of me smoking upset my mother. She'd much prefer it if people didn't think I did that, and now there was proof. Was there proof of my homosexuality yet? (Did I even have proof of it yet?) I wondered if the paparazzo was crouched behind the fence, overhearing my side of phone conversations with Ann when I would sit outside and smoke and talk to her about my therapy sessions. I talked to Ann about therapy and other important life-changing things. Ann had recommended I go to therapy and had also recommended the therapist. Ann listened to my panic and my confusion and to most of my dramatic statements like, "If I get into a relationship, if I even try, then people will find out I'm gay!" She replied, "What's so bad about that?" Which was ridiculous, of course. Everything was bad about that.

The episode with the scene of me in my underwear aired in New York three hours before it would air in LA. So I told Ann to watch it and call me immediately.

"Hey."

"What did you think?"

"I thought the show was great. You weren't in it as much this week."

"Ann! What did you think of the scene? How do you think I looked?"

"Great."

"What do you mean, 'great'?"

"Sexy. You know, great."

"Did I look thin?"

"I thought you looked like a normal, healthy woman."

Normal. Healthy. Woman.

My mother told me a long time ago that "healthy" was a euphemism for "fat." She'd say to me, "Don't you just hate it when you see someone at the supermarket and they tell you, 'You look healthy'? They clearly are just trying to tell you that they think you look fat." She'd tell me how she'd handle the backhanded compliment by smiling and pretending she was receiving a genuine compliment all the while ignoring their attempt to be insulting. After all, it's in the way an insult is received that makes it an insult. You can't really give offense unless someone takes it.

All of the words Ann used were euphemisms for fat. *Normal* just meant that I was fat. Since when did anyone ever go to the doctor's and feel good about being in the weight range that's considered normal? A normal size for women in this country is a size 12. Models aren't "normal." Actresses aren't "normal." She may as well have told me that I'd just embarrassed myself in front of 15 million people. If she didn't want me to think that, she would've used words like "overworked" instead of "healthy," and "girl" instead of "woman." How could the image of a woman, with her big voluptuous hips and round thighs and big, heavy breasts be applied to me if I was the skinny, straight-up-and-down, shapeless girl I was starving myself to be?

Message received loud and clear, friend.

You can't give offense unless somebody takes it.

10

BOUGHT A treadmill and put it in my dressing room. That way I was able to run during my lunch break on the set. I also bought another treadmill and put it the guest bedroom in my new apartment. With two treadmills, I didn't have an excuse not to work out. Because I had started to bring my Maltese dog, Bean, to the set with me, it was hard to get to the gym after work, and having a treadmill in my dressing room allowed me to run for the entire lunch hour instead of taking time out of my workout to drive to the gym and park. Although I hadn't had exercise equipment in my dressing rooms prior to *Ally McBeal*, I didn't invent the concept. Many of the cast members had them.

I got a nutritionist. Her name was Suzanne. I met her during a routine checkup at my gynecologist's office. She worked out of a small office in the back a couple of days a week and helped women change their diets to decrease their weight and increase their fertility. My doctor introduced her to me after I'd complained about my inability to maintain my weight. I told him that there were weeks when I'd gain and lose seven pounds from one Sunday to the next. After doing tests for thyroid disease and other medical problems that might have explained my weight fluctuation, he decided that the fault lay with me, that I didn't know how to eat. I agreed with him and hired Suzanne to be my nutritionist.

I loved the thought of having a nutritionist. It made me feel professional, like I was considering all aspects of my work in a thoughtful and serious way. Before my first session with Suzanne, I made the decision to do everything she said. Like a faithful disciple, I would follow her program without question the way a top athlete would drink raw eggs if his coach told him to. This was the kind of private, customized counseling I needed to be a working actress. Like a top athlete, I needed this kind of performance-enhancing guidance. I needed a coach. But mainly, I loved having a nutritionist because Courtney Thorne-Smith had one.

"Hi! Come on in. Mind the mess." Suzanne was a tall, thin woman with a sharpness to her movements. She dressed blandly and conservatively and was almost sparrowlike with long, thin arms and bony hands that would dart back and forth. I wondered why a woman like that, who was naturally thin, would be drawn to nutrition. I knew there were reasons to be interested in food other than weight loss, but I couldn't imagine those reasons being compelling enough to make nutrition your life. Instead of seeing her at the gynecologist's office where we met, I met with Suzanne at her home in Brentwood. When we'd first met she was wearing a white lab coat, and although the meeting was brief, from behind a desk she seemed officious, judgmental, bossy. But a layer of expertise and officiousness was immediately removed just by stripping her of her white coat and placing her in a different setting, in her home with her child's toys strewn about, her family in photographs looking at me. They were conservative-looking folk, poised to judge me for being so much fatter than she was. Then again, I felt they were judging her for being so messy. The fact that she was a black sheep made me feel a lot better.

"So from what the doctor tells me you have trouble maintaining your weight and knowing what to eat. Please know that you are one of millions of people who struggle with this, which is why people like me have a job!" Suzanne was no longer a skinny bird poised to judge me. She was caring and concerned. It was off-putting.

"Tell me why you think you can't maintain a healthy weight." She looked at me with kindness and openness, but there was a fragility to her that I found disarming, perhaps because I recognized a similar vulnerability in myself. Did she starve and binge and purge, too?

"Well . . ." I was surprisingly nervous. I really hadn't planned on opening up to someone about my eating habits, and all of a sudden it seemed like no one else's business. It seemed too personal. It seemed strange and a little idiotic to talk about food, like I was a five-year-old sitting cross-legged in a classroom learning about the five food groups.

"I don't know. I guess I just never knew of a really good diet that I can do every day so my weight doesn't fluctuate."

"Well, Portia. I'm not going to teach you a diet, I'm going to teach you a way of life. We'll talk about what you like to eat, and then I'll devise an eating plan that will be healthy and help you lose weight."

Sounds like a diet to me.

She talked and I listened. She had a lot to say about the kinds of calories one should eat, the value of lean protein, the dangers of too many carbohydrates, the difference between white and brown carbohydrates, and the importance of choosing the "right" fruits without a high sugar content.

"I like bananas. What about bananas?" Bananas were a staple in my "in-between" dieting phase. After starving myself by only eating 300 calories a day, I would often eat a slice of dry wheat bread with mashed banana.

"Well, Portia. Bananas are the most popular fruit, probably because they're the most dense and caloric of the fruits, so you'll have to be careful not to have them too often."

That explained why my "in-between" diet packed on the pounds. Bananas. Of course, the only fruit I liked was the only fruit this big fat country likes. I'm so typical.

"What are your eating habits now?"

"Now? Well, unless I'm getting ready for something, like a photo shoot or a scene like I just did on *Ally* where I had to be in my underwear, I guess I eat pretty normally. But you know, with the occasional binge."

"What do you mean by 'getting ready'? What do you do to 'get ready' for a photo shoot?" She leaned in slightly toward me. What I was saying seemed to intrigue her. I was wrong in thinking that maybe she starved, too.

"I eat three hundred calories a day for a week." I was shocked to see that her eyes widened with disbelief as she registered the information. It made me angry. She was judging me.

After a pause, she asked, "What do you eat to make up the three hundred calories?"

"Dry bread, mainly. Crackers. Pickles. Mustard. Black coffee."

"What happens when you're done with the photo shoot?" She asked like she didn't know the answer. It annoyed me.

"I binge, I guess. I eat all the foods I didn't eat while I was dieting, and then sometimes I eat too much and well, you know . . ."

Should I continue? Should I tell this conservative woman who already looked slightly shocked by my eating habits that I vomited? She's looking at me with anticipation and encouraged me to continue with a slight nod of her head. "I throw up."

I could see that she was uncomfortable, but I felt compelled to continue. "If I feel like I haven't thrown it all up, I'll take twenty laxatives to make sure it's all gone." Why would dieting and throwing up be so surprising to her? Really, as a nutritionist, she should have heard all that before. It made me wonder if she was qualified to help me. Maybe she helped really fat people take off a little weight, not someone like me who really needed to be taught the "way of life" that she was pitching. It made me mad because I didn't want to talk about myself and feel judged, I just wanted to learn about the five food groups like a five-year-old and take home a weekly eating plan.

I knew that I was being overly dramatic and that maybe she didn't need to know about the purging, but her reaction to my eating habits embarrassed me and that's what happens when I'm embarrassed. I get mad and I punish. And in response to my aggression, she leaned back in her chair and held a book up to her face, like a shield in between us.

"Have you seen one of these?" She waved it around. "It's a calorie counter. It'll help you figure out which are the healthy foods you can enjoy so that you'll never have to feel like you need to do those kinds of things again." Her eyes and her voice lowered as she lowered the book, her defenses. "Portia, it's really important that you understand food and stop this unhealthy cycle of yo-yo dieting."

Yo-yo is an inaccurate way to describe weight fluctuation. It is not the term anyone would use to describe the highs and lows that were the basis of my self-esteem. Yo-yo sounds frivolous, childish, disrespectful. Yo-yo sounds like a thing outside of yourself that you can just decide to put away and not pick up anymore. It suggests that there are end points, predetermined stopping points where the highs and lows end, because the string of a yo-yo is a certain length that never changes. My "bottom" would always be 140 pounds, my "high" 115. But it isn't like that. There's nothing predetermined about gaining and losing weight. Every day of my life I woke up not knowing if it would be a day on the path to a new bottom, a new big number that I'd never before seen on the scale, or if I would have a good day, a day that set me on the way to success and happiness and complete self-satisfaction. Since I was a twelve-year-old girl taking pictures in my front yard to submit to modeling agencies, I'd never known a day where my weight wasn't the determining factor for my self-esteem. My weight was my mood, and the more effort I put into starving myself to get it to an acceptable level, the more satisfaction I would feel as the restriction and the denial built into an incredible sense of accomplishment.

After introducing me to the calorie counter, Suzanne was all business. As well as teaching me how to count calories, she taught me to weigh my food. She told me that portion size was very important and to ensure I was getting the right portions, I had to buy a kitchen scale. She told me what to put on that scale for which meals. She told me that I should eat six small protein-enriched meals a day. She told me to keep a journal of what I ate.

Chicken, turkey, orange roughy, tuna, egg whites, oatmeal, blueberries, nonfat plain yogurt, steamed vegetables, brown rice, wheat bread, bran muffins, nuts—all weighed and documented—were my stable of foods I was allowed to eat. Most other things were not part of the program.

As I left her house that day I felt an overwhelming sense of relief. I had heard that in order to know how to overcome difficulties, you needed the "tools" to do it. Suzanne had given me a program with tools. A no-fail system of calorie counting, weighing, and adding up my daily intake so there would be no guesswork to my weight loss. Now that I had my curriculum in the form of my "allowed" foods, homework assignments in the form of a diary, and weekly exams when Suzanne would evaluate how I'd performed, I could be a good student.

11

WAS OFFERED the cover of *Shape*. *Shape* is a health and fitness magazine that depicts lean, physically strong women. Its articles explain the secret to killer abs and each month it unveils the no-fail diet. On the cover it displays a fit woman, a celebrity if they can get one, who promises to tell you her strategy for weight-loss success. They take pictures of their cover girls in skimpy outfits, like a bikini or spandex shorts, and then interview them about how they achieved optimum "health." I knew why they picked me. It wasn't for my lithe body or killer abs, and they certainly didn't see the underwear scene before offering it to me. I was simply the new girl on the hot TV show. I doubted anyone making the decision had even seen me on the show. Of course, I panicked and gave a million reasons why I shouldn't do it, but my publicist and manager thought it was a great opportunity. A cover is a cover.

It was hard to argue with my publicist and manager. My publicist and manager knew better than I did. The cover of *Shape* complemented the clean-living, fresh-faced image they were trying hard to create. They had subtly written a character for me to play in public, gently coercing me to play the role of an ingénue, fresh but glamorous and with an ounce of naïveté. They guided me into the character by favoring romantic dresses over sexy dresses for red carpet events and to most questions about the show or my life, they smiled with approval when I answered that my journey from law student to Hollywood actress was "a dream come true." It seemed effortless and surprising: a Cinderella story. I understood their reasoning. I needed an image to sell; the truth of who I was needed to remain a secret and Portia, the young, heterosexual, self-confident Australian actress needed to emerge. Besides, most of the successful, leading-lady actresses had graduated from this rite of passage. However, the ingénue was a difficult role for me to play—more difficult in fact than a commanding, self-assured attorney. Even if I ignored the fact that I was gay, at twenty-five I was too old, too cynical. I played the ingénue once in *Sirens* when I was twenty, and even then I felt more like Dorothy Parker than the character of Giddy, the gullible artist's model.

I didn't know how to play that character for the *Shape* interview. With neither health nor fitness being of interest to me, I didn't know what to talk about. How could I possibly explain my weight maintenance when it was attributed to starving and bingeing?

SHAPE: *Portia, tell us how you stay in shape?*

PORTIA: *I eat three hundred calories a day for as many days as I can before a photo shoot. The rest of the time I binge and purge.*

SHAPE: *What's your favorite workout?*

PORTIA: *I'm afraid to work out at all because I'm worried that muscle definition makes people look bigger. I hate the look of fit, muscular women. I prefer the long, waiflike look of models who are most likely just as sick as I am.*

Suzanne had stopped me from crash dieting. It was a cycle of loss and gain, she explained, that once started, could never be stopped. It was true. After shooting the scene in my underwear I had gained a lot of weight. Reluctantly and fearfully, I put my new diet into practice for the week leading up to shooting the cover of *Shape*. I was extremely nervous that because I'd not starved myself the way I usually did before a shoot, my body wasn't really in good enough shape to grace the *Shape* cover. Walking into my trailer that was sitting atop a hill at the location they'd chosen for the shoot, I felt unprepared and anxious. I had weighed in at 125 pounds that morning—not a number on the scale I was used to seeing the morning of a photo shoot, much less a cover shoot wearing a bikini. I had already eaten, too, another abnormality before a shoot. I had eaten my individually packaged oatmeal sachet with antioxidant blueberries and Splenda, a sugar substitute that Suzanne said was so healthy she gave it to her baby. Although I knew that I was being a good student and following the only program that had a chance of actually working for me, the guilt and unworthiness I felt by not starving myself in preparation for the shoot were unbearable. I was embarrassed to shake the hands of the picture editor and the executive editor of *Shape*. I was ashamed that even though I had a gym membership, I rarely used it. Although I'd never really liked the "fit" look, I wished that I could drop my robe to reveal muscular arms and legs and a defined abdomen and waist. I was dreading dropping my robe and showing them the exact opposite of what I knew they were expecting to see. During the shoot, and in a fit of insecurity, I asked one of the photographer's assistants, an unattractive guy who looked sandy and sunburned, like he'd spent the morning surfing, how my body compared to the other girls who'd modeled for the cover. I'd been watching him all morning, not because he was interesting, but because he looked so bored, so uninspired by working on photo shoots, or perhaps this shoot in particular. He was the perfect person to ask because I knew he'd answer with complete honesty. He wouldn't care if he hurt a girl's feelings. His expression changed the second I asked the question, as if the question were like a plug inserted into his brain that reanimated him and sent energy flooding to his face. With a big, dumb smile he responded slowly, giving more weight to each word than was necessary to make the point. "We photograph some women with really sick bodies."

I got what I asked for. Honesty. I knew my body couldn't compare to the other girls; I just needed to confirm it. This dumb guy said what all the other guys out there were thinking. And if I were going to have a career, I would need to impress men just like this one. If I couldn't be the *Maxim* girl with big breasts and a tiny waist, I could be model-like. Unattainable. I could be elegant. Graceful. Thin.

I would just have to get myself one of those sick bodies.

"Morning, dear. How was your photo shoot?" Vera, the costume designer, looked exhausted and like she really didn't care to hear the answer. I was the fourth actor she'd seen that morning. But because she was very polite, she added, "What did you do again?"

"I did the cover of *Shape*."

"*Shape*? What's that?"

I told her that it was a fitness magazine and as I told her how important it was to me because I was passionate about exercise, I sounded like the well-versed liar I had been trained to be. My agent and manager would've been proud.

As I slipped into a navy skirt, I thought about my plans for the summer. I created a picture in my mind of me lying by a pool overlooking the Caribbean ocean, the most beautiful girl on the lounge next to mine. In my mind, the girl turned her head and smiled a sleepy smile, her eyes full of love for me. I had an uncanny ability to escape the present moment and into my fantasy world whenever I wanted to. I especially liked to think about other things during a wardrobe fitting. It made the inevitable comments about how the tailor can let the waist out a little, "just to make the skirt more comfortable," somewhat bearable, knowing that I could choose a happier moment in another place and time. But I was going to be in the Caribbean with the girl of my dreams, so my daydream was borne more from excitement and a little wishful thinking than it was from a place of complete fantasy. Only a few more weeks of wardrobe fittings and my fantasy would be a reality. I held my breath and sucked in my stomach as the zipper closed the gap to the waist. I felt the pinch of the waistband and held my breath again, this time for the conversation between the costumer and tailor that would inevitably ensue.

Go to hell.

As I stood in the fitting room, I almost laughed out loud as I remembered the first words I spoke to Sacha, the girl I was going to be with over summer in St. Barths. It was my first day of Melbourne Girls Grammar School and a stunning black girl who I later knew as Sacha, had left the group in the corner of the quadrangle to talk to me, the new girl. Sacha looked as if I'd slapped her across the face. I didn't know why. "Go to hell," was the only thing I could say. She had strutted up to me with no prompting or subtle invitation and said to me, "You have such pretty hair you should wear it down. Take it out, I want to see it."

The All Girls Grammar School was extremely strict and had a policy about hair, among many other things. The uniform had to be worn with a blazer when off campus, the socks had to always be pulled up to the knees, and the hair must always be neatly pulled back off the face. So you see, she was definitely just having a go at me. She was trying to get me in trouble—or worse. She was trying to get me to pull my hair out of my rubber band and shake it all around like a shampoo commercial so that the pack of girls she was standing with who dared her to come tell me to let my hair down could laugh their asses off at the new girl. I knew girls like that—mean girls. Besides, I was an easy target. I was a model who recently changed her name from Amanda Rogers to Portia de Rossi, so I was prepared for that kind of bullshit. So you see? "Go to hell" was the preemptive strike needed at the time and really the only thing I could say. I can't really remember what happened after that, or how Sacha and I became friends, but we did. Over a period of weeks, we became inseparable. We would spend weekends at her parents' home, staying up all night watching MTV and eating loaves of white bread, butter, and apricot jam. We borrowed each other's clothes. We went out to nightclubs together and flirted with men. For years we were good friends, best friends. Until one day, long after we'd left school, I fell in love with her.

I fell in love with her the day I left home to audition for the movie *Sirens*. I was nineteen years old when I left law school and flew to Sydney to audition for a career I didn't even think I wanted. I had spent my life studying to go to law school, and with one phone call from my modeling agency asking if I'd like to do a movie, I was prepared to ditch law and become an actress. By the time I disembarked and collected my baggage at the terminal, I had fallen in love with Sacha. She was no longer just a friend; she was the reason I had to get the movie. If I was successful, I could win her, seduce her with money and power just as Martina Navratilova and Melissa Etheridge had won their previously heterosexual girlfriends. By their actions, these powerful, famous lesbians told the world that straight women were more desirable than gay ones and if you were rich and powerful enough, you could snag one of your own.

Sacha was not a lesbian. But then, neither was I. I just liked to sleep with women.

My girlfriend had to be heterosexual because I didn't want to be a lesbian. If she was heterosexual, then it suggested that I was also heterosexual. Also, I was scared of lesbians. In fact, I would cross the street if I saw one coming toward me. One time I didn't cross the street and I ended up sleeping with a lesbian because I felt sorry for her. She had just lost her girlfriend in a car accident and I was devastated for her. Nothing sounded worse to me than losing your girlfriend; that the one precious connection that you had made in your whole life was gone, wasted, lost in a car wreck. It sounded so much worse to me than a wife losing her husband—it was worse than anything. I found this woman to be quite unattractive. She was overweight and had a shaved head and facial piercings. But I had to sleep with her. It was only polite.

My girlfriend would have to be someone I already knew, someone I could trust. The last thing on earth I needed at the end of my first season on *Ally McBeal* was to be outed by some girl who just wanted to date me because I was on TV, who just wanted to sleep with me so that she could tell people that I was gay. The career that I once didn't think I wanted was now something that I couldn't live without, and a rumor that I was gay would be enough to end it. As it turned out, I loved acting. During the filming of *Sirens* I discovered that while in character with the camera rolling, I couldn't do anything wrong, that there wasn't a right way to deliver a line, merely a different interpretation. I loved interpreting meaning from words. My happiest moments of learning in school or in college were spent deciphering poetry, reciting John Donne or Shakespeare using inflection with my voice to convey my interpretation of the poem's meaning. I discovered while filming *Sirens* that acting was transformative. I discovered that you could be someone other than who you were and get attention for it, be applauded for it. And all of that was very appealing to me—especially the part about being someone else.

I had planned this vacation for us years before I could afford it, when I began to travel and thoughts of an island and Sacha and I together living on it, if only for a short time, kept me company. Over the years, each time I was away from home, I would write her long, romantic letters that explained my feelings, what our lives would be like together, and how I would take care of her. When I lived in London to complete postproduction after *Sirens* and then hung around to try to find a reason not to go back to law school—like a play in the West End or another movie—I would go down to the coffee shop in the morning to begin writing, and I'd finish the letter in the evening, sitting alone at the corner table of the local pub just off King's Road in

Chelsea, close to where I lived. Writing to her, I was no longer lonely. I had someone waiting for me across the world in Australia. I could tolerate anything as long as I had a notepad and a pen and could pour my heart out to her in these letters. In airport lounges, thoughts of her would engulf my senses to the point where I'd almost miss planes, and in Los Angeles, thoughts of her would numb the pain of losing a job, of hearing no after an audition. My fantasy life with Sacha was as helpful to me as it was adjustable. For when I was in a relationship with Mel, or had a crush on Kali, Sacha would again revert to being just my best friend. Sacha also had relationships of her own, long-term, serious heterosexual relationships. Because of that, I never sent her any of the letters that I had written. But she knew how I felt about her. I'd told her that I loved her after long drunken evenings of partying and making out with her on nightclub dance floors. I knew that given the chance to move to Los Angeles and be with me, she would no longer want to be tied down by these demanding, serious boyfriends. So none of that really mattered to me.

Besides, I had a boyfriend, too. His name was Erik.

Erik was Kali's ex-boyfriend. He became my boyfriend when I invited him to be my date at a Hollywood event. Although he didn't see why it was necessary for me to hide the fact that I was a lesbian, he assured me that he would play the role of my boyfriend to the best of his ability, so I made Erik my permanent beard. The fact that he agreed to be my beard proved his affection for me. Hollywood events were something he had no interest in attending, and in fact, as a budding novelist, he had expressed contempt for the whole industry. His idols were Hemingway and Vonnegut, not Cruise and Gibson.

I had adored Erik from our first meeting at Kali's apartment in Santa Monica. He was deeply thoughtful, attractive, and intelligent. If I could have, I would've slept with him just to show him how much I adored him, but on the one occasion when he crashed in my bed and sex had crossed my mind, the smell of him took the thoughts away. He didn't smell bad. He just smelled male. All men do.

Although Erik quickly learned his role, our first public outing as a couple was nerve-racking. I had never walked a red carpet with anyone before and his attitude toward the media was not helping to quell my nerves. To Erik, a television camera was an opportunity to be a wiseass. (He had told me that if he were to ever appear on *Letterman*, he'd give a shout-out to all the black people in the audience.) As usual, I'd left nothing to chance. I had memorized answers, this time to the right questions: What was I wearing? What are my workout tips? What is my must-have beauty item? In the rented stretch limousine on our way from my apartment to the event on Rodeo Drive in Beverly Hills, Erik and I rehearsed answers to possible questions the two of us might be asked.

"So, if they ask something like, 'How long have you been dating?' just say something vague like, 'just a few months.' "

"I think it's funnier if I say that we just fucked for the first time on the ride over here."

"Erik! This is serious! Don't be a dick."

It was all very funny to Erik. There was nothing on the line for him. He wasn't gay and trying to appear straight. He could attend the event like a spectator, listen to Bocelli, observe this weird Hollywood charade, and drink wine and eat food without concern of getting fat. He wasn't going to have to face the press and pretend that all this was real; he just had to say one easy thing or nothing at all.

"Please say nothing at all."

He shot me an unnerving wink from underneath his mop of blond hair as he got out of the limo, straightened his jacket, and stood with his back to me like a statue, offering his arm like the gentleman escort role I had asked him to play. Despite the fact that he was a smart-ass in my ear all the way down the red carpet, he managed to obscure his disdain from the photographers, and my little plan worked. I was asked if he was my boyfriend and I decided that by answering coyly ("We're just friends"), I would pique their interest more than by announcing that we were dating. Plus it carried the added benefit of being the truth. Because of him the event felt less like work. As someone who wasn't particularly smitten with the world in which I lived, he gave me perspective on my job as an actress, served up with a drink and observations that made me laugh. The women at work assumed he was my boyfriend, and I did everything in my power to keep that assumption alive.

I had a boyfriend called Erik. He was smart and handsome and tall, and he was mine. Except Erik had a girlfriend. Erik left me for a woman who would have sex with him because he didn't smell strange to her. He left me because I was never his to leave. It was a devastating breakup.

12

"COME ON in, Portia. How have you been doing this week?" Suzanne was holding an unwashed dinner plate in her hand as she opened the door. I assumed she'd noticed this dirty plate on her walk from wherever she was, through the living room and to the front door. She was surprisingly messy for such a thin woman. I said hello to her, but in my mind I was thinking how funny it was that I would equate thinness with cleanliness. That observation triggered a memory of being in art class when I was asked to describe how Kandinsky painted and to explain why I didn't like him. "He paints like a fat person," was all I could think to say at the time, as his painting was messy, nonlinear, disorganized, as opposed to Mondrian, a painter who worked in the same period and used colors sparingly, modestly, and who stayed within the lines. He was orderly, clean, and thin.

By the time I left art class in my head and joined Suzanne, I was on the couch. I was beginning to trust her despite my initial fears and wanted to talk to her about my past. From my first session, I had become more aware of the abnormalities of my eating habits as a kid, and it felt good to talk about it out loud. I had considered going back to the therapist who had helped my husband and me realize that our relationship was doomed to failure, but food and eating seemed to be more of a nutritionist's area of expertise than a couples' therapist's, so I told Suzanne everything. I no longer cared whether she was shocked.

I told her that from the age of twelve, starving and bingeing and purging had been the only way to reach my goal weight. That starving was easy because there was always an end in sight. Junk food was around the bend just after the photo shoot or the round of go-sees. But by the age of fifteen, I needed to devise a plan to not only lose weight but to maintain my weight loss. At the end of the school year, I'd convinced my mother that the strict girls' grammar school I attended was "getting in the way of my education" and that I needed to take a year off to model, make some money, and then enroll in a more progressive private school the following year. The fact that I needed to lose weight was nothing new. Ever since I'd begun modeling, I'd always needed to "get ready" for a photo shoot. Me losing weight before a job was like an athlete training for a competition. But if I was going to take a year off school to model, I had to figure out a more permanent solution to the weight problem. I couldn't starve and binge and purge like I had always done. By the time I was fifteen, the purging and the laxatives had become part of my everyday life, and although I wasn't concerned about the possible damage it could cause to the interior of my body, it was a drag to have to spend so much time in the bathroom. Plus, there was only one bathroom in my house.

I told Suzanne that I had asked my mother to help me. Every time I was booked for a job that I had to drop pounds quickly for, I'd beg her to help me the next time so I'd never again be in the predicament of having to starve before a job. I'd say, "Please don't let me eat chocolate." And, "If you see me eating too much of anything, just remind me what I go through every time." This request bothered my mother because, like an addict, when I was in the throes of eating, I could get quite angry and yell at her if she commented on my habit. "You don't want to eat that," was the most common thing she'd say as I was stuffing a chocolate-covered cookie in my mouth. She was wrong. At that moment, eating that cookie was all I wanted to do and I told her so in many different ways over the course of that little experiment. In sober moments, I'd apologize for my hurtful words and plead with her to continue to help me. I told her to hide the cookies. Then when I found them underneath the living room sofa, I'd angrily eat them, saying that all she cared about was how thin I was. That she didn't really care about me. That all she cared about was my modeling career.

"That sounds like a difficult situation for both you and your mother."

"It was."

Using my mother's watchful eye as a deterrent to bingeing was probably the worst thing I could have done. While I'd always binged, it had never disappointed my mother as much as it did during this time. It had worried her greatly that I had left school to model, and if I wasn't thin enough to book jobs, then leaving school didn't serve any purpose. Since I'd asked her to help me maintain my weight, we were in it together. We had a problem that we could overcome together. The list of taboo foods got a lot bigger, too. In the past, while I may've hidden the occasional chocolate candy bar, now eating any food that wasn't diet food sent the message that I was not helping myself. That I'd given up. It was simply heartbreaking to see the disappointment on her face as I sat the plate down on the dinner table piled high with the same food she'd once encouraged me to eat to make me big and strong. It disappointed me, too. Because a simple meal that my brother, mother, and grandmother would eat was never something I could eat. Models don't eat mashed potatoes with butter. And as my mother kept pointing out, I was the one who wanted to be a model.

So I stopped eating in front of her. In front of her, I'd eat steamed vegetables. In the back alleys of restaurants, sitting in between two Dumpsters, I'd eat anything I liked. If my mother wasn't home and lack of pocket money forced me to make do with the food that was in the kitchen pantry, I'd keep one eye on my grandmother as she sat in the living room and hastily get to work on half a loaf of bread and butter with apricot jam. I'd then walk to the supermarket with a butter knife, buy bread, butter, and apricot jam, throw away the few slices of bread to make it look like the untouched original loaf, then use the knife to remove the portions of the butter and jam to make it look like everything was just how I found them. Or I should say, just as she left them.

My mother thought there might be a medical solution to the weight problem in the form of a prescribed appetite suppressant. A drug called Duromine was well known in Australia. It is phentermine, the *phen* in Fen-phen, and was similarly heralded for its effectiveness in weight control. I was prescribed Duromine after a physical examination by a doctor and started taking the drug.

I lost weight. I lost weight and was thin—bony, even. I was ready for any modeling job without concern and was the envy of my school peers. The only problem with the drug was that I couldn't sleep. If I took it every morning with a cup of tea, I felt jittery all day long, speedy almost, and that feeling of restlessness and anxiety stayed with me throughout the day and continued into the night. I could take it daily for only a couple of weeks before I felt like I needed a break from it. Instead of being the answer to helping me with consistent, steady dieting, the Duromine became like a yo-yo in itself. It became another wagon to fall off. It was yet another way to disappoint myself with my lack of willpower, of toughing it out. I just couldn't hack it, just like I couldn't hack dieting. I'd stop taking it, claiming that it affected my studies and my overall health, but secretly I missed eating. I missed the comfort that tasting and chewing and swallowing gave me. I missed the warmth in my belly and the feeling of wholeness; I was incomplete on Duromine, and on food, I was whole.

I realized during the sessions with Suzanne that it almost didn't matter who I was talking to, it was good to talk. And while I talked, she listened. She gave me my program for the week, gave me some helpful tips for the upcoming holidays, and sent me back into the world with my homework.

13

I SURVIVED SEASON TWO OF *ALLY MCBEAL!*

THAT WAS the slogan on a T-shirt that was given out to the cast and crew by a cast member. I survived season two—but barely. Since beginning the show I had felt a constant indescribable pressure, a lurking threat of being fired, even though there was no evidence to suggest that I was displeasing the executive producer. While it was a good place to work and people were generally respectful, there was an eerie stillness and a certain kind of silence to the set that felt like a breezeless summer day, and while there were no insects, there were no birds chirping either. During the last four weeks of the season, every night after wrap, I would get into my car, smile and wave good night to hair and makeup, and like clockwork, I would burst into tears once I made the right turn from Manhattan Beach Studios onto Rosecrans Boulevard. And I would sob, not just cry. I made loud wailing noises that sounded more like "ahhhhhh" than the kind of crying I'd done over other things. In fact, I sounded like Lucille Ball as Lucy Ricardo when she would cry loudly, embarrassing Ricky to the point where he'd do anything she wanted just to shut her up. No one could hear my wailing, however. I wasn't doing it for effect. I was doing it to soothe myself, to comfort myself. And I didn't know why I was crying either. I would cry just as loudly if I'd spent the day performing a wordy two-page closing argument to a jury as if I'd been propped up on a chair in the background of the law office with no dialogue at all.

With the end of the season came the holidays. I had booked the trip with Sacha to St. Barths. While I was excited to realize my dreams of being with her, there was no doubt that I was nervous to see it through. I was worried that by embarking on a romantic journey with Sacha, the journey could come to an end, taking my romantic fantasies with it; the daydreams that lulled me to sleep smiling, the fantasies that filled otherwise empty hours, and the soothing thoughts that took pain and loneliness away would all go with it. These thoughts gave me both anxiety and hope toward the end of the season. Finally, for better or worse, our romance would become a reality.

In St. Barths, however, reality was shocking. It ruined romance like an annoying little brother. It was a pestering ever-present element in our conversations, especially as the conversations featured her boyfriend, Matt, to whom she was considering getting married. Our precious time alone in that tropical paradise was not filled with longing glances and passionate lovemaking, but rather it was spent with our heads stuck in our respective books and in arguments. A conversation about the book I was reading, in fact, ended all arguing, as reality punched me in the face and knocked illusion out cold.

"What's that book you're reading?"

"Ellen DeGeneres's mother, Betty, wrote it. She tells her story about what it's like to have a gay daughter."

"Who's Ellen DeGeneres?"

Her having a fiancé in Australia didn't deter my quest to make Sacha my girlfriend, but not knowing who Ellen was two years after she made international headlines for coming out on her show suggested to me that being gay wasn't even on Sacha's radar, despite her willingness to make out with me on a dance floor from time to time. From that moment on, I knew that I was alone without my imaginary life to keep me company. So I swallowed my disillusionment in the form of cream sauces, piña coladas, and pastries, served up to me by the private chef I'd hired to help me seduce Sacha into a life of lesbianism. Now the chef's role was to reward me for my hard work on *Ally* for the season. I ate my way into relaxation in St. Barths. And I got really fat.

The fact that I got fat was unfortunate as I was scheduled to shoot the cover of *Rolling Stone Australia* two weeks after my vacation ended. I went back home to Melbourne to my mother feeling more like a deserter than the war hero I had dreamed of. I thought I'd be paraded around Camberwell, the town where my mother lived, as the American TV star triumphantly returning. To be honest, there was still some parading, some walking up to the Camberwell shops with my mother to talk to the shopkeepers about my adventures overseas, but it felt wrong. The pounds were evidence of the pressure. Heaviness overshadowed the levity of talking about what I wore to the Emmys or what Calista was like as a person. People could sense my depression and discomfort, and that really ruined the fun for everyone. So my mother dutifully hid her chocolate-covered cookies, and I starved and cried and went back and forth to the gym I used to go to for aerobics classes back in the eighties.

ROLLING STONE AUSTRALIA. ISSUE 566, OCTOBER 1999

There are two rumours about Portia de Rossi . . . So which rumour would she like to address first?

"Oooh, I love this," the 26-year-old says in her peculiar LA via Melbourne accent. "It's just like truth or dare!"

OK, the first rumour is about the hair. We know it's real. We know she's a natural blonde because her mum has shown us the baby photos. Even as a four-year-old her white-blond hair was worn long and girly. So that's that out of the way . . . The second rumour is that De Rossi was spotted in clubs around Melbourne recently cosying up to other girls. So does that mean she's bisexual? A lesbian? A long, delighted squeal

comes down the telephone line. "Ooooh, how fun! I love that question!"
she says, shouting now . . .

"Let's just say every celebrity gets that rumour and now I feel like
I've joined the club. Hooray!"

Hooray indeed. Not only were they "on to me," a phrase that my
mother would use when my secrets were being pried out of their vault
and into pop culture, but the photo shoot exposed another terrible
secret, possibly worse than being gay. It told the world, or at least the
people of Australia, that I was fat. I tried as hard as I could to get the
weight off, but whittling down from 140 pounds in two weeks proved
to be too much of a feat even for this crash dieter. If only Sacha had
fallen in love with me, none of this would've happened. Now I was on
the cover of a magazine, fat and looking like a hooker in a chainmail
boob tube and leather hot pants. Over the previous six months, I was
told that I had ranked highly in the polls featured in men's magazines
as being "hot," mainly because of the icy, untouchable nature of my
character. Nothing was more of a foil for my real, gay self than to appear on the cover of men's magazines as a sexy, man-eating young
actress. Another difficult role to play, I was discovering who I was while
desperately trying to convey the image of the woman I wasn't.

When Portia de Rossi looked at the clothes we'd chosen for this
month's cover shoot—leather hot pants, chainmail boob-tube, handcuffs,
G-string, she only had one thing to say: "Oh fuck!" Several cigarettes
later and a few soothing words from her mum and her aunt Gwen
(also at the shoot), she was happily admiring herself in the sexy clob-
ber. "Mama, do you think it's too kinky?" she asked. "No," her mum
replied. "You look very pretty."

After the photo shoot, I went to the airport. I had to fly back to Los
Angeles to meet with executives from L'Oréal to discuss being their new

spokesperson for a hair product. I knew that people thought I had nice hair. I knew it was special because I was often told that it was the reason for my success. The fact that I played the title role in the Geelong Grammar School production of *Alice in Wonderland,* for example, was because of my hair, according to all the girls at school. Occasionally, on modeling jobs I was singled out to be featured in a campaign because of my hair, and on *Ally McBeal* toward the end of my first season, my hair acted out more drama than my character did. It went to court to showcase how women use sexuality to get ahead in the workplace, it indicated when my character's walls were up, and it even performed a few stunts, notably when John Cage "wired" my hair to remotely shake loose from its restrictive bun when he wanted me to "let my hair down." So the fact that my hair had garnered some attention from people who sell hair products wasn't surprising to me. In fact, it was the only thing that had made sense for quite a while. The fact that I didn't like my thick, unmanageable hair was irrelevant.

I didn't write letters to Sacha in the airport terminal. I ate. There was nothing left to say, no fantasies I could act out on paper of how we would be happy together in a tropical paradise, so I ate. I ate English muffins with butter and jam. I ate potato chips and cookies and gulped down Coke. I threw up. I left the first-class lounge to shop for food in the terminal. I ate McDonald's burgers, vanilla milk shakes, and fries. I threw up again. Then I got on the plane.

"Can I get you a drink, Ms. de Rossi?" The American stewardess had a lipsticky mouth and overpronounced the syllables, as Americans tended to do. It was strange to hear the American accent after being in Australia. It reminded me that I had an accent, too. It reminded me that Australian-born Amanda Rogers was now American-seeming Portia de Rossi. If magazines didn't say otherwise, I could definitely pass as a Yank. My dad had called Americans Yanks. I thought it was funny when I was a little kid. He'd also sung me to sleep with a passionate, out-of-tune rendition of "The House of the Rising Sun."

"Baileys Irish Cream, if you have it." Of course I knew they had it, it just sounded more polite, more whimsical. I was aware that the stewardess would think that an after-dinner cream liqueur would be a ridiculous drink to order before dinner, and I needed her to know that I knew it was ridiculous, too, so I said: "I've been looking forward to some Baileys. I always have it on planes." That made it better.

When I refused dinner and asked for my sixth Baileys, the stewardess got weird again. Of course, she served it to me; I was a first-class passenger after all, but I could detect concern in her pour, more than just the concern that comes with pouring liquid into a narrow-rimmed glass on a moving vehicle that is subject to bouts of turbulence. She was judging me. She looked disgusted. She was worried for me. She had reason to be worried, I guess. I had spent a lot of the plane ride quietly crying, as I often do because I hate hovering between one place and another. "Neither here nor there" was an expression my grandmother would use to describe confusion and displacement, and it is a disturbing place to be. This state of hovering during the fourteen-hour journey was once filled with fantasy scenarios of being Sacha's obsession or having a beautiful body on the cover of a major magazine. Now I had no choice but to fill the time by bringing a glass of thick, creamy liquid back and forth to my lips. I was neither in LA nor in Melbourne, neither straight nor gay, neither famous nor unknown, neither fat nor thin, neither a success nor a failure. My Discman played the soundtrack for my inner dialogue—rare recordings of Nirvana and so here we were, Kurt Cobain and I, displaced, misunderstood, unloved, and "neither here nor there"—he being neither dead nor alive, both in his life and in his death. It occurred to me as I listened to lyrics like "and if you killed yourself, it would make you happy" that if I were at the end of my life, I wouldn't have to keep running the race. If I were really old and close to dying, I wouldn't have to do another season, another magazine cover. I could be remembered as a successful working actor, a celebrity, even. I had been given the challenge of life and beaten it. The pressure I had put on myself to excel in everything I did made life look like a never-ending steeplechase. The thought that I had fifty more years of striving and jumping over hurdles and being the one to beat in the race was enough to make me order another drink.

After my seventh Baileys I threw up. I made myself throw up, but it took a long time to do it, and because I was drunk, it was sloppy. I've never liked airplane toilets. They've always disgusted me, so the unclean, smelly toilet made me nauseous and the nausea made me think there was more food and liquid in my gut to get rid of. A lot of dry heaving and coughing followed. My fingernails had cut the back of my throat where my gag reflex was and I was throwing up saliva, maybe bile, and a trace of blood. Several times, I heard knocking on the door. I ignored it. It didn't bother me at all, actually. I deserved to be on this plane and in this bathroom just like they did. By the time I had unlocked the door, there was a guy in a uniform waiting for me. He looked officious and slightly angry, which made me angry. There are other toilets on the plane, for God's sake.

"There's some concern that you're not feeling well. Is there anything I can do to help you, Ms. de Rossi?"

"No. I'm fine." The purging session had given me a colossal headache. So I added, "Maybe some aspirin."

As I walked down the aisle, I noticed a contraption in the way. It was in the aisle blocking access to my seat. It was silver, and looked like a cylinder on poles with wheels attached. The stewardess stood next to it and as if reading my mind she replied, "Oxygen. I think it'll make you feel better."

Something shifted. As I looked into the face of the stewardess, I no longer saw expressions of judgment and disgust. I saw concern. The once angry, officious-looking man in the uniform returned from getting aspirin for my headache and gave it to me with a smile. I looked at my two uniformed nurses, and their caring, nurturing expressions, and quietly sat in my seat and attached the oxygen mask to my face,

When I woke up to the plane preparing for landing in Los Angeles, the silver contraption, and my headache, were gone. I was in Los Angeles.

My name is Portia de Rossi. I'm an American actress about to embark on my second season of a hit TV show. I am here and not there. I am here.

14

THERE ARE a few places in Los Angeles where art meets up with commerce for a drink and the Four Seasons bar is one of them.

As I walked in from the lobby, I saw little plays being acted out at nearly all the tables—the actor, writer, or director presenting himself as something to invest in, the producer or executive sizing them up before deciding to purchase or pass. Sometimes, like a chaperone, the manager or agent will be present at one of these sales meetings. The manager tends to lubricate things with friendly, ice-breaking conversation. Also, the manager orders lunch or drinks for the table and plugs the awkward silences by asking after the producer's kids. Most times, their kids play soccer together. Or attend the same school. Hollywood is a club. And with the help of a couple of referrals, I got to fill out my application.

I walked through the bar to the assortment of floral lounge chairs that would serve as the site for my success or failure. I was meeting with the L'Oréal executives. I was a potential new product. I approached them in the dress and heels I'd agonized over wearing for a week. Did the dress convey respect and excitement and downplay desperation? Or did it somehow expose the truth: that my self-esteem hinged on their decision? Was it too low-cut or too high-cut? Was it too tight? Did it display my wares in an attempt to arouse interest in a cheap, throw-in-everything-you've-got way? I led with my hair by running my hand across the nape of my neck to scoop up the thick blond "product" and dumped it over one shoulder for inspection: cheap, but effective.

"Hi. I'm Portia."

Handshakes all round. They looked interested. They looked like they liked what they saw. I prayed that it would go well. I prayed they would pick me.

I really needed that campaign. My ego needed it. During the course of my first season on the show, I felt like I was blending into the background. The initial thrill of writing for the new character, Nelle Porter, had given way to the thrill of writing for an even newer new character, Ling Woo. I really couldn't believe what happened. Instead of introducing one cold, calculating woman, David Kelley had split one character and given it to two people. He'd given us half a character each. If Nelle was given one cutting comment, Ling would take the other. Nelle would romance one boss at the law firm of Cage and Fish, Ling would sleep with the other. As always I had to wonder if it was something I had done wrong. Maybe I wasn't vicious enough? Maybe my vulnerability shone through the austere exterior? Maybe I wasn't sexy enough for the kind of nasty-in-a-good-way attorney he had in mind? Maybe I was just nasty in the bad way because no matter how hard I tried I didn't give off a flirty, sexual vibe. I'd signed up to play an intelligent professional, not a sex kitten. And when I'd tried to break through the icy veneer to find the sex kitten, I tended to just look like a kitten: vulnerable, fragile, in fear of abandonment, and needing to be held.

Maybe I looked too fat in my underwear.

The L'Oréal campaign would fix all this. A beauty campaign would be an opportunity for me to restore my dignity, my uniqueness. Apart from gracing the cover of *Vogue*, I couldn't imagine anything in the world more glamorous than a beauty campaign. A beauty campaign had the power to validate. Like becoming a model, it was a way to convince people beyond a doubt that you were, in fact, attractive. Selling shampoo serves up an answer to a question that's vague and subjective.

It tells you what beauty is, that the face selling this product is a beautiful face.

There's nothing like external validation. I craved it. It's why I went to law school. The theory of objectivism claims that there are certain things that most people in society can agree upon. A model is pretty. A lawyer is smart. Our society is based upon objectivism. It's how we make rules and why we obey them. That was perhaps the only thing I learned in law school. I was too busy modeling to go to class.

The L'Oréal bigwig was a pleasant, smiling man and he ordered a Heineken from the server. I could tell he was the bigwig, because no one else who sat in a floral lounge chair would have had the gall to order alcohol in a meeting. It bothered me slightly that he did that. It seemed like meeting with me wasn't terribly important. That he didn't need to impress me, win me away from Garnier or any other competitive hair care brands that might be offering me a similar deal. But what bothered me most about the Heineken was the thing he said as he picked up the icy green bottle and pointed to it with the index finger from his other hand.

"No more of this for you, Portia."

Now, I liked beer. I especially liked Heineken, and I didn't like that anyone would say something like that to me. If he'd been a doctor who was explaining my impending liver failure while demonstrating what caused it at a bar, or if I was that Olympic gymnast I'd pretended to be in summer as a kid, who was celebrating her last night before going to a foreign country to compete for gold, I might have been okay with such a statement. At least, I would've understood it. But why did he not want me to drink beer? Could it be because alcohol is fattening? Aging? Makes you stupid if you get drunk? I didn't understand. But what I did understand from that comment was that I had just been offered the job of being the new face of L'Oréal.

A fitting followed a week after the meeting, and with it all the excitement and beer drinking that came with celebrating my new, prestigious job. The fitting for the commercial took place at the Four Seasons again, and I figured the hotel served as a kind of L'Oréal office base away from the home office in New York. The executives took their meetings in the bar, conferred in a conference room, slept in their individual suites, and lavished their new star with a room full of beautiful clothes to try in the presidential suite. My manager came with me to the fitting and both of us were excited.

After the initial meetings and greetings of the stylist and her assistants and tailors, I wandered into the main room of the presidential suite wide-eyed and my mouth agape. All the furniture had been removed and the walls were lined with racks and racks of clothing. Hundreds of suits hung on the racks and on every rack, on the north, south, and west walls, was the same gray suit.

"Great. I was just looking for a gray suit! Now I know where they all are."

The mood in the room was quiet and not jovial, so I put my smartass personality to rest and took out the pleasant, compliant, easygoing one I've been using at work since the day I started. I knew this kind of client, the kind where every little detail mattered; I'd modeled for them for years. I'd just never worked for this giant of a company at this level. My experience with clients who tested every little detail in a think tank of consumers who'd been randomly collected from shopping malls was limited to the smaller companies in Australia. And nothing says, "You're in the big leagues" like two hundred near-identical suits in the presidential suite of the Four Seasons in Beverly Hills.

I looked at a gray suit with a short jacket and a pencil skirt with a side slit. Then I looked at a gray suit with a pencil skirt and a short jacket with a slightly different lapel than the one I'd looked at five minutes prior that had a pointier, larger lapel and a skirt that was slit on the opposite side. Some of the fabrics were a different weight than others with a different ratio of cotton to wool. It was clear to me that my opinion or preference of suits didn't matter at all, and so I went into the dressing room and tried on jackets and skirts as they were handed to me.

Undressing in front of my manager was embarrassing. I didn't feel quite thin enough to be standing around barefoot in my G-string, but I didn't want to tell her to leave the room. After all, the only reason for her to be here was to help me navigate through the sea of suits, and I knew she'd have much preferred to be somewhere else with another of her bigger, more famous clients. She was a busy woman whose time was important, so I couldn't have her wait in the living room. Besides, there was no furniture anywhere else in the hotel suite. Comfort had been cleared away for productivity. And the skirts that were passed in and out of that dressing room from the stylist's assistant to the stylist to the tailor and then back to the stylist's assistant to be hung back up on the rack of suits that didn't fit looked like a production line in a factory—an unproductive factory. So far, not one of the suits had fit. The skirts either didn't zip up in the back, or if they had Lycra or another synthetic fabric helping them to stretch, the skirt did that telltale bunching that looks like ripples on a lakeshore between two gently rolling hills that were my thighs. They didn't fit. None of them. I tried on suit after suit until it was obvious to the stylist and the tailor that the fitting should take place skirt by skirt. It was pointless to try the jacket if the skirt was so small it couldn't be zipped up in the back.

They were all a size 4. My modeling card measurements—34, 24, 35—had put me at a size 4. And it seemed like the more expensive the suit, the tighter it was. A size 4 in Prada was a size 2 in the type of clothes I'd wear for *Ally*. I could've argued that the European sizing was different. I could've made a case for myself, but none of that was important when I couldn't zip up the fifteenth skirt in a row. None of what I could've said would be important.

You can put on a brave face for only so long. I put one on for about three hours before it cracked. After three hours I fell silent. There was nothing to say. We all knew what was going on. I was unprofessional.

I didn't deserve the campaign. My manager had slid down into her chair with her hand on the side of her face, exhausted, no longer willing to go to battle for me. The stylist, who had lacked a personality in the beginning, found one toward the fourth hour of the fitting, and it wasn't pleasant to be around. She'd stopped addressing me directly. Everything she said in front of me was to her assistant or tailor: "Go get the Dolce skirt. Let's see if she can fit into that." Or "What if you let the skirt out as much as you can. She might be able to get away with it."

She stopped cold as the door of the suite was knocked upon and opened simultaneously. It was the L'Oréal executives come to see what was taking so long. They had been in the conference room taking meetings but had been expecting to see some pictures of Portia de Rossi in several gray suits. We were supposed to have given them Polaroids of all the options by now. We had given them none.

"Hi."

I didn't bother to smile or go to them in the hallway. My manager didn't even get up.

"What's going on in here?" The female executive had a smiley yet accusatory voice. The kind of pissed-off yet polite voice one would expect from Hillary Clinton if she had the sneaking suspicion that someone was trying to pull the wool over her eyes.

There was an awful silence. It was a silence full of thwarted hopes, a stale-air kind of silence.

The explanation they were seeking was summed up with a simple statement from the stylist that everyone seemed to understand.

"Nobody told me she was a size eight."

Like a dead man to the galley, I walked with my manager to the Four Seasons parking garage. When I'd driven in that morning, I'd been given the option to self-park or to valet park and, quite honestly, I didn't know which one was the cool thing to do. I thought maybe it said more about the type of person I was if I did away with all the ceremony of a valet. It said that I was self-sufficient, that I could see through artifice, that I wasn't falling for it. I was happy about that now because the vast gray parking structure was empty of people, except for my manager and me, the emptiness echoing the clicking of our heels as we walked through it. It occurred to me as I was walking miles to my car (valet parkers got all the good spaces) that the parking garage held up the rest of the building and was its true nature, that all the floral lounge chairs and Hollywood dealings were like costumes and a character to an actor; another kind of empty shell that needed a good stylist and a purpose. I'd been given another fitting two days from now, a time and address scratched on a piece of paper. That would give the stylist time to find bigger sizes. The second fitting would take place in the rented space of the stylist in a not-so-good part of Hollywood. That's what you get for drinking beer.

My manager walked me as far as the elevators, but that was as far as she'd go. We'd come down the stairs, tried to find my car around that area, and then started walking because I thought that maybe my car was at the other end. I have no sense of direction. If I haven't been to a place before, I'll get lost. In the car, if I haven't traveled the exact route, I'll get lost and almost force myself to go the wrong way to prove that I knew it was the wrong way. I deliberately go the wrong way so I can predict the outcome with confidence.

At the elevators, as she was trying to leave me and get back to her pretty Jaguar and her pretty office with the ocean breeze, I showed her the big gray empty space inside me. I didn't mean to; it's just what happens if I disappoint someone I'm trying to impress. The crying seemed to come abruptly and from my stomach and as I cried, it folded in half and bent over and couldn't be straightened back up. My head was somewhere past my knees and my heels could no longer balance the weight of my head and torso—all of it making heaving, sobbing motions and so I sank to the cold gray concrete. I was on the ground. It was a brief moment, but for that moment I was on the floor of the bottom floor of the Four Seasons: from the presidential suite to the floor of the bottom floor in four hours. My manager yanked me up by the arm with the super-human strength that comes with embarrassment, the way a mother yanks up a child who's thrown a tantrum in a department store.

"I can't do this, Joan. I'm too fat. They don't want me. They want someone else. I think we should get out of it. I don't want to do this anymore. Joan, I'm too fat. They told me that Heather Locklear was a size zero and Andie MacDowell was a two!"

She looked around to make sure no one could see us. She made sure none of her producer friends whose kids play soccer were anywhere around to see this spectacle and then she said:

"Honey. You have big legs."

I stopped crying. I was shocked into stopping. I'd never heard that before in all my years of modeling. I was hoping for some bullshit reassurance about how the stylist should have had more sizes and how women my height shouldn't be a size 2. Instead I was told the truth.

Yes. Of course, I have big legs. I have big thighs that make all the skirts tight no matter how much I weigh. Everything makes sense now. In fact, Anthony Nankervis, the boy who told me I had slitty, lizard eyes also told me I had footballer's legs. I don't know how I could've forgotten that.

With a dismissive hand gesture to punctuate her point, she said it again. She announced it with certainty, the way that any fact would be stated, requiring no qualification and inviting no rebuttal.

"Just face it, honey. You have big legs."

. . .

"What part of your body do you like?"

The Jenny Craig counselor is talking to a jovial woman at the two o'clock spot in the group circle. She is a very fat woman with dull brown hair.

"My hair?" Laughter all round.

"Well, that's not exactly a body part, now is it, Jan."

The circle has about twelve people in it, and I am at six o'clock. While Jan consults her list of several of her body parts that she likes, I look at the blank sheet in front of me and try to think of one of my own. Hands? No. I hate my hands.

"I like my hands," says Jan, looking down at her fatty, pasty hands. I wonder how she can like her hands because even if she thought that her right hand was graceful and slender, her wedding band on her left hand, barely visible through the mounds of flesh suffocating it, tells the story of the big fat body attached to it. As she waves them around to help her mouth make a point, I wonder who put that band on her finger with a promise of being true to her through thick and thin. I wonder if that promise is diminished now, relative to the sliver of band now visible: a once-thick gold band now seemingly thin: a seemingly happy bride now thick with disappointment. But I guess if you only looked at her right hand and heard her laughter, you might still think she was happy. And maybe her husband's fat, too.

Three o'clock likes her eyes. That would've been an obvious one for me because my eyes can't gain weight, but I don't like my eyes. They're too small and close together. Four o'clock likes her calves. They're strong and lean apparently, although I can't see them through her pant leg so I'll have to take her word for it. My calves are my least favorite *part of my body because after years of treating my local ballet class like it was the Australian Ballet Company, they are enormous. You can't see them, so you'll have to take my word for it. Five o'clock likes her arms. Really?*

"Portia?"

"Has everyone met Portia? She's a newcomer to the group and is the youngest Jenny Craig member we've ever had. Tell us your favorite body part, Portia."

My workbook is blank. My mind is blank and yet racing through thoughts. I am fifteen years old and 130 pounds in a room filled with people twice my weight and age and yet I can't think of a thing. My feet have crooked toes, my ankles are too thin, my calves are too thick, my knees are dimply, my thighs are too big, my ass is droopy, my hips are too wide, my stomach is round and has rolls, my rib cage . . . ? No. My ribs stick too far out at the bottom and that makes my whole torso look wide. My breasts are tiny and disproportionate to the rest of my body . . .

"Portia?"

"Umm. I don't know."

What about my arms? My back? My shoulders? My wrists? Wrists. No, my wrists are too small for my forearms and my hands, and so because of my wrists, my hands and arms look bigger.

"There's nothing I like."

The room falls silent. We were all laughing a second ago and complimenting three o'clock on her mauve eyes that looked like Elizabeth Taylor's and now we're all silent, all around the clock. All the fat people sitting from twelve right back around to eleven are looking at me at six o'clock. I know that look. It's the look of the thoughts that run through your mind when you're looking at a smart-ass. I was the joke to them— the kind that makes you not want to laugh.

"Come on, dear. There must be something that you like?"

There was an ounce of anger to her tone. My lack of an answer probably looked like unwillingness to play along, but in truth I was still running through all my parts trying to find something to say.

"Well, if you don't think you have any good body parts, then I guess we're all in trouble!"

That was the kind of joke that makes people laugh.

PART TWO

15

AWOKE TO a strange silence and shafts of light stabbing into the room from the corners of the blinds. The light carried millions of tiny dust particles, which I guess were always there yet only now visible because of the soupy, thick air with its beams of light illuminating them. I was eerily calm when I awoke. I was aware that I had cried myself to sleep over the L'Oréal incident; my eye sockets felt misshapen and water-logged, as though they could barely keep my sore, dry eyes in my head. But it felt like I had cried for the last time. That I was never going to cry myself to sleep like that again. Despite the heaviness of my head, with its headache and sinus pressure, there was a levity to it, a lightness to it, like everything inside of it that made the world I lived in a place of peace or a place of torture, was weightless—quiet, floating. I felt over-taken by a sense of peace, by the feeling that today was truly a new day.

I got out of bed and immediately started stretching. An odd thing for me to do, but I wanted to feel my body. I wanted to "check in" with it, acknowledge it. As I stretched, there was a certain love I gave to it, an appreciation for its muscles straining and contracting. I liked the way it felt as I touched my toes and straightened my back. I felt like I was sud-denly self-contained. Like the answers lay within me. Like my life was about to be lived within the confines of my body and would answer only to it. I didn't give a shit what anyone thought of me.

As I stretched my arms out to the sides, I ran my fingers through the beams of light, cloudy with the dust that swirled around my bedroom. I saw the beauty of my messy bedroom and inhaled the summer air. All the clothes I'd tried on and discarded on the floor before going to my L'Oréal fitting were looking up at me, wondering what they had done wrong. Despite the mess and the dust, it smelled sweet and I felt myself smiling as I inhaled. I liked that smell. It was the smell of the imported Italian talc in the yellow plastic bottle that I had bought to pamper myself but only now enjoyed as talc and not a status symbol. As I walked barefoot on the painted concrete floor of my bedroom toward the bathroom scale I felt confident that what I was about to see would make me happy for the rest of the day. I felt empty and light and I didn't care what number the scale told me I was, today I was not going to define myself by it. Today I knew that despite what it said, it was unimportant. Today I would start my new life.

I had the answer to my problems.

I would always be prepared.

I was about to make everything easier.

The scale confirmed what I'd suspected. It read 130. The weight I had always returned to no matter the effort to get beneath it. In the past, this number had invariably plummeted me into despair. It reminded me that no matter what I did, I could never win—that my body with its bones and its guts and its blood weighed in at what it felt comfortable being as a living organism with its own needs. It hated me and thought I was stupid for attempting to change it with my tortuous rituals of forcing regurgitation and starving it of food. It always had the upper hand, the last word. And the last word was 130.

Today being the first day of my brand-new life, with its sunshine and its soupy air, 130 was a beautiful weight. It was my weight. It was Portia, a straight-A student who earned a place at the most prestigious law school in Australia, who had an exciting modeling career and the courage to try her hand at acting in a foreign country. It was the weight of the girl who was a successful actress, who made money, who was independent. For the first time in my life, I didn't view my body as the enemy. Today it was my friend, my partner in all the success I'd accomplished. As it stepped off the scale and over the pile of discarded clothes, onto the wooden floorboards and toward the food journal on the coffee table, it expressed its strength and joy by lunging, deep and controlled, thighs burning, stomach taut. And with an outstretched arm the hand flicked through the pages of lists of food items and calories and wrote in big, curly pen strokes something the journal had never before seen: my weight.

130

I was hungry and yet unusually unafraid of being hungry. I went to the fridge and then the pantry and proceeded to line up all the possible breakfast foods on the counter. Sitting on the counter in a row, equally spaced and looking like *The Price Is Right* game show items, were the foods Suzanne, my nutritionist, had given me to eat. The breakfast options of oatmeal, egg whites (you can buy them in a jar, you know), bran muffins, wheat toast, and yogurt were all looking at me and available, but Suzanne had preferred me to eat oatmeal and egg whites because the combination of the two gave good amounts of carbohydrates and protein and because the two-part process of cooking and eating, she believed, made you feel as though you were eating a big, satisfying meal. I made the decision to eat egg whites and oatmeal. I read the calorie contents of the single-serving prepackaged oatmeal sachet: 100 calories. I wondered what 100 calories meant to my body, what it would do with it. Would it use it just to drive to work today or could it drive to work, sit through hair and makeup, and act out a scene all on 100 calories? Would it gently prompt my mind to produce feelings of hunger when it was done burning the calories or would it ask for more food before it was done using the energy from the food I'd given it? If the body was so clever and knew what it needed for health and survival, how come obese people got hungry? The body should use the stored fat to sustain itself to prevent diabetes or heart failure. If it was so clever, it should take over the mind of a self-destructive obese person and send out brain signals of nausea instead of hunger. I came to the conclusion that no matter what my body said it needed, I could no longer trust it. I couldn't rely on my body to tell me what I needed. From now on, I was in control. I was its captain and would make all the decisions.

I decided that I didn't need the full 100-calorie oatmeal packet. It was clearly a common measurement for a normal common portion of food that ordinary people would eat. Obviously, it wasn't a portion that was meant for a person who was dieting. If the average person who wasn't going to lose weight ate a 100-calorie packet for breakfast, then I should eat less. I immediately felt so stupid that I hadn't seen that before. Of course you couldn't lose weight if you relied on Quaker to allot your portion; I had to take control of it. I calculated the grams of food that would deliver an 80-calorie serving on the kitchen scale, and after being careful to give myself the exact amount of oats, I poured it into a bowl. I added hot water and a sprinkling of Splenda. I ate it slowly, tasting every morsel of oatmeal and its claggy syrup. Then, instead of randomly pouring a generous dollop of egg whites from the jar into a hot pan coated in oil, I got out the measuring cup. I measured half a cup of egg whites and poured it into a pan coated with Pam—a no-calorie substitute for oil. I added a sprinkling of Mrs. Dash and salt. Next step was coffee. A mindless consumption of calories in the past would now be another thing ingested that needed measuring. How many additional calories I could spare in my coffee would be determined by the rest of my meal; if I was particularly hungry and needed a large portion of egg whites with my oatmeal, for example, I would take my coffee black, but if I came in under my allotted calorie consumption for the morning, I could measure out a tablespoon of Mocha Mix, a nondairy creamer, to add to it. In the past I would just randomly pour calories into a cup, not caring that a generous pouring of Mocha Mix could run 50 calories. Fifty calories. That was more than a third of my actual food for the morning. After drinking the coffee and eating the egg whites and the oatmeal, I had never felt more satisfied. I was full. I was clever. I had halved my morning calorie intake. I planned on re-adjusting my whole program. I would take my diary everywhere I went and record each calorie that went into my mouth. Suzanne had taught me to weigh, calculate, and document like a mathematician solving an equation, and with my new education I was ready to solve the weight problem.

Suzanne had set my calorie intake for optimum weight loss at 1,400 calories a day. I reset it to 1,000.

Problem solved.

16

"WELL, HELLO there. I'm a big fan of your show. What a delight to meet you."

A middle-aged gray-haired man sat behind the desk of the Granville Towers lobby and practically sang his greeting to me in a gently lilting Southern accent. He seemed genuinely excited to meet me, and his happy demeanor was contagious. I shook his hand and smiled an involuntarily broad smile and I realized that I hadn't really smiled in awhile, that his sparkly nature was in stark contrast to my dullness. Everything about the Granville made me happy. Situated at Sunset and Crescent Heights, the location was perfect, and the building was historic and beautiful. A true example of 1920s architecture, the penthouse apartment that I was about to see had the potential to saddle me with a mortgage. It was time to buy a home, to invest in my life in Los Angeles. I needed a place of my own and a penthouse apartment in an Old Hollywood building on Sunset Boulevard sounded like a place an actress should live.

As I waited in the lobby for the real estate agent to arrive, the doorman, who introduced himself as Jeff, got up from his station and walked around the desk, talking excitedly as if I was the only visitor he'd had in months.

"Mickey Rourke lived here. He just moved out, oh . . . what . . . it'd be a couple of months now. He had three little dogs, Chihuahuas I believe." It annoyed me that people find celebrity so impressive that they have to talk about it. What annoyed me more was that I was impressed. Somehow the building was instantly more valuable to me just because a celebrity had lived in it.

"I'll show you his apartment if you like, but don't tell the agent—I'll get in trouble." Jeff spoke from the corner of his mouth in an exaggerated whisper even though there was no one else in the lobby to overhear. It was dramatic and I would usually have found it annoying, but I liked the fact that he'd invited me to share a secret with him. It felt warm, welcoming.

"It's on the ground floor, but I like it more than the penthouse you're going to see because it has the beautiful coffered ceilings, you know."

On our way see Mickey Rourke's apartment, Jeff told me of other celebrities who had lived at the Granville: Brendan Fraser, David Bowie, and Amy Locane. Michael Michele, an actress on *ER*, was a current resident.

"You know, the place was built in 1929 and it was called the Voltaire. It was a hotel back then, but sometime after that it was made into apartments and apparently, though there's no real proof of this, Marilyn Monroe lived here with Joe DiMaggio."

Jeff wore a jacket and tie. In fact, everything about him was old-fashioned. He seemed to be part of the history he so loved to talk about, as if he lived in a black-and-white movie. If he weren't so enamored with movie stars, I could also picture him living in the South before the Civil War. I could see him as a gentleman on a plantation in Georgia in his hunter green library dwarfed by ceiling-high shelves filled with leather-bound books. But Jeff clearly loved Hollywood, and he loved his job. He was the doorman, the gatekeeper of the Granville Towers, and his excitement over me made me feel as though I could be one of his movie star stories, just as Mickey Rourke and his dogs and his ceilings will forever be one of his stories.

The penthouse apartment wasn't spectacular. It didn't have the molding on the baseboards or the high coffered ceiling that Mickey's had. It wasn't particularly spacious, and the views, although beautiful from the east window, were blocked on the north side by the Virgin Megastore building at Sunset 5, the shopping complex next door to the Granville. In fact, from the first floor of the apartment, looking out the floor-to-ceiling windows on the north side created the optical illusion of a scorching desert. The yellow paint on the Sunset 5 building looked like sand and the heat that spewed out from the air conditioning vents on the roof created that warped-air look of a heat wave. After seeing the small galley kitchen and the modest bedroom and living room, we took the staircase next to the public elevator that led to the attic above the penthouse apartment, while the real estate agent explained to me the resale potential if I connected the penthouse apartment to the attic with an interior staircase. I hadn't planned on renovating, but when I saw the view from the spacious high-ceilinged attic I no longer had a choice. I had never been so excited in my life. On the north wall were thirty or so large windows in rows of three, pitched in an A-frame, and beyond the windows, instead of the desert that I saw from the floor below, was the vast industrial roof of the Sunset 5. Clouds of smoke billowed from the metal chimneys and swirled in the wind, occasionally clearing to show the enormous steel tubes in a cross-section of right angles looking like the indecipherable circuit boards my brother as a kid used to spend hours soldering wires onto to make LEDs light up. The space was currently being used as a studio for the portrait photographer who owned the unit, and the tungsten lights and paper backdrops clamped onto C-stands made the apartment even more loftlike. I felt as though I had been transported to an artist's loft in a city like Philadelphia, which was much more exciting to me than where I actually was. Where I was, was predictable. But the apartment made me think there was more to life than being an actress on a David Kelley show. It made me remember who I used to be and where I had wanted to live if I had stayed in law school in Melbourne: in a nongentrified artist neighborhood off Brunswick Street, the place that made me happier than any other place on earth. For on Brunswick Street I was gay. I wore motorcycle boots, had slightly dreadlocked hair, and wrapped leather around my wrists. I drank beer at the Provincial and ate penne Amatriciana at Mario's and saw indie bands with my best friend, Bill.

"I'll take it."

I left my new apartment with its own industrial city and flew past Jeff, the doorman, in a hurry. I had to get back to my sublet in Hancock Park in time to make dinner. Since lowering my calorie intake to exactly 1,000 calories a day, I discovered that the best time to eat dinner was at exactly six o'clock to give my body a head start in burning the calories. If I ate at six, I still had five or six hours to move around before I lay still for six hours. If I ate any later than that, I worried that overnight the unused calories would turn to fat. I discovered that although I didn't want to lower my calorie intake to under 1,000, as anything lower would be the equivalent of crash dieting, I could speed up the weight loss by increasing the amount of exercise and eating at the right times. Occasionally, if I felt particularly energetic, I could squeeze in a quick workout before bed and if I didn't actually get on the treadmill, I would do sit-ups and leg lifts on the floor next to my bed.

When I got home, I prepared four ounces of lean ground turkey and a spattering of ketchup, cooked with Pam and lightly sprayed with I Can't Believe It's Not Butter spray. As annoying as the name of the product was, every time I doused my food with the stuff I would silently congratulate the marketing team behind the brand. For yes, I too, couldn't believe it wasn't butter. More than that, I couldn't believe something that delicious didn't have any calories. I sprayed it on everything. It tasted great with my morning oatmeal, mixed into my tuna at lunch, and was a perfect partner for my ground turkey with ketchup at dinner. It even tasted delicious as an ingredient of a dessert I concocted: Jell-O, Splenda, and I Can't Believe It's Not Butter spray all mixed together. At 10 calories per serving, it satisfied my sweet tooth and was my favorite new recipe that I had created. I had never thought of myself as a chef before, but I was quite impressed with my cooking. I was impressed that I had the ability to take foods that weren't usually paired and put them together for a delicious, low-calorie meal.

I picked up the phone before deciding which number to dial. Kali? Erik? Would either of them care about my new apartment? I had originally wanted to live with Erik. I wanted to buy an apartment that was big enough so I could have Erik as my roommate. But the thought of what the pantry in the kitchen would look like stopped me from pursuing it. Erik would buy food. All kinds of food would assault me as I opened the cupboard to reach in for a can of tuna. And I would have to prepare myself mentally every time I opened the refrigerator, as maybe one of those foods would tempt me enough to trigger a binge. On Sundays he might invite friends over to watch a game, eat pizza, and I would be left alone cleaning up the kitchen with the tortuous decision of whether to eat the remaining slice or throw it in the trash. Even if I threw it in the trash I couldn't be certain that the thought of eating it wouldn't keep me up all night, worried that I would retrieve it and eat the cold discarded piece despite the fact that it smelled of cigarette ash and beer. I would certainly get up out of bed and eat it. Then, knowing that I'd blown it, I'd have to keep going. I'd eat every bit of his food, his potato chips, and his leftover Chinese food, his breakfast cereal, and those chocolate cookies he eats when he needs to be comforted. My kitchen would be a dangerous temptress—and she would constantly flirt with the fat slob inside.

In my new apartment my fridge will be sparse. My cupboard will be bare. My house will be safe.

I picked up the phone to dial Ann in New York. I couldn't help but feel like a conversation with her would feel more like the second round of a boxing match than a celebration of my new apartment. Since the underwear episode on the show, Ann and I had barely spoken. Upon further evaluation of her comment about my looking like a normal woman in my underwear, I was quite sure she wasn't aware that she was insulting me. However, I was sure she was careful not to compliment me, either. She had expressed her opinions about not emphasizing looks and weight and had tried to get me to read feminist literature like Naomi Wolf's *The Beauty Myth*. No, Ann didn't mean anything by it. Nevertheless, I couldn't let a comment like that slip by again without retaliation. My gloves were on, ready to strike if Ann was being insensitive.

"AC. PdR"

"PdR!"

For some reason, when Ann and I first became friends, I had to call her by her full name, Ann Catrina, when I was referring to her. Then I had to say her full name to her face. Eventually it got so tedious to call her Ann Catrina, I shortened it to AC. She reciprocated by calling me PdR. So now we have that.

I excitedly told her about my new place while pouring my fourth Diet Coke; a low-calorie substitute for the wine I used to drink with dinner. Not drinking was yet another healthy change I had made since taking nutrition and fitness seriously. I told her about what had happened in St. Barths with Sacha. She said she was glad because she seemed to think there was a great gay girl out there who could really love me. That if I kept chasing Sacha as she was busy chasing men, I would miss this wonderful, proud-to-be-gay girl as I ran right by. What she couldn't quite tell me was how this self-confident, happy gay woman was going to meet a closeted Portia and be perfectly okay with going back into the closet to be her secret girlfriend. Where would I meet her? Would it occur at a supermarket when our shopping carts accidentally collided and we telepathically exchanged the information that we were gay, available, and interested? Ann Catrina needed to understand that there wasn't a solution to this problem. To shut her up, I told her the most disturbing information:

"There's a morality clause in the L'Oréal contract."

"A . . . what now?"

"It states that if I'm caught doing something that damages the image of the company, I'll have to pay all the money back. I'll have to pay back the advance, everything."

My agent and manager had called me to go over the contract just before the fitting. Remembering how I sat in the car with the cell phone to my ear, having to pull over in order to calm myself, I felt as sick telling Ann about it as I had when it was told to me. The clause cited examples like public drunkenness, arrests, et cetera, but I knew that it would include homosexuality. The wording of the contract was vague, and I was unsure exactly what would constitute a breach of the contract and how "morality" was defined. The whole thing made me sick. I was so scared about the morality clause I didn't want to even talk about it. I just wanted her to stop talking about how easy it would be for me to live my life openly. I just wanted her to shut up about it.

Before she could ask any questions or try to reason with me, I told her about my nutritionist.

"She has you on one thousand calories a day?"

"Yes. Well, no. I modified the diet a little. She told me to eat fourteen hundred for weight loss, but I wasn't really losing weight so I got rid of some extra calories here and there."

"She thinks you need to lose weight?"

"Yes. Oh, I don't know. We haven't really talked about that."

"What do you talk about, then?"

"Eating healthily. You know. Not gaining and losing all the time like I've been doing."

The more I talked, the more concern I could hear in her voice. Which annoyed me. She didn't understand the pressures of being an actress, of showing up to a photo shoot where the wardrobe was nothing but handcuffs and a strip of chainmail. She didn't know what it was like to try to find a dress for the Golden Globes and having only one good option because it was the only sample size dress that fit your portly body. She didn't know what it was like to hear that you have a normal-looking body after starving for weeks to get a thin-looking one, hoping that your friends would admire it. "Normal" isn't an adjective you wish to hear after putting that much effort into making sure it was spectacular.

"Ann. I gotta go."

"Go pour yourself a glass of wine and relax about it all. You've always looked great, PdR. There's nothing to worry about."

Right. Like I was going to drink wine two days before the L'Oréal shoot.

"Okay, AC. See you later."

"Oh! Before you go, can I stay with you in a couple of weeks? I'll be in town for a few days. A friend from UCLA just got engaged, so I thought I'd come to LA for the party."

No. No, you can't stay. Even if you come after I shoot L'Oréal, I need to keep going now this diet has started working for me. I need to eat at exactly six o'clock every night, and I can't drink alcohol with you like we used to. I can't go out to dinner anymore. I don't get to take a night or two off where I can eat whatever I want. I'm about to look good for the first time in my life, and for the first time I know I'm never going to gain it back again. So I can't take a few days off. If I eat and drink, I'll gain again. Besides, I don't even have the room anymore. I need to work out on my treadmill at 10:00 at night and 6:00 in the morning in the spare bedroom where you're expecting to stay.

"Yes. Of course you can. When?"

"Around the fifteenth. I'll email you."

I hung up the phone. The fifteenth was twelve days away. So I gave myself a new goal. Over the next twelve days, I would eat 800 calories a day. I needed to give myself a cushion so I could enjoy my time with Ann and not worry about gaining weight. If I lost a little more than I'd originally planned to lose, I would regulate my weight loss again after she left because I knew that weight lost too quickly was sure to return. Suzanne told me that. So I opened my journal and in the top right-hand corner of every dated page for the next twelve days I wrote 800. I would be ready for Ann's visit. I even looked forward to it.

I weighed myself first thing. I was 120 pounds. Actually I was probably a pound more, but my mother once showed me a trick to play on the scale where you set the dial a couple of pounds below the zero, but in a way that isn't very obvious to the logical part of your brain—especially from standing height looking down. If the needle sidles up to the zero, sitting next to it but not quite touching it, your brain is tricked into thinking that the needle needs to start in that position or the reading will be inaccurate. In fact, if you tap your toe on the scale the needle often resets itself to zero anyway, so to me lining up the dial perfectly with the zero was like sitting on a fence. Like I should've picked a side. Shall I choose denial of truth on the side that reads heavier but with the comfort of knowing that in reality I'm lighter, or shall I choose the immediate thrill of weighing in under the real number, to help with incentive?

I hated that zero. The zero is the worst part of the scale because the zero holds all the hope and excitement for what could be. It tells you that you can be anything you want if you work hard; that you make your own destiny. It tells you that every day is a new beginning. But that hadn't been true for me until recently. Because no matter what I did, no matter how much weight I lost, I always seemed to end up in the same place; standing on a scale looking down past my naked pro-truding belly and round thighs at 130 pounds.

But I was 120. It was the day of the L'Oréal commercial shoot. I should've been happy and yet I felt disturbed. My stomach was pro-truding very badly. It looked distended, almost. Or as my mother would put it, it looked like a poisoned pup. I hated it when stupid phrases like that popped into my mind. I hated that I had no control over my thoughts. But I especially hated that my stomach looked bloated and yet the rest of my body felt thinner. What was the point of dieting like I'd been doing, if on the most important day, my stomach was sticking out like a sore thumb?

I walked to the shower and punched my stupid stomach as I went. What could have caused this? The night before I ate only 200 calories of tuna with butter spray and mustard. How could I still see so much fat on my stomach? I stood under the shower and watched the water run between my breasts and over my stomach, cascading onto the shower floor from just past my navel because of the shelf that the protrusion of bulging fat had made. I picked up inches of fat with my fingers. It wasn't just bloat, it was fat. It was real fat; not something that I could take away by drinking water and sitting in a sauna. I'd ignorantly thought I wouldn't have any fat at 120 pounds.

I felt sick. I felt like I couldn't face the L'Oréal executives and the stylist again after what had happened last time. My suits were at least bigger, but with my stomach puffed out like this, I didn't know if that would even matter. What if I didn't fit into anything again? I started to cry. Stupid weakling that I am, I had to cry and make my eyes puffy to match my puffy body. I had finished shampooing my head when I realized that I used the wrong shampoo. With all the crying and obsessing about my stomach, I accidentally used cheap shampoo instead of the L'Oréal shampoo I was supposed to use the morning of the commercial. Now I would have red puffy eyes, a fat stomach, and hair that felt like straw to bring to the set. A derisive laugh escaped my throat as I realized that I was the spokesperson for the new shampoo but didn't use the shampoo that I'm selling because subconsciously I didn't believe the famous L'Oréal slogan, "Because I'm worth it."

"Because I'm not worth it." I said it out loud looking at a zit on my chin in the mirror using the same inflection the other L'Oréal girls use to tell the world that they are worth it: the same inflection that I'd use that day. It sounded funny so I kept saying it as I walked around the house.

"Because I'm not worth it," as I looked for pretty underwear that I didn't have among the ugly, stretched-out panties in my drawer. That I didn't think to buy some pretty, new underwear for the shoot was unbelievable to me.

"Because I'm not worth it," I said as I sipped my black coffee, wishing I were thin enough to have creamer in it because the strong black coffee tasted putrid and assaulted my taste buds. I skipped breakfast altogether because I wasn't worth it.

As I picked up my cell phone and walked to the door, I was aware of the time for the first time that morning. I was late. I should've been at the set already, and I didn't even know where I was going. With a surge of adrenaline, I rushed out the door and down the stairs, trying to decipher directions from the map. I was the star of the commercial and I was going to be late. All those people would be waiting for me. The L'Oréal executives, the director, the hairstylist and makeup artist who were both so renowned they had published books and signature product lines—all of them were waiting for me. Maybe that was a good thing. Maybe that's what stars were supposed to do. They're supposed to display their power by making other people wait for them. As I caught one red light after another, I had a choice to be in a frenzy of anxiety or relax into a character that keeps people waiting—like an R&B diva or a rock star. The lyrics of "Pennyroyal Tea" came to my mind. "I'm on my time with everyone." It was easier to play that character than to care.

17

WHEN ANN arrived I was still not at my goal weight. Although I had worked hard and I was ready to eat and drink with her, I still had weight to lose. I was 115 pounds and my goal was 110. I still had big thighs. I still saw round bulging thighs when I looked in the mirror. I didn't know if getting to 110 would take the bulges and the roundness away, but it was worth losing the extra pounds to try to make them straight. I just wanted them to look straight. Still, I needed to at least allow myself to have a drink with Ann Catrina, as it had been a while since I had seen any of my friends and I needed to have a little fun. Besides, I knew that depression caused weight gain because of some kind of chemical in your body that is released if you're unhappy and that can slow down your metabolism. Cortisol? Something like that.

Eating 800 calories a day was difficult. Not because it was too little food but because it was too much. One thousand calories divided perfectly into my daily meals, but no matter how I tried, I couldn't quite get 800 to fit. I removed the egg whites from the breakfast menu, opting to eat a serving midmorning, which left me with just the oatmeal. I had gotten used to eating the reduced portion of the prepackaged single serving of oatmeal and now it weighed in at 60 calories a serving. I added some blueberries, Splenda, and the butter spray so with the teaspoon of Mocha Mix I got my 100-calorie breakfast. I ate 60 calories of egg whites at around ten o'clock. One hundred and fifty calories of tuna with 50 additional calories for tomatoes, pickles, and lettuce was ample for lunch. Three ounces of turkey with butternut squash was around 300 calories and then an additional 40 calories for miscellaneous things—like gum or Crystal Light and coffee throughout the day—brought my total in at around 700. Quite often, if I was working and didn't have time to prepare the egg whites, then the daily total would be somewhere in the low six hundreds.

I fine-tuned my workout regimen. On days when I didn't have to go to the studio, I would begin my workout at exactly 6:00. On days I worked, I got out of bed at 4:15. I ran for forty-five minutes on the treadmill at 6.0 on a 1 incline. I didn't like running uphill. It did something weird to my lower back, but I felt I had to run harder and with my stomach tight to make up for it as most people run on an incline. I did sit-ups after my run. I did exactly 105 sit-ups. I wanted to do 100, but the 5 extra sit-ups allowed for some sloppy ones during my ten sets of ten reps. If I had time, I would do leg lifts: 105 with each leg. In addition to my workouts at home, I went to Mari Windsor Pilates and got a Pilates trainer. A costar had gone there and I'd read about Pilates in magazines so I thought I'd try it. It seemed that most celebrities were doing it, and I felt it was a particularly appropriate body-sculpting workout for me because it was originally designed for dancers and I used to be a dancer. It was slightly intimidating, however, because the other clients there were so thin and toned. It was a new goal to be thinner and more muscular than the other women at the Pilates studio, which ultimately was a good thing, because I have always thrived on healthy competition. After I was confident that I had the best body of all the paying customers, I would set my sights on the trainers.

Round Three: I was in my corner and Ann was in hers. Ann, a featherweight from New York City takes on Portia, the middleweight from sunny Southern California. Ann rang the bell by saying:

"Okay, I understand that you want to lose weight, but you should have some perspective on how much you're losing—like some way of measuring that isn't necessarily a scale. I know for me, there are clothes that are tight when I've gained weight and a little loose when I've lost weight. Certainly you have that, too. Like if you can fit comfortably into your skinny jeans, or if they're just a little loose, you're done losing weight, right?" She took a sip of wine, stroked my dog sitting in her lap, and waited for my response. I could tell that this conversation wasn't easy for her. And while I was quite chuffed that she'd care enough to have it with me, I wished she'd just shut up.

According to her laws, I guess I had no perspective. But what's perspective when you started out fat? Why would I ever want those jeans to be a little loose when they were a 28 waist? I couldn't tell her this, of course, because then we'd have to talk about how now I was on TV and that the "normal" life I lived at my "normal" weight no longer applied. I couldn't sit there and brag about how I was different now because I was on TV. I just wished she understood that without me having to explain it.

I was losing weight, though. I ordered a pair of 26 waist pants that took four weeks to arrive, and they were too big, too big by at least a size, maybe even two. I was really disturbed by this because I thought I'd looked good four weeks ago. God, I did a photo shoot for *Flair* four weeks ago and the magazine hadn't even come out yet. How disgusting that that was what people would think I looked like.

I guess some time had slid by without a response and Ann didn't like silence in a conversation, so she continued:

"I have to tell you something."

Here it comes, I thought. Here comes the part where she tells me I drink too much and right now I'm too drunk to take it well.

"You're too thin."

It was all I could do not to laugh. Really. The laughter was in my torso somewhere waiting to escape, but I stuffed it down because her face was so serious, plus I was enjoying it so much—the thought of being too thin. That's funny: too thin. Just this morning on the set I had to clench my buttocks as I walked through the law office on a full-length lens because if I walked normally the part where my hips meet my thighs bulged out rhythmically with each step: left fat bulge, right fat bulge, left fat bulge, and cue dialogue, "You wanted to see me?" Too thin. She continued talking about my arms being sinewy and veiny and how I looked like an eleven-year-old and that it wasn't attractive, but I just wanted to laugh. Oh, why not just enjoy this surreal moment and laugh? My face was contorting to control it from escaping anyway. I knew my face well enough to know that it's a traitor to my mind. It gives away all my secrets. And so I laughed. I laughed really hard.

"I'm sorry. It's not funny. I don't know why I'm finding it funny. It's not funny. It's just . . . you're so serious!"

"This is serious! You didn't have dinner tonight. And you don't look good, P. I think you've lost perspective."

My laughter died away. Not because what she was saying made sense to me but because I knew it was just an illusion created by my clothes or the way I was sitting.

It's not real. I'm not really thin. Should I show her my stomach and the rolls of fat? Or do I sit here on the floor and keep the pose that's making her think that I am thin so I can enjoy this moment longer?

I never wanted it to go away. I knew the minute I stood, it would be over. Or when I changed out of these magical jeans and into my pajamas. I was jutting out my collarbone subtly and separating my arm from my body to make her not feel stupid or wrong. She was going to realize it tomorrow, but for right now I knew she needed to be right and I needed to hear that I was thin. So I kept posing as a poor, starved waif until she stopped talking.

"Does any of what I'm saying make sense to you?"

What could I do? Answer her honestly? Say, no, AC, none of this makes sense because none of it is true. Even if you think you are telling me the truth, that I'm too thin, it's just your truth, your perspective. It's not society's perspective, the clothing designers' perspective. If it was, then models would have curves and actresses would have round faces and designers would make sample dresses bigger. What did she know? She was at NYU getting her master's in . . . something. Business? Besides, I'd never gotten so much attention for having a good body. I had just been featured in *In Style* for having the "Look of the Week." *US Weekly* gave me the "Best Dressed" accolade for the Rick Owens dress I wore to the Fox party. And last week Vera told me that I was her favorite actress to dress. I'd never gotten so many compliments. Everyone told me I looked fantastic.

"P, I'm just concerned, that's all."

"And I appreciate it, but there's nothing to worry about. I ate dinner."

"You didn't have dinner."

I had dinner. I ate grilled vegetables. I did stop eating them, though, because I could tell that they had used a lot of olive oil to cook them. I didn't wear any lip balm because I wanted to make sure I could detect if anything I ate was cooked with oil. I couldn't tell how much oil was used unless I had nothing waxy or oily on my lips. Besides, who knew whether the shea butter in lip balm contained calories that you could accidentally ingest? I had to worry about all the incidental calories, the hidden calories. Oil has a lot of calories and is a hidden ingredient in so many foods.

Oil is really my main problem right now.

"Look." I thrust my wineglass in her face. "I'm drinking alcohol! Plenty of calories in that."

God. I've drunk my weight in wine and she thinks I have a problem?

Ann shifted Bean slightly on her lap and looked around the room. She looked intently into each of the living room's corners as if searching for a way to change the subject. Her eyes settled on the open kitchen door. They remained there and I realized that my kitchen scale and a calorie counter were probably what she was looking at. While it oc-curred to me that there was a slim chance she actually thought I was too thin, I had decided moments ago that she was just jealous. Who wouldn't be? While I knew I wasn't skinny, it was obvious that I had gained control over my weight, which is a huge feat worthy of jealousy. Everyone wants to be in control of their weight.

"So. How was the L'Oréal shoot?"

"Great . . . really fun, actually. I think it'll be a pretty good commer-cial. I had to do that classic 'hair shot.' You know, where they fan out your hair? I felt pretty stupid doing that, but it should turn out okay." I took a sip of my wine. I wanted to tell her that I fit into my clothes and that most of them were even too big, but I couldn't. Usually, that would be the kind of thing we'd talk about, but after her rant about my being too thin, I had to keep quiet about the one thing that made me really happy. I wanted to tell her that they kept testing me by telling a PA to ask me if I wanted to eat or drink anything, like lunch or cof-fee, and I passed the test. I didn't eat all day and everyone was really impressed because they kept talking about it and asking me over and over again if I wanted food. I wanted to tell her that I got back at that bitch of a stylist for announcing to the L'Oréal executives that I was a size 8, by being too thin for her precious clothes. I wanted to describe the tailor's facial expression when she had to rush to take in the skirts that she once said didn't have "enough in the seam" to take out. But I couldn't. So I told her that I had fun and everyone was really nice. It was the kind of answer I'd give in an interview.

Just as I began to feel sorry for myself for having to lie to everyone, including my best friend, I remembered something that I thought she'd find funny.

"Well, there was one thing that was pretty funny. At one point the makeup guy and his assistant started talking about whether I could do makeup as well as the hair products—if I had good enough facial features . . ."

"That's great," she interrupted. "L'Oréal wants you to sell makeup as well?"

"No. No. They don't. My God, Ann—it was hilarious. They went through every part of my face—in front of me—tearing each feature apart like, 'What about lips?' And then the assistant would say, 'Well, she has lovely lips, but her teeth are a little crooked and not that white.' And then they got to my eyes. They almost agreed on mascara because I have really thick eyelashes until one of them mentioned that my eyes were too small."

I already knew that I had small eyes. *Us Weekly* told me. Thank God for that because before the article I thought my eyes were fairly normal and I treated them as such. Without their proper diagnosis, I couldn't apply the correct antidote to disguise this flaw. It was a piece on beauty and how the reader, if she identified with a particular flaw that could be seen on a celebrity, could deemphasize the problem. I had, "small, close-together eyes." I took their advice and have since applied dark swooping upward lines at the corners to lessen the appearance of the smallness and roundness of my close-together, beady little eyes.

"Anyway. It was pretty funny."

"That doesn't sound funny to me."

By the furrow in her brow, I could tell that unless I left the room I would be listening to another lecture—this time about how the L'Oréal executives aren't the experts and how I'm perfect the way I am. I would have had to nod my head and pretend to agree with her even though we both knew that I wasn't perfect and that L'Oréal clearly are the experts.

"I'm so sorry, AC, but I gotta go to bed because I have to get up early. You got everything you need? You good?"

"Yeah. I'll go to bed in a minute. And I won't see you before I leave, I guess, but I'm here if you want to talk. Call me anytime, okay?"

"Okay. Good night." I bent down and hugged her. I adored AC. She had only ever wanted the best for me. Unfortunately, she didn't understand that what was best for me before getting the show and what was best for me now were two different things.

I glanced at the treadmill as I passed the guest bedroom door on my way to the bathroom. *Get on the treadmill.* I couldn't even imagine how many calories were in those three glasses of wine. The voice in my head told me that I was lazy, that I didn't deserve a day off, but there was nothing I could do about it and so I brushed my teeth and slipped into bed.

Lying in bed was always the worst time of the day. If I hadn't done all that I could do to help myself, I imagined what the insides of my body were doing. As I lay motionless and waiting for sleep, I stared at the ceiling and imagined molecular energy like the scientific renditions I'd seen in science class as a kid, shaped like hectagons and forming blocks of fat in my body—honeycomb parasites attaching to my thighs. Or I'd see fat in a cooling frying pan and imagined the once vital liquid energy slowly coagulating into cold, white fat, coating the red walls in my body like a virus. The unused calories in my body caused me anxiety because I was just lying there, passively allowing the fat to happen, just as I had passively allowed myself to keep ballooning to 130 pounds. But did I have the energy to get out of bed and do sit-ups? The wine had made me lazy. I had the anxiety, but I was too lethargic to relieve myself of it by working out. I could've thrown up. But if I threw up the wine, Ann might have heard and then she'd never get off my case. If I threw up, then she'd feel validated and I'd feel stupid because that's not what I did anymore. I was healthy now. I had the willpower not to crash diet and then binge and purge. I had solved that problem.

I got out of bed and onto the floor to start my sit-ups. I couldn't think that I had solved the problem of my weight fluctuating if I just lay in bed allowing the sugar in the wine to turn into fat. As I began my crunches, I heard Ann getting ready for bed. I could hear her checking her messages on her cell phone and I could vaguely make out a man's voice on the other end. As she turned out the light and got into the bed that I'd moved against the wall to make way for the treadmill, I couldn't help but wish I were her. I wished I were a student living in New York, dating and going to parties. I wished I could travel to another city and stay over at a friend's house without worrying about what I was going to eat. I wished I could just eat because I was hungry. I wished my life wasn't about how I looked especially because how I looked was my least favorite part of myself. I wished I had a life where I could meet someone I could marry.

18

What did you eat last night?

I awoke to this question in a room that was still slightly unfamiliar even though I had lived in the new apartment for over a month. As I calmed myself by running through the list of foods I'd eaten the day before, I noticed a crack on the bedroom ceiling where it met the wall and was beginning to run toward the window that faced the yellow desert that was the wall of the Sunset 5. Not only was the bedroom still slightly unfamiliar to me, but the whole downstairs level also, as I only ate and slept on the first floor, spending most of my waking hours upstairs in the attic. My treadmill was upstairs in the attic and it was beckoning me as it always did after I had completed my mental calculations of calories in and out. The treadmill was really the only thing up there and was perfectly centered in the attic, between the wall of windows that showcased the industrial city that was the roof of the Sunset 5 and the east windows through which I could see all the way downtown. The wall opposite the smokestacks acted as a bulletin board where I had taped pieces of paper. Because the walls would soon be replastered and repainted, they were not precious; they had no value other than as a place to put my thoughts. Mostly the pieces of paper were exaggerated to-do lists. I say "exaggerated" because they said things that were more like goals that I wanted to achieve than things that needed to be done. The largest piece of paper with the boldest

writing stated, I WILL BE 105 POUNDS BY CHRISTMAS. Another
stated, I WILL STAR IN A BIG-BUDGET MOVIE NEXT SUMMER.

Starring in a movie had only recently become important to me, as
Lucy Liu had just gotten *Charlie's Angels*. Suddenly being a cast member on *Ally McBeal* didn't seem to be enough anymore. Everyone at
work was reading movie scripts and going on auditions. I often recited
my audition lines while I was on the treadmill. I recited them out loud,
loudly, over the noisy whirring and the thud of my footfall as I jogged
at a 5.5/1 incline. I also put a TV up there with a VCR so I could
run and watch movies, which was so much better than sitting to watch
them. I had discovered that I could do a lot on the treadmill. I could
read books and scripts and knit on the treadmill.

As I began my morning workout, I looked over at the cards on the
left of the to-do list which ran down the length of the wall.

111
110
109
108
107
106
105

I was 111 pounds. Each time I lost a pound I took the card off the
wall. It helped keep me focused and it helped me to remember that
once I'd achieved the new lower weight and the card stating my previous weight was gone, that I could never weigh that much again; that the
old weight was gone. It was no longer who I was. It was getting more
difficult to lose weight as I got thinner, so I needed all the incentive
and motivation I could muster. Putting my weight on the wall was a
clever thing to do as it always needed to be in the forefront of my mind,
otherwise I might've forgotten and walked on the treadmill instead of

run, sat instead of paced. I once saw a loft where a famous writer lived, and all over the wall was his research for the novel he was writing. He described the book to me as his life's work, his magnum opus. I felt like controlling my weight was my magnum opus, the most important product of my brain and was worthy of devoting a wall to its success.

I liked doing my morning workout in the attic even though I lived next to a Crunch gym. When I first moved into the apartment I went to Crunch often, but I discovered that I didn't like showing my body to the other patrons who were no doubt looking at me as critically as I was looking at them. I hated the thought of them recognizing me and telling their friends that Nelle Porter had a round stomach or that when I walked on the treadmill the tops of my thighs bulged out from side to side. What I hated most about going next door to Crunch was the possibility of paparazzi finding me on the way home after a workout, when I looked bloated and my sweatpants were clinging to my thighs. So instead of subjecting myself to the worry of being seen by people and cameras, I preferred to use my treadmill in the attic or to run up and down the stairs next to the elevator for exercise. Sometimes, if I felt particularly energetic, I would time myself as I ran the six flights that connected all the floors of my apartment building. I would run up and down, all the way from the penthouse to the ground floor and back. I could do this mostly unseen by the other tenants, as most of them were lazy and only ever took the elevator.

As I ran on the treadmill in my attic, however, I occasionally felt paranoid. Although it wasn't very likely, I sometimes felt that it was possible that a photographer was taking pictures of me from the in-dustrial roof, that through the smoke he could get clear shots of Portia running on the treadmill in a big empty room. Or he would take video of me lunging from one side of the room to the other, as I had decided I would lunge instead of walk, since lunging would maximize the number of calories I could burn and help tone my legs at the same time. What made the possibility of paparazzi finding me in my loft even more frightening was that I wore only my underwear when I was at home because I liked to stay as cold as possible to burn calories and because, since I was always running when I was home, if I wore workout gear I'd just have more laundry to do. It terrified me to think of that tabloid picture: Portia in just her underwear, running and lunging, a wall of numbers and weight loss goals behind her.

My paranoid thoughts were interrupted by the shrill sound of Bean's bark. Although I would've loved to ignore her and finish my workout, I knew she needed to be taken out. I had only been running for forty-five minutes and I had to leave for work very soon. Reluctantly, I got off the treadmill and went back downstairs to clothe myself and collect her. Having to travel between floors in my underwear using the exterior public staircase was interesting. I had planned on renovating shortly after owning the apartment, connecting the floors and making it more my taste, but I couldn't find the time to search for the perfect architect and designer in between working and working out. I kind of liked it separated, too. I liked that I was hard to find in this secret room that no one, not even a housekeeper, knew existed. I could hide in the attic. And while I didn't like the beige carpet and the previous owner's bed frame and cheap dining table on the first floor, I couldn't be judged for my apartment's decor since it wasn't mine, it wasn't my taste. It was liberating, actually, to live in a space that I owned yet it didn't announce my personality. I could still be anything I liked. I didn't have to live with my previous conclusions of who I was reflected all around me in furnishings and paintings, fabric and stainless steel appliances. I lived in a blank canvas, albeit an old and sullied blank canvas, upon which one day I could create a tasteful masterpiece. While I waited to create my space, however, I had barely any furniture. I had no chairs and no sofa, no coffee table. The only indication that someone lived there was my large collection of antique mannequins that were propped up around the living room. While I had always enjoyed them as an expression of the female form, the mannequins became useful as sometimes

I measured them and compared my body measurements. I had just started measuring my body parts as a more accurate indication of my weight loss. Mannequins represented the ideal form. By comparing myself to the mannequins, I could take an honest look at how I measured up to that ideal. But mostly I just liked to look at their thin, hard limbs.

As I pulled out of the parking garage of my apartment, I checked the time. It was 9:02. It took a long time to drive to work from anywhere in Los Angeles, since Manhattan Beach was far from the city. I didn't get to finish my workout, as Bean took an inordinately long time to go to the bathroom on the lawn of the garden terrace on the second floor. While I could have left her there on her own and come back to collect her on my way down to the parking garage, I decided to wait with her, however impatiently. Although the garden was walled and looked quite safe, I couldn't risk losing her. She was my best friend.

I seemed to catch every traffic light on Crescent Heights Boulevard. As I sat and waited, staring at the big red light that was preventing me from moving, I began to feel lightheaded. My palms were sweaty. I was feeling nervous and anxious and yet I couldn't attribute these feelings to being late for work—I'd given myself plenty of time for the long drive. I realized that I felt anxious solely because I wasn't moving. When the light finally turned green, my stomach continued to feel fluttery, my palms still slipping slightly on the steering wheel, my sweaty hands unable to grip it firmly. Sitting behind the steering wheel, pinned to the seat with a tight strap, I felt as though the cabin were closing in on me; the faux-suede roof was barely tall enough for the loose knot of thick hair that was held on top of my head by a chopstick. As I turned my head to the right to check on Bean who had jumped from the passenger seat and into the back, the chopstick scraped against the window; a sound that shot through my nerves, filling my mouth with saliva that tasted like metal. I tried to shake it off. I shook my hands and pumped my arms. I made circles with the foot on my left leg. I lit a cigarette to counteract the metallic taste and to calm my nerves, but the wisps of blue smoke curling up into the windshield looked poisonous, which cigarette smoke sometimes did to me when I was in confined spaces and forced to look at what I was actually inhaling. It looked very blue trapped between steering wheel and the windshield before turning white and making its way through the front, turning clear as it reached Bean in the back. I painstakingly extinguished the cigarette, careful to be sure that it was completely out, and I wondered when I was going to use up the calories I'd eaten for breakfast as I hadn't had time to do my full one-hour run. As I followed the last wisp of smoke from the ashtray as it meandered upward and collided with the passenger window, I saw a beautiful tree-lined street on my right named Commodore Sloat. The name struck me as being very odd as it sounded more like a street name you'd come across in London than where I was, south of Wilshire in Los Angeles. I checked the time: 9:20. It occurred to me in a flash of excitement that I had time to get out of the car and away from this anxious feeling of being trapped, stale, and inactive. I would take a quick run up and down that street.

"Good morning, Portia." Vera smiled as I walked into the fitting room. She smiled and shook her head. "Could you get any thinner? Look at you! Every time I see you, you just keep looking better and better. I hate you!" Vera laughed and wheeled in a rack of clothing. I started to undress in front of her and stood proudly in only a G-string and platform shoes. I felt liberated. I felt free because I no longer had to worry about how I looked, or whether the clothes would fit, or if I deserved to be on a hit TV show. I didn't have to worry what people were saying about me. Anyone who looked at me could see that I was professional.

The first suit was too big, as were the second and the third. My mind didn't wander to a happier time and place like it usually did during a fitting. I simply couldn't have been happier than I was in the present moment.

"Can you get twos and fours for the Skinny Minnie from now on," Vera called out to her assistant. "And maybe get her some shorter skirts. Let's show off those long legs of hers."

Skinny Minnie. As stupid as that name was, I felt delighted that someone would attach it to me. She handed me sweaters rather than jackets because, as she explained, the jackets she pulled for me would all be too big. To my amazement and delight, everything was too big. We set a time for another fitting the following day.

She shook her head again. "I wish I had a tenth of your discipline."

"Well, I had help. I have a great nutritionist." I looked at Vera's body. She was chubby. I'd never noticed before. "You don't need to lose weight. You look great."

Conversations about weight are practically scripted. There are only a couple of things to say in response to a woman complaining about her weight, and the response I just gave Vera was probably the most popular.

"I need to lose twenty pounds—at least! Seriously, will you tell me how you did it? Like, what do you eat? What's, like, your average day?"

She admired me. She really looked as though she was a little in awe. She thought I could teach her how to be disciplined, which was ridiculous. You can't teach someone self-control any more than you can teach them common sense.

"I'd love to, but it's really tailor-made to what my body responds best to. I really don't think it would work for you."

I wouldn't have ever told her my secrets. This was mine. I was successful at the one thing almost everyone wants to be good at, dieting. Besides, I couldn't tell anyone what I ate. I could just imagine her face when I told her that if she wanted to achieve this level of success then she'd have to eat two-thirds of an oatmeal sachet for breakfast, tuna with butter spray for lunch, a spoonful of ground turkey with butter spray for dinner, and for a treat, Jell-O mixed with butter spray.

"Okay then, Skinny Minnie. Fine. You're done losing weight now though, right? 'Cause you look perfect—but any more and you'll be too thin."

"Yep. Hard part's over. It's all about maintaining it now."

I wasn't done losing weight. Although I thought I looked good, I knew I could look even better. When I turned sideways to a mirror, I could see that the front of my thighs were shaped like a banana from my knee to my hips. At 105 pounds, my goal weight, they would look straight. I still had six more pounds to go.

"Gotta go to work. They need me on set. See you tomorrow." I left the wardrobe rooms feeling elated. I didn't even need to smoke a cigarette. As I walked to the set, I felt calm and in control.

"Morning, Portia." Peter greeted me as I walked into the unisex bathroom set where my one half-page scene would take place. I didn't have any dialogue. I seemed to be used less and less, which was annoying because I'd never looked more camera-ready. I'd never looked more like an actress should look.

"Hi. Good morning. How's it going here?"

"You know. Same old stuff. I'm in court again this episode." He rolled his eyes. He was always in court.

"Better you than me." I said it, but I didn't mean it. I was extremely jealous that David Kelley gave Peter his clever cross-examinations, his brilliant closing arguments. I thought that I had proven my chops as an attorney the previous season, and yet I was relegated to the odd scene in the background of the law office. I had even lost my status as the sexy, untouchable love interest that had me revealing myself in my underwear. It seemed ironic that since I had spent hours a day sculpting my body, preparing myself for scenes that I used to be unprepared for, I no longer had the scenes.

Although I was acting in the scene with him, it felt like I was watching Peter perform, just as the crew was watching him perform. He walked into the unisex bathroom, saw me in the character of Nelle, yelped, and walked back out. In every take he was hilarious. I did nothing. I just had to stand still and in a very specific spot so the mirrors in the unisex set didn't reflect my face into the lens. I was told that if the camera saw me, I would ruin the joke.

After I finished my one scene that morning, I met my brother for lunch at Koo Koo Roo. I usually ate lunch alone, preferring to eat my canned tuna and butter spray in the privacy of my dressing room. I had made a makeshift kitchen in the shower of my bathroom where I stocked spices and bottles of Bragg Liquid Aminos, canned tuna, and Jell-O. I also kept all the tools I needed—a can opener, chopsticks, and bowls. One bowl, however, I had to take back and forth with me because I used it to help me measure portions. It was a cheap Chinese-looking footed bowl with fake pottery wheel rings on the inside, and the first ring served as a marker to show me how much tuna I should eat. If for some reason, when I was mixing my portion of tuna with the seasoning and butter spray it went over the first ring, I tended to throw it away and start over. Usually, if it went over the first ring when I was mixing it meant I was too anxious to eat and I was hurrying out of sheer greed. As I ate approximately a third of a can of tuna per meal, there were three chances to get it right.

I didn't like to eat out or with other people, but I hadn't seen my brother in a while and so I made an exception. He had been asking me to celebrate with him for some time as he had quit working for the biomedical product company and started his own helicopter company, Los Angeles Helicopters. I chose the venue. Koo Koo Roo was the only restaurant I would go to, as they seemed to use very little oil or fat. When I walked in, my brother was already sitting down, a plate full of food in front of him.

"Sorry, Sissy." He gestured to his food. "I have a meeting at two o'clock." He reached into my bag where he knew he'd find a silky white head to pet. "Hi, Beany." He whispered his hello to my dog who illegally went everywhere with me in that bag.

"Don't worry about it," I told him. "Clearly Mr. Bigshot Pilot is too important to wait for his sister."

My brother is a pilot and I am an actress, I thought. Two kids from Australia and here we are in LA, both living our dreams.

"I'll go order."

I was secretly very relieved that he had gotten his lunch before me. Ordering the four-ounce turkey dinner at Koo Koo Roo in Manhattan Beach could be tricky. Only the one in Hancock Park near my old apartment weighed my turkey under the four-ounce portion because they knew I liked it that way. At other locations, like this one, the people behind the counters argued that I would have to pay the same price for the full four ounces so I might as well have the full four ounces. It was a tiring argument for me and a confusing one for them as they thought I was presenting them with some kind of riddle. I liked the restaurant chain, but because the one closest to my home was difficult for me to frequent, I tended to eat there less. I couldn't go to the Koo Koo Roo on Santa Monica near my home because it was in the middle of boys' town, the gay part of town, and I was terrified that if I were seen there, people would know I was gay. Although sometimes I thought that was ridiculous, mostly I thought staying away was the right thing to do. After all, everyone in there was gay, so why wouldn't I also be gay? Would I be the only heterosexual in the whole place looking for turkey? Would the customers look at me with surprise and concern, having had a rare sighting of a heterosexual who has clearly lost her way, and offer to give me directions to get back to the straight side of town? Or would they quietly snigger and congratulate themselves for having a finely tuned gaydar, for knowing that I was gay all along, as they stood in line to place their orders?

I sat down with my plate of turkey all four ounces of it despite asking for three—and immediately began feeding Bean from the plate. She loved turkey and she helped keep my portions down. She loved Koo Koo Roo as much as I did. I was so busy feeding Bean, it wasn't until my brother spoke that I realized that he had been watching me in silence for quite some time.

"You gonna eat any of that yourself?" I looked up at my brother and was surprised to see that he looked almost angry. His arms were folded tightly across his chest. His lips looked thinner than usual and his eyes seemed shallow, like he'd put an invisible shield behind them that blocked out the kindness in his soul that he'd shown me only moments before.

"You're giving your lunch to your dog, Porshe." Now my brother sounded angry. He never called me anything but Sissy unless he was pissed.

"Chill out, would ya? What's wrong with you?" Now I was getting pissed. "I don't eat all four ounces of it because it has too many calories, okay?"

"And how many calories do you eat?"

"Fourteen hundred a day, like everyone else." I hated lying. I found myself doing so much of it lately. I couldn't tell anyone the truth anymore.

"Bullshit. You can't be eating that much. You look really thin."

It was all I could do not to smile. What with Vera calling me Skinny Minnie and now this, I had had a really great day.

"That's not a compliment, idiot."

Damn. I must have smirked.

"I know." I knew he didn't mean it as a compliment because of the tone of his voice, but how could anyone ever take "you look really thin" as anything but a compliment?

"Okay—I'll gain a little weight. Jesus." When attacked, defend by lying. "It's not deliberate. I've just been working too hard lately." I was watching him become more relieved, but there was obviously something more that he needed to hear.

"I know I'm too skinny."

That did it. He looked happier, his lips fuller, his eyes not so cold. His arms fell to his side.

"Don't you have a meeting?" I asked him.

He nodded.

"Okay then. Bugger off." I kissed his cheek and smiled.

He reached into my bag to pet Bean. He started to leave but then turned back toward me.

"Just because you work with someone who's skinny, doesn't mean you have to be skinny, too."

19

SAT ON Suzanne's couch. Seeing Suzanne had become a pretty exciting ritual for me as I got to show her how well this little student was doing with her homework. I had certainly lost weight on her program, even though I had to lie about how many calories I was eating. I never went back to 1,400 calories a day because I didn't need to. After Ann's visit, I actually never went back to 1,000. There was no point in increasing my daily calorie intake when 600 to 700 was working so well for me. My weight loss had slowed down slightly since going under 110 pounds, and that was even more reason to stick with the lower calorie consumption.

"How many calories are you eating, Portia?"

"Fourteen hundred." I answered her with a slightly incredulous tone in my voice, hoping that the tone would convince her that I was telling the truth.

"Can I see your diary?"

I reached into my bag for the journal, careful to pull out the right one. There were two journals in my bag at all times, the real one and the one for Suzanne. Not only did the real one show my actual calorie consumption, it had notes and messages in it as incentive for me to stay on track. I used the same motivating techniques in my diary as I did when I was a kid striving for high honors in my ballet exams, but whereas I wrote, "You will not get honors" on a sheet of paper for the ballet exams, now I wrote "You are nothing," on every page of my diary. I don't know why, but that statement filled me with fear and then the desire to be "something." I always used the thoughts of being nothing and going nowhere to help me achieve goals. When I was a teenager studying to get into law school, I would repeatedly listen to a Sonic Youth song called "Song for Karen" about Karen Carpenter, who died from anorexia. In the song, the phrase that Kim Gordon repeats, "You aren't never going anywhere. I ain't never going anywhere" was like a mantra for me and pushed me to study longer, to try harder.

But I knew my motivating techniques weren't conventional and I couldn't share them with Suzanne. Especially because in my diary I referred to my homosexuality, which was something she didn't know about. I could imagine how horrified Suzanne would be if by accident I pulled out the real diary and she saw YOU ARE A FAT UGLY DYKE written all over it. She probably thought she'd never even met a lesbian. It made me smile just thinking about the expression on her face if she'd known there was one in her living room.

I handed her the fake journal. It was very time-consuming having to make up the "proper" amount of food with its weight and calories. Thank God for the calorie counter. But the most annoying thing was putting variation in my pretend diet. I had to pretend to be interested in a wide variety of foods, which I wasn't. Most people aren't. My mother ate practically the same thing every day. In fact, I only ate seven things: turkey, lettuce, tuna, oatmeal, blueberries, egg whites, and yogurt; eight if you included Jell-O. She looked over it as I sat opposite her feeling like a schoolkid who cheated on a test. Only when she handed it back to me was I aware that I had been holding my breath.

"What does your exercise program look like, Portia?"

"You didn't tell me to write it down." Even though I had wanted to brag to her about the amount of exercise I did, I didn't write it down. At least not in the fake diary I made especially for her.

"No. I'm just curious. What kind of exercise do you do?"

"I run, mainly. Pilates, sometimes. But running, I guess." I told her about the amount of time I spent on the treadmill and that I'd found a way to run on it for my entire lunch break at work without ruining my makeup. I told her about my long drive to work and how I liked to break it up with a run. I knew she'd be proud of me. It must be heartbreaking for a nutritionist if her clients are too lazy to increase their exercise to help her do her job. I bet they'd blame her, too, if they didn't lose weight.

"I found this nice, tree-lined block just south of Wilshire where I can run because sitting for too long kills me."

"What do you think will happen if you sit for too long?"

"I'll get fat, Suzanne! Diet is only half of it, you know."

She looked concerned. The look didn't surprise me because she always looked concerned when I spoke. I had decided that that was just how she looked all the time. I learned to ignore it.

"Portia, can I ask, do you get your period regularly?" She looked slightly embarrassed at having to ask the question.

"Sure, I guess." I'd never really thought about it. Because I wasn't scared of getting pregnant, I didn't really pay attention to it. I thought back over the last couple of months and realized that I couldn't remember having it.

"No, actually. Now I think about it, I can't remember the last time I had it."

She nodded her head repeatedly, but the movement was so small it was almost imperceptible. If I hadn't have been looking directly at her, I wouldn't have seen it. But her silence commanded my attention. I found myself breathlessly waiting for her next word, yet I didn't know why.

"Portia, have you ever seen anyone . . . like . . . a counselor . . . who could help you deal with your weight issues?"

I was confused. Wasn't she helping me deal with my weight issues?

"You mean, in the past?"

"Yes. Did your mother have you see anyone when you were a teenager?"

I went to Jenny Craig and Gloria Marshall. I guessed I could tell her about that.

"When I was fifteen—the year off school to model—I went to a couple of weight-loss centers."

I told her that after the Fen-phen-type drug didn't work, my mother and I decided to consult the dieting professionals. Jenny Craig was first, with its eating plan and meals in cans purchasable at the counter after each group session with fat women in chairs sitting in a circle. I didn't lose weight. I gained it. I stopped eating the canned food and became too busy with homework to attend the scheduled meetings. But my mother and I discovered Gloria Marshall, with its flexible schedule and gymlike atmosphere and so I joined that as well.

The Gloria Marshall center closest to my house was two train stops and a short walk away and I could go there any time I liked. I would pack loose-fitting clothing into my bag and stop by on my way home from a modeling go-see. I would change, weigh in, and get to work, kneeling on one knee while placing the length of my thigh on a wooden trundle machine that looked more like a wheel used for spinning wool than workout equipment. While my thigh was being pummeled by the wooden spinning wheel, the radio would play "A Horse with No Name." Always. There was no exception. The song made me very depressed that the man was a nomad with no attachment, no home. I didn't think he was free and had chosen to forgo all the other ways humans make themselves feel falsely purposeful and safe. I thought he was lost. And that his survival depended on the horse and that he could care for the horse but not have attachment to it scared me and made me feel empty. But I've always read too much into songs. When I was eight years old, the song that would play to call us in from the playground at the end of afternoon recess was, "Those were the days, my friend, we thought they'd never end," and every day I became instantly nostalgic for the moment that had just ended, knowing that I'd never be eight again, that I'd soon be burdened with knowing more than I did at that moment when I had two loving parents and no responsibility.

I was received by the patrons of Gloria Marshall in a similar way to those at Jenny Craig, with disdain, only the Gloria Marshall counselor used me as an example of how effective their program was so the ladies regarded me with hope and a little awe. They didn't know that 128 pounds, the "target" weight to which most of them were aspiring, was my starting weight. When I became the model Gloria Marshall client, I hadn't even started the program.

It was clear by the look on Suzanne's face that what she was hearing wasn't normal to her. I had never before thought of myself as abnormal in my approach to food and weight. As a young teenager I was surrounded by models who would drink only watermelon juice for two days before a shoot, or eat a big dinner, do cocaine, and go wild on the dance floor of a nightclub to burn the calories from the food. But I didn't need to be a model to surround myself with diet-obsessed unhealthy people. School was full of them. Suzanne's shock made me think she lived in another world, an unrealistic world where teenage girls were happy with their bodies just the way God made them and nourished them with the home-cooked meals their mothers made so they could grow up to pursue a career knowing that what a girl accomplished was of far greater importance than how she looked. And maybe that world did exist, although I have never even briefly visited, much less lived in it. There was a moment in the session with Suzanne when I thought about law school, how everyone seemed to place value only on grades, not looks, and how I had carried over from high school the idea that somehow my personality would help my grades. That if I mooted with sarcasm and wit, I would win the mock trial by being the most entertaining. I also thought that hair, makeup, and wardrobe would win quite a few points. I thought that if I rolled into a lecture on Rollerblades flush from a modeling job, I could be the teacher's pet, that I'd get more attention, more private tutoring. None of that happened for me. Instead I felt vacuous, frivolous, a dumb blonde who didn't belong. There was nothing cute about an obnoxious girl flitting around from modeling jobs to lectures on Rollerblades. I became deeply ashamed just thinking about it.

It felt strange, all of a sudden: sitting there, exposed and abnormal. I'd said too much. After all, Suzanne was just a nutritionist. I had come to learn what to eat and how to stay on track with my diet, not to spill my guts about my childhood and my insecurities. I realized at that moment what she was referring to when she asked if I'd seen a counselor at the beginning of the session. And in the silence following my rambling, I could see by her smug expression that I had confirmed to her that I was in the wrong place.

"Portia. I want you to be healthy and happy, but I don't know if I'm helping you achieve that. I don't think I'm qualified to help you."

I looked down past my manly hands that were sitting on my lap to a stain on the carpet.

Of course you can't help me. I'm losing weight on my own.

The fact that I had to write a pretend journal should've been an indication to me that I knew more than she did on the subject of weight loss.

I looked at her and smiled sweetly.

She went on to tell me that I had issues that were best handled by a specialist. She told me she would research eating disorder therapists. Then she asked for my mother's phone number in Australia.

20

WITHOUT HAVING an assistant go to the Beverly Center to run my errands for me, I was forced to pull into the parking structure of the dreadful shopping mall on my way home from work to take care of a couple of items myself. I had been contemplating whether to get an assistant, but it was hard to justify such a self-aggrandizing hire. I could certainly afford one, but I wondered how that would look to my friends and family. How would it look to my co-stars when most of them didn't have one even though they worked a lot more than me? As my character seemed to be appearing in fewer and fewer scenes as the weeks and episodes rolled on, Nelle Porter required hardly any of my time at all, which gave me all the time in the world to shop.

I hated going shopping. I always tended to feel lonely, even with Bean in a bag by my side. I hated being surrounded by people and yet having no one to help me make a purchase other than the person trying to sell it to me. I hated feeling the desperation of sales assistants and knowing that the commission from my purchase could make or break their day. I also hated people looking at me, I hated children screaming, I hated loud, distracting music, I hated the pet stores with the sick tiny puppies in hot glass cages, and I hated who I was. I discovered how pathetic I was in a store. I defined myself by the items I chose. I could find what I was looking for in black and in pink, and for twenty minutes I would try to decide if I wanted the black one or the pink one. I would think that I was more of a "black" person but that getting it in black was too ordinary. It made me wish that I were a "pink" person when I'm not a "pink" person. This kind of thinking was amplified in a clothing store because invariably I would be overwhelmed by everything I was not only to discover that who I was didn't even have a place in the store. That in all of Barneys, there wasn't a tank top or a pair of cargo pants that let me know that I was a welcome member of their society; that they have covered the fashion needs of the upwardly mobile young women who can afford to shop there while sending a message to me that I was not welcome. I didn't belong there. It told me that their young women wore short skirts and heels and delicate tops with small straps and elegant, tiny necklaces. Their young women were delicate, with soft manners and good bone structure because these young women had inherited the delicate, tall, thin gene from their beautiful mothers who, twenty years prior, were seduced into making offspring by their wealthy, powerful fathers. The Barney's clientele had no need for tanks with thick straps, boots, and cargo pants. "Go to the Gap with the average, ordinary, people" is the message the store was sending. "You'll find something for yourself there."

As I boarded the escalator and rode down into the bowels of the Beverly Center shopping mall, I became paranoid that my activities might be recorded by the paparazzi. It wasn't that I feared being caught doing something wrong, it was that I feared being caught doing something so ordinary. I hated paparazzi. Paparazzi made me feel like I was a criminal under investigation for insurance fraud, stalked by photographers who were hired to provide the evidence. Paparazzi are the ultimate hunters. They are patient, prepared, and precise. There's a wordless exchange that occurs between the hunter and the hunted. They tell you that while you may have gotten away with your life this time, they'll take away your life next time. They'll ruin the illusion that is your fake life—the life that you show to the world while keeping all the secrets of your real life hidden. The photographers and you both know that it's only a matter of time; that with persistence they will expose you for the fraud you are. They told me with one glance that they knew I was gay, that I was fat under the flattering shirt I was wearing, that I was Amanda Rogers, a no one from nowhere. Having an assistant would lessen the chance of being caught as I tended to play the "maybe I can get away with it" game. I would let my guard down, feeling stupid for having an over-inflated ego and thinking that people cared about me enough to take my photo, only to discover that indeed they did.

As far as I could tell, there were no paparazzi at the Beverly Center. After buying a black exercise mat and nude underwear, I headed back to the car. I decided that because I hadn't eaten for many hours and my calorie count was fairly low that day, I would allow myself to have a piece of Extra chewing gum. I always allowed myself to have the gum, but at 5 calories a stick, I had to add it to my daily calorie allowance because it was these kinds of unrecorded calories that could build up and cause you to gain weight. I put my seat belt on, reached into my bag for a piece of gum, and put it in my mouth. The sweetness and coolness of it filled my body with a current of ecstasy, and a rush of syrupy water flooded my mouth and my belly. After what seemed like only seconds of chewing, the initial surge was over and I could almost feel my endorphins screaming for survival as they slowly faded back into the blackness of my empty body. Worse than feeling depressed that the rush was over was the feeling of ravenous hunger ripping through my head and my gut. It was a pain that I had never experienced. As if under hypnosis, I reached into my bag again. Robotically, I unwrapped the gum and fed a piece into my mouth. I fed another piece into my mouth. I spat the wad of chewed gum into the ashtray and fed one more piece into my mouth. And then I shoved the pieces into my mouth two at a time. I spat them out. I repeated the frenzied feeding, chewing, and spitting. And then it was done. There were no more sticks of Winterfresh gum left. I slowly came back into my mind only to realize that I'd just consumed 60 calories. I sat in the car unable to turn the key, terrified by what had happened. There was no reason for it, no upsetting situation that had sometimes triggered me to binge in the past, nor was it a conscious decision to blow my intake for the day. It was a normal day, pleasant even. Without an indication, how would I know when this might happen again? What if it happened once a day? How the hell was I not in control of the only thing I thought was possible to control in my life?

I had been abducted. I was not in control. Now I would live in this state of constant anxiety that I would be overtaken by this vacancy of mind. I would hover there, in this place of helplessness and uncertainty, waiting to be abducted again.

A surge of fear and anger rushed through my body, and I ripped off my seat belt and got out of the car. In the crowded parking structure of the Beverly Center, I started running. If I couldn't control the intake, I could control what happened next. I could eliminate it. I could run it off. I started sprinting. I ran as fast as I could to the concrete wall at the end of the parking structure, slapped the wall with my hand like a swimmer at the end of a lap, and like a swimmer I used the energy to turn back in the direction I came with ferocious speed, getting faster and faster with each pump of my arms and legs. When I ran past my car, I could hear my dog barking, her barking getting fainter as I sprinted to the other end of the parking structure, dodging the occasional car that pulled out of a space, and slapped the opposite wall, catapulting myself off the wall in the other direction to repeat the exercise. I was aware of loud screeching noises as cars passed me, their tires making that sound as they struggled to grip onto the slick concrete through the turns, some of them bulging into the oncoming lane to avoid running into me as I sprinted from end to end. But I couldn't worry about that. I had to stay focused and keep running. I could eliminate half of these calories if I kept running.

"Stop running!"

A young man holding the arm of an elderly woman on a ventilator yelled at me as he crossed my path and attempted to put her in a medical van. He was angry. Maybe my running made him angry because seeing someone freely express their desires by doing whatever took their fancy made him feel trapped, tethered to the ventilator as if he himself depended upon it for life and not the old woman. Although I thought he was very rude to yell at me so loudly, there was something about the tone in his voice that startled me and made me slow down. Once I slowed down it was hard to get the speed back in my sprint.

I became aware of my footwear, too, and wondered how I could have reached that speed in five-inch rubber platforms. They were my work shoes, my "off-camera" shoes. They were purchased, as the name "off-camera" suggests, for use on the set of *Ally McBeal* when the camera couldn't see my character's feet, but I had given them a leading role. For although they were plain and from Payless, they made my legs look thin. Because their height gave my body the perfect proportion, they were the last things I took off before bed and the first things I put on in the morning. I'd started not to wear any other shoes, even to workout or hike, and I never walked barefoot in my house anymore for fear of passing a reflection of myself in a window. But to be able to sprint in them . . . that's something that I didn't think I could do.

I hated that stupid nurse for breaking my concentration. How dare he interrupt me as I was trying to fix this awful situation I found myself in. It was hard to understand the importance of something like this unless you were desperately trying to lose weight, but I couldn't say that to anyone for fear of it sounding trivial. No one knew that my whole career hinged on its success.

I got in the car to drive home. I was angry and riddled with anxiety. If I waited too long to finish burning off the calories consumed by chewing the gum, the calories might turn into fat. At the red lights, I took my hands off the steering wheel and pumped my arms furiously while holding my stomach tight. I alternated putting my left foot and my right foot on the brake so as to bend and straighten my legs an equal number of repetitions. I sang loudly the whole way home while thrashing my head around. I was not a huge fan of Monster Magnet, but there was one song I played repeatedly in the car because it helped me expend energy while driving. I couldn't get home fast enough. I turned onto Crescent Heights from Beverly and started thinking about a strategy to burn the excess calories. I would park, take the elevator to my apartment, drop Bean off, change into workout gear, and go next door to the gym. No. I would park, drop Bean off in the garden, run up the six flights of stairs, take the elevator back to the garden floor, get Bean, run back up, and then get on the treadmill at home.

I got myself and Bean out of the car as quickly as I could and started running with her to the garden floor. I hurriedly put Bean outside in the walled garden and took off up the stairs. She would be okay there for a minute. It was an enclosed garden and she needed to stretch her legs. I took the stairs two at a time so I could feel the burn on my thighs. When I reached the fifth floor, I went back to running one stair at a time, but fast, so it felt like I was running in place. I admired my coordination and athleticism. Running that fast up stairs is tricky, especially in platform wedges. I liked wearing the shoes for these tasks, though. I felt as though they burned more calories because I was forced to be aware of protecting my ankles from spraining. Perfect balance was required to land each step with my weight spread evenly on the balls of my feet between my big toe and my little toe, and perfect balance, as I had learned at Pilates, requires energy. And after putting 60 unwanted calories into my body, I had energy to spare.

When I reached the top of the seventh floor and there were no more stairs to climb, I faced a decision. Would I take the stairs back down to the second floor to get Bean? Or would I take the elevator down and run up the whole staircase one more time? Going down stair by stair couldn't really do much to burn calories, and it seemed that it would be smarter to take the elevator down and run back up in the time that I had to burn it off before it settled on my stomach and thighs. I got into the elevator, hoping Bean would forgive me for leaving her out there alone for another five minutes, but I had no choice. In the quiet space inside the elevator, I started to comprehend what had just happened to me. I'd binged without reason. I had lost control. I'd lost control and I could do it again without warning. If I lost control again, I could get fat again. I would have to start this thing over again. I would fail at the one thing I knew I was good at.

I went all the way down. I was at the bottom floor and I ran fast, two stairs at a time, past Bean, past exhaustion, past the memory of what happened in the parking structure of the Beverly Center. I took my hands off the rail and just used my legs to propel me two at a time up the tubelike staircase, with its forgotten wallpaper and its unappreciated carpet. I reached the top, hit the elevator button, and furiously ran in place, crying now as I figured that crying has to burn more calories than not crying. The elevator door opened and I rushed in. I realized after I was in the elevator that a man had been exiting. Could that have been my only neighbor? I'd never met him. The doors closed and my crying seemed to get louder perhaps due to the confined space or the fact that I had stopped jumping up and down for fear that the jumping would cause the rickety old elevator to break down.

I shook my hands and twisted my torso from side to side. I thought about the fact that I had to eat again soon. It was getting dark outside probably, and I liked to eat dinner before it got dark so I could digest my food before I went to bed. If I just ate egg whites, just pure protein, I'd probably be okay. But I should do it soon. I should run again and go make food.

I started back up the stairs, a little more tired now, and took them one at a time. It was still better than sitting on my sofa, worrying. I started a breathing exercise. Inhale four stairs, exhale four stairs, inhale four stairs, exhale four stairs. It helped me keep the pace I needed to reach the top of the seventh floor in two minutes. I started noticing how long it took to get from the bottom to the top on my second trip up the stairs and I could still do it in the same time as it took when I first started. Since I was obviously not as tired as I thought I was, I decided to do it again. Dinner could wait five more minutes. This time in the elevator, I visualized the food entries in my notebook and calculated my calories for the day. My heart leapt out of my chest not because it was straining to pump oxygen to my overworked body but with panic. My notebook was still in the car! My bag was still in the car! Where were my keys? Did I leave them in my bag?

When the elevator hit the bottom floor I ran past Jeff, the doorman, and into the parking garage in search of my bag. As I opened the heavy steel door of the parking structure I saw my black Porsche, the driver's door wide open. I was embarrassed running to get my things and close it, but there was no need for my embarrassment because no one was around. I felt stupid anyway. I felt stupid because I was sure someone saw that I'd forgotten to close my car door. Everyone in the building knew whose car that was and now someone who lived near me knew that I was "scatty." Scatty was the word my second-grade teacher used to describe me to my mother. "Amanda is a bright girl, and has potential to be a good student, but has trouble focusing in class and is scatty." I was scatty, unfocused, forgetful. I was the kind of girl who would drop out of law school to pursue acting, the kind of girl who would leave her car door open with her keys in the ignition and her purse on the seat. The kind of girl that couldn't maintain her weight.

I could see through the barred windows of the above-ground parking structure that it was dark outside, and although it would be harder to run up the stairs with my heavy bag, I knew it was my last chance before I had to start preparing food. I started back up the stairs again, two by two again, this time using my bag as a weight to add difficulty to the climb and to make balancing on my platform shoes harder. I held the bag with both arms out from my chest and climbed the stairwell with its ugly lighting and stained wallpaper. I climbed slower this time but because of the weight I could feel the burn and so as I got to the top I decided to repeat the whole exercise one last time. It was the only time I had used a weight to aid in burning the calories, and if I did it one more time I felt pretty confident that I could forget that the little mishap with the gum had ever happened.

I arrived at my front door. It had beckoned me at the end of the climb all six times in the last thirty minutes and now, because of my hard work and determination, I got to walk through it. I got to be home. I could finally rest. I turned the lights on in my cold apartment without furniture and threw my bag on the floor. Under the glare of the bare bulb hanging from the ceiling, I saw all the little round stains on the carpet where Bean had previously gone to the bathroom. It wasn't her fault, and I was just about to pull up that carpet anyway. She was a good dog. It's just that sometimes I didn't have time to take her out.

Shit! I had forgotten Bean.

I ran out the door, and down the stairs frantically hoping that I would find her where I left her thirty minutes ago in the garden on the second floor. Bean! My sweet little friend was alone and in danger of being stolen or of getting out onto the busy street and I was the idiot who left her there. God! I hated myself! As I ran down the hallway to the glass door that led to the garden I saw my little Bean. I saw a little white face with big black eyes, scared and shivering from cold and fear, squished onto the glass of the door as if trying to push through it to be in the safety and warmth of the hallway on the other side. I scooped her up and held her close to my chest as I slid down the hallway wall and onto the floor with relief. She was my baby and I had left her. My obsession with weight loss had made me neglectful of the things I cared about. I looked in her big, trusting eyes and stroked her silky white head and said:

"Beany. I'm so sorry. I'll never do that again. I love you so much." I noticed for the first time in weeks that her eye stain had gotten really bad. There were mats in her fur.

"Come on. Let's go home."

Clutching Bean and with tears streaming down my cheeks, I was again faced with the choice of taking the stairs to my penthouse apartment or the elevator. I found myself in a small crowd of people who were waiting for the elevator, some of whom had acknowledged me by asking, "Are you okay?" I knew the elevator would be more comfortable for Bean and I really should've been thinking just about her. She needed to feel calm and safe, not jolted around as I ran up stairs. But it might be quicker to take the stairs and what Bean really needed was to eat and feel safely tucked away in her bed at home, and so I started the journey up the seven flights of stairs. I watched her head bob up and down with each stair and I felt so bad, but it would be over soon.

As I reached my apartment door, left wide open, I remembered that my purchase from the Beverly Center was still in the trunk of my car. A black exercise mat lay in the trunk of my car. How typical of me to buy exercise equipment and never use it. How typically disorganized of me to forget that I bought it so I could begin my workouts with my trainer at home. She would be here first thing in the morning.

It was clear I needed an assistant. I was overwhelmed with all the things that needed to be done. I needed an assistant to help me remember Bean, that she needed to be groomed, walked, and taken downstairs so she wouldn't go to the bathroom on my rug. I needed an assistant to go to the convenience store and to remind me of my workouts. But mainly I needed an assistant to go to the Beverly Center so that this would never happen again.

21

THE NOISE of the escalators as they took people to the gym was a strange one. It was dull and barely there, like the hum of a refrigerator. It was a backdrop to the screaming of the coffee grinder coming from within Buzz Coffee and the music that would blurt out of the Virgin Megastore as its glass doors spat out another customer or sucked one in. But the escalators were beckoning me, politely but relentlessly inviting me to the gym as I sat and waited to interview an assistant. Now that my body was thinner, I wondered if I wouldn't mind the other women in the gym seeing it. Maybe I could ignore their critical looks long enough to work at defining my muscles now that they're not buried underneath layers of fat? As I waited for her to arrive, I watched the escalators go up and down regardless of whether there are people on them or not. They took people to the gym and then they took nobody to the gym. The movie theater was on the second floor also, and I was trying to spot the people who were going to the midday movie, wondering whether the blackness of the theater would fill the void or exasperate it. I would never see a movie on a Tuesday afternoon. Everyone knows workdays are for working.

By the time Carolyn arrived I had come up with a few immediate reasons for needing her, although sitting motionless and watching people go to the gym had made me quietly anxious. I had begun to move my legs up and down to get rid of some of that anxiety, but I found that most of it was thrust at Carolyn, as I began telling her what I needed even before she had time to settle into one of the uncomfortable iron chairs that circled the bolted-down outdoor table. She responded immediately by whipping out her notebook and pen and seemingly matched my anxiety by writing hurriedly and responding to every grocery list item with "What else?" I'm not sure we really made eye contact until the frenzied listing and recording of the to dos was over.

"I need for you to go to a Ralphs to get the yogurt because only Ralphs carries the brand that I eat." "What else?" "I need you to take Bean to the groomer's." "What else?" "I need you to schedule Pilates." "What else?" "I need you to oversee the renovation of my apartment." "What else?" "I need you to go hiking with me because I hate being alone." "What else?"

I'm gay and I need you to be okay with that. What else? I need you to make me okay with that. What else? I need you to keep all my secrets and not tell anyone that I'm a phony.

"That all?"

She signed a confidentiality agreement drafted by my business manager, who knew of no real reason why I should need one, and became my assistant.

"I like to work out. Do you?"

"Yes. I do."

When Carolyn and I finally sat back and breathed each other in, we were already committed. I noticed a few striking things about her. Carolyn was colorless. She had depth to her hair because it wasn't white, yet it had no color. She had a pale, colorless face. She had thin, bony hands that were also colorless except for a thin blue vein that meandered its way from the end of her wrist across the back of her hand to the start of her little finger. Her bony hands matched her thin, bony frame. Among all the round people on the escalators and at Buzz Coffee, Carolyn struck me as straight. I wasn't envious of Carolyn's weight, but instead appreciated it. I appreciated that someone other than me cared about weight loss, and as I instinctively knew that weight loss wasn't a new thing to her, I appreciated that she cared about weight-loss maintenance. And so from that moment on, Carolyn and I would be united in our goal to maintain. With her help, I would maintain my hair color, my nail length, my dog's whiteness, and my car's cleanliness. I would maintain my clothes and my friendships by politely remembering to send apology notes to Kali or Erik explaining how my work schedule conflicted with their dinner parties. And because Carolyn would bring me food and schedule my workouts with my trainers, I would easily maintain my weight.

I returned home after my meeting with Carolyn and was immediately struck by the cold that had crept into my apartment through a crack in the window. I usually left the window slightly open because I liked the idea of fresh air. Actually, it was more than just the air I was wanting. It was the sounds of traffic on Sunset Boulevard, the noise of the industrial air conditioner on top of the Sunset 5. I could sit in my dining room to face another meal alone and yet feel connected to the world around me. I could imagine the actresses rushing to auditions reciting their lines as they waited for the light to turn green at the intersection of Sunset and Crescent Heights. Thinking about actresses driving around to auditions prompted me remember my favorite quote from Mae West when she was asked if she had any advice to give young actresses in Hollywood. "Take Fountain," she said exhaling the smoke from her cigarette. There was so much traffic outside my apartment on Sunset, I wished more actresses took her advice.

I walked into the kitchen to prepare my meal. I would eat 50 calories of egg whites. I found that alternating the egg whites and the tuna for lunch helped with weight loss, as egg whites would cut my lunchtime calorie intake in half. I had been eating egg whites instead of tuna a lot more lately for this reason. Plus, I liked to cook. I never really enjoyed it before, but it was very satisfying preparing a meal, cooking and eating it. I felt quite obsessed with food. It was all I ever really thought about. I was worried that my passion for it would lead to my failure to abstain from overindulging, but I took comfort in the knowledge that people who love to cook are quite often obsessed with food. Cooking was a hobby, an artistic expression, and for me, the ultimate control of what I put in my body. I washed the small mustard plate with the black swirl pattern that I used for egg whites. I washed all the dishes before I ate from them to make sure they were clean. Occasionally the dishes felt greasy when I took them out of the dishwasher and I wanted to ensure that I wasn't ingesting any residual grease or oil that might be on them.

Dishes and utensils were very important. I couldn't just eat from any dish. Each dish had meaning. Each dish helped me in my quest to achieve the perfect body. If I felt anxious about eating, my anxiety was always instantly allayed when I saw my little white bowl with the green flowers, as it had a faint hairline crack that helped me to figure out portions. I had to see the crack at the bottom of the bowl at all times, plus the crack is particularly helpful when I didn't want foods to touch. I also ate every meal with my second favorite tool—chopsticks. Chopsticks were useful for obvious reasons. I'm not Asian, nor am I coordinated. They were unnatural and awkward for me and as a result, the food fell through the little obtuse triangles making me eat slower. If I ate slowly, I didn't eat as much.

I sat down at the dining table to my mustard-colored plate of egg whites. Then I got up and closed the window. The wind had kicked up making it colder, and now the sounds of Sunset Boulevard, once soothing and connecting me to the world at large, were intrusive and grating on my nerves. Horns blasting and muscle cars accelerating reminded me of all the impatience, pretension, and aggression in society that lay beneath my penthouse loft apartment. I was very safe in there with my scale and my schedule. I closed the window, but I turned the air conditioner down to sixty degrees. I hadn't really proven my theory, but it just made sense that if you were shivering and trying to stay warm, your body was burning excess calories. It had to. As I hadn't yet begun to eat the egg whites, it occurred to me that maybe my body was burning fat, not calories, as I probably used up the 100 calories from breakfast on my morning Pilates workout. I liked that thought. Although I didn't have to lose more weight, I definitely had a little more fat to burn. My thighs were still big. My stomach still had about an inch of fat on it and, as it was summer during Christmas in Australia, I wanted my stomach to be flat and perfect when I went home. If it wasn't flat, then all that effort would've been in vain. When I went to Australia for Christmas, I wanted my mother to see a determined girl, a girl in control of her life, and a fat stomach doesn't exactly convey that message. A fat stomach said that no matter how hard I tried, it got the better of me. I failed. I couldn't finish the job.

I decided not to eat the egg whites. I didn't need them. As they slid off the plate and into the trash, I felt a surge of adrenaline. I felt invincible, powerful. Not eating them was incredibly difficult and by not eating them I had just proven to myself that I was stronger than my basic instincts, that I could deny them. I wouldn't give in to the desire to eat, because after all, isn't that what fat people do? They give in to desire? They know they shouldn't eat the brownie, but they just can't help themselves. For the first time in my life, I felt like I was helping myself. Although I didn't want to lose any more weight, I certainly couldn't gain any back, especially before Christmas. I wanted to go back to Australia, the hero my mother wanted me to be. I wanted to show my mom that I'd finally conquered the demon. I'd wrestled the beast that threatened our sanity, our relationship, and our self-worth, and I conquered it. We would no longer go to a photo shoot with a sick, sinking feeling in our guts hoping that I was good enough to pass; pass as thin, pass as pretty, pass as a model, pass as a TV actress, pass as worthy of getting attention. Now when I got attention, I knew I deserved it. I'd worked very hard for it.

The kind of attention I had been getting from the press was widespread—from high-end fashion magazines to supermarket rags. I was almost always included in big, splashy tabloid stories about "stars in their dieting hell!" Paparazzi were everywhere I went all of a sudden and I knew the only reason for that was because I was thin. They had been including me in these cover stories about thin actresses and almost every week was another story. Society is obsessed with being thin and a handful of actresses, me included, were showing them that with hard work, it was an achievable goal.

Some of them said that I was anorexic. It wasn't true. At 100 pounds I was way too heavy to be anorexic.

I'd achieved 100 two days earlier. It was a crazy feeling of elation. I wanted to take pictures of my naked body to document it but decided against it just in case I hadn't reached my lowest weight. I didn't want to look at pictures in the future knowing that the image I saw in them wasn't how I'd really looked. I didn't want to have to remind myself that I was actually thinner than the picture showed.

I wanted to document my success because I secretly knew that I couldn't keep this up forever. I knew that one day I'd be looking at those pictures talking about my thinness in the past tense. I just knew that the fat, lazy, overeating piece of shit with her period and her sweat glands and her body odor lurked under the surface of this clean, pristine machine of a girl that I was currently.

With the three hours between lunch and my snack of Jell-O, I had planned to check out a local ballet class in a little courtyard off Sunset. I had seen the studio the previous week when I walked into the courtyard to smoke a cigarette where the Sunset Boulevard traffic couldn't see me. Through the window, I could see that the instructor was an old Russian man with a cane that he banged on the floor in time with the music. I could see his mouth opening wide and his neck straining as he instructed his students: fat, sloppy, middle-aged women in full makeup and tights. I could see an old woman in black on the piano belting out the music, keeping time, playing a two-handed chord to accompany a tondue and a plié. I wanted to go talk to him about joining the class. It would be a good way to exercise and socialize. But mainly I wanted to join it because it would remind me of a time when I was happy, when life was simple and uncomplicated. I could be eight years old again: a skinny, happy girl in a leotard, joking with her best friend behind the instructor's back, our friendship pure and untarnished by sexual desire. It would remind me of a time when I was the best. And I would definitely be the best—and the thinnest.

Look at that inch of fat.

I changed my mind about going to the ballet school when I changed my clothes. When I was naked I could see fat on my stomach and I couldn't imagine showing it to people through a leotard. I knew that I was thinner than the ladies in the class—I was thinner than most people—but also had imperfections, and I just didn't want to reveal them to the other women. It was so bizarre to me to think that these women were extending their big fat legs in the air and prancing around half naked when most of them wouldn't be caught dead in a bathing suit at their next-door neighbor's pool. Or maybe they didn't care. Maybe I was the only one who cared. In any case, going to ballet class would be something I could do when I no longer had to worry about feeling the fat fold over at the junction of where my hips met my thighs in an arabesque. I'd go when I knew that if hypercritical paparazzi found me in the little glass box of a studio, I would be prepared. I would know that they couldn't get a shot of the fat that sat just above my hip bones. I'd go when I knew that the worst the press could say was that I was too thin.

As I lunged my way across the floor to my treadmill to run down the time to my next meal, I wondered if you could really ever be thin enough to be too thin. Even if the tabloid headlines pretended to be disapproving of a girl who was supposedly "too thin," I could always detect envy in the text—that in the tone of the article, there was always the underlying element of awe. And I knew the readers were reading it jealously, wishing that they could be just like us—determined, controlled, not needing anything or anyone to feel special or successful; we'd created our own ultimate success. We had won the battle that the whole world was fighting.

22

WOULD YOU like anything to drink, Ms. de Rossi?"

The airline stewardess spoke softly as if to conserve energy, no doubt gearing up for the ensuing fourteen-hour flight to Melbourne. She already looked tired and we hadn't even taken off yet. She looked old, too. And fat.

"Water, please." I was extremely proud of myself that I was no longer a gross, disgusting pig of a bulimic, downing Baileys Irish Cream and throwing it up in an airplane toilet. I was so glad that I wasn't doing that.

I waved away the mixed nuts that accompanied the water (I asked for water, and yet they assumed I meant water and nuts?), leaned back in my chair, and took out my food journal. There would be no tears on the plane today. I would return home to Melbourne in triumph. I opened the journal and wrote the date, December 19, 1999, and underneath, in big curly writing I wrote something that impressed even me—and I was the one who accomplished it.

95

On December 19, I hit 95 pounds. It was poetic, really, that the day I returned home was the exact day I accomplished this amazing feat. Ninety-five pounds gave me the cushion that I needed to go home for Christmas and eat and drink with my family. Ninety-five pounds would impress them. It might also slightly concern some of them, no doubt, as I had recently become aware that there are certain body parts that looked a little strange. I was okay with that, though. They needed to know that my life wasn't a never-ending Hollywood party; that my money wasn't just given to me, that I had to work hard for all of it. I had been worried that my friends and family might feel jealous of my success. As long as I worked really hard and made sacrifices that were obvious to other people, I wouldn't feel guilty that I made more money than my brother or had a more exciting life than my Australian friends could ever dream of having. Mostly though, they seemed to be more interested in Hollywood at large than they were in my success. I was tired of telling stories about the celebrities I'd met. I'd started to feel like my mother had sent me out as a spy or an undercover reporter to mingle with the special people and bring back the news of what it was that made them special when all I really wanted was for her to think that I was special. Sometimes, if I found a celebrity to be abrasive or rude, she'd disagree with me, citing a tabloid story about the kind acts they did or the fact that other people seemed to like them. She'd always laugh and agree when I told her how ridiculous it was that because of a tabloid she thought she knew better than I did, but her comments came with a subliminal warning: the written word is a powerful thing. The perception of who you are is more important than who are. You are what other people think of you.

The aging stewardess came back, eyes cast downward at her notepad while surfing the tide of turbulence like a pro.

"Can I take your lunch order?"

Something happened to me when flying. I felt that either the calories were impossible to quantify and so that meant that the food had no energy or matter so I could eat everything, or because the calories were impossible to quantify, I could eat nothing at all. Another factor was time. If y equaled 300 calories consumed over a 24-hour period, then what was x if I left Los Angeles at 10:00 p.m. and after fourteen hours of travel I arrived in Melbourne at 6:00 a.m. two days later? How many calories and how many days should I account for? Eating nothing was really my only option.

"I'm not eating lunch today. I had a big meal already."

Why I had to tell her about having a big meal I don't know. I hate it when I do things like that.

When the stewardess came around to deliver the meals, she asked again if I wanted anything, perhaps thinking that the smell of hot beef would send me into a frenzy of regret that it wasn't going to be plopped down in front of me. I reassured her that no, I really didn't want anything. I could resist dead rotting cow on a plastic plate.

After lunch the stewardess rolled a silver tray of cookies and ice cream down the isle.

"Dessert, sir? Would you like some dessert today, ma'am? Dessert, sir?"

She made her way through the seated strangers up the aisle to where I was sitting. She stood in front of me with her cart full of sugar and lard and instead of simply asking me if I would like dessert, she decided to inject some personality into it.

"I'm sure you don't, but . . ." Her sentence trailed off. She had an apologetic look on her face like she was sorry for me that I didn't get to partake in this joyous activity, that being an actress precluded me from all the fun that cookies and ice cream bring. Her droopy eyes seemed to say, "I'm sorry you can't have this. Actresses don't eat cookies." Maybe she was sure I didn't want a cookie just because I'd not eaten any lunch. Then again, what if I had skipped lunch just so I could eat the cookie? How could she have known what I wanted?

By the time dinner came around, I was asleep. Actually, I pretended to be asleep. I didn't want anyone to know that I didn't eat anything during the fourteen-hour flight. Something like that could leak into a tabloid. And while I enjoyed the speculation that I was too thin, I didn't want them thinking I was sick. I wanted people to admire my tenacity and self-control, not to feel sorry for me for starving myself into the shape of an actress.

The long, sleepless night of listening to the drone of the engines was punctuated by the stewardess asking if I'd like to have anything to eat with a cute smile and a "How about now?" in half-hour intervals, which finally trickled down to a raised eyebrow and a quick glance every two or three hours. As breakfast was being served and I asked for black coffee, she could no longer contain herself. I could see that she was gearing up to say something and I thought it would be along the lines of how in her twenty-year career as a mile-high waitress, she'd never before seen a person refuse food. I had clearly made an impression on her and that was something I really didn't want to do. I didn't want her telling anyone that the Australian actress on *Ally McBeal*, the "thin one" (I could just hear it now, "No, not Calista, the other one!") didn't eat and is therefore sick. But to my surprise, her expression changed as she leaned in slightly to speak to me. Her face went from a tired, concerned expression to a hint of a smile. Her droopy eyes became animated.

"You're being so good!"

Yes, lady. I'm always this good.

"Oh! No. I'd love to eat, believe me, but I have this slight stomach virus and you know how awkward that could get on a plane!"

She laughed. Why does everyone think toilets and what goes on in them are funny?

"Well, I hope you feel better." She refilled my coffee cup and I wondered if someone with stomach flu would drink black coffee. I wondered if I'd blown my cover. I pulled out my diary and wrote an entry. I told it that I had eaten nothing and if I weighed more than 100 pounds in Australia it was because of water retention. That's what happens with plane travel. It was good to write it down to remind myself, and the explanation could come in handy if I found myself in a panic in my mother's bathroom on her old pink and black scale.

To say that I hit the ground running isn't an overstatement. When I got off the plane, I began a slow, steady jog through the terminal. There was nothing wrong with that, I thought, as I could just as easily be running to make a connecting flight as exercising my body, limp from sitting for fourteen exercise-less hours. I ran to the airport bathroom to begin my ritual of trying to look fabulous for my mother. I always tried to make a good impression with my hair, makeup, and wardrobe for my mother, as I knew that seeing me looking great always made her happy. But this time was even more special because this time I was skinny. I had the thinnest body I'd ever had to show off to her and so I didn't feel as though I needed the extra-special hair and makeup to counteract my ordinary, girl-next-door body. The package had to say "star" and now my body was helping me deliver that message. After I changed out of my loose clothing and into my skinny jeans and a tight tank, I headed home.

"Mama!" I got out of the cab and ran into my mother's arms, leaving my luggage in the trunk for the cab driver to deal with.

"Bubbles!" My mother dubbed me that when I was a little kid. She still calls me that sometimes. I really like it.

"Darling." She pulled away from the hug and looked me up and down. "You're too thin!" She blurted it out in a way that seemed un-controlled yet premeditated, like her nervousness had built with hours of rehearsal and had culminated in an explosive delivery.

Clearly, she had been lying in wait for me. She was ready for me, armed with evidence. A month ago, Suzanne had called her and tipped her off to my weight loss. According to my mother, Suzanne said my weight loss was extreme and that due to her lack of being qualified in the field of eating disorders, she was racked with guilt and feeling re-sponsible that she had helped cause me to have one. I told my mother that if Suzanne admitted that she was not qualified in the field of eating disorders, how could she possibly diagnose them? It was my mother's lack of common sense that irritated me at that moment standing before her in the driveway, because I knew that she couldn't possibly be concerned by how I looked, only by what she'd heard. Even if I convinced her that Suzanne was wrong, then she would eat up those goddamn tabloid stories about how I was starving myself. She was just waiting for me to arrive so she could levy the insult after a cursory up-and-down glance, a feel of my back when she hugged me, a quick confirmation that the tabloid journalists had once again got it right. This was not the reaction I was hoping for. I wanted her to hug me and look me up and down and tell me that I looked great. I wanted her to tell me that it was obvious that I was working hard, that I had finally got it together after all the years of hell my weight had put the two of us through. Instead she looked horrified.

"Miss?" The cab driver was waiting for me to collect my luggage or pay him or something.

"Sorry. Here." My mother put a bright yellow plastic, Australian fifty-dollar bill in his hand and waved her thank-you at him as he pulled away. She turned to face me as a tram rattled down the busy main road just past the iron gate of our driveway. Several cars sped past in both directions, and the noise and speed of the background made my mother's stillness and silence in the foreground quite surreal. She became aware that she was looking at me strangely and for too long and so she averted her gaze; she wanted to look at me and yet she knew that she shouldn't, as if she were passing a roadside accident. She stood there in silence looking like a little child, her arms dangling limply by her side.

It was clear to me then that she was very worried. I was no longer irritated or angry or disappointed. I was shocked. Did I look emaciated? There had been times when I looked in the mirror and thought I was too thin, but most times all I could see were the inches I still had to lose. If I still had fat on my thighs and hips, surely there was nothing to be concerned about. But her reaction did make me wonder because worry was something that I had rarely felt from her. While I was sure she had a lot of it while raising two kids as a single parent, she never wanted my brother and me to see it. When our dad died and left us in chaos, she rebuilt order with a stiff upper lip. She told me that I was smart and that she had nothing to worry about with me. I made sure I didn't do anything to make her worry. When I was a teenager and all my friends were smoking pot and sneaking out of their bedroom windows to go to nightclubs, I told her that I tried pot, hated it, and in which club she could find me. I was never the kid that gave her trouble. I was the mature and independent one who aced the test and won the race. I was the entertainer, the one who made things exciting with my modeling jobs and my acting and my overseas adventures.

Now, at twenty-five years old, I had made her worry. I took a deep breath, and my eyes welled up with tears. I hated seeing her so uncomfortable, not knowing where to look or what to say, and yet simultaneously, it felt good. I had traveled thousands of miles in search of the opposite reaction, yet I suddenly felt myself preferring the one I'd received. Her concern felt warm, comforting. It seemed as though she was afraid of losing something very precious, and that something was me. Because I'd always been so strong and independent, her concern about me prior to this moment mainly seemed to be about the things I could produce, like a modeling job or a beauty contract. I felt so happy I wondered if I had deliberately lost this much weight in search of that reaction. All of a sudden, I felt worthy of care. I was the one to worry about. Caring for a weak, sick child required a different kind of love. And in that moment in the driveway, I discovered that that was the kind of love I preferred.

I love you too, Mom.

I didn't say that. I really wanted to, but it was too abstract, too heavy and emotional.

Sometimes it's better to keep things happy and superficial.

She obviously thought the same thing because she straightened up and put a smile back on her face as if the incident had never happened.

"Bubbles, you're home!" She'd been looking forward to my return for weeks, getting her petunias in the garden ready for the holiday. Christmas was a special time for her since my brother and I moved to LA. She wanted to dismiss her worry so she could enjoy her daughter's homecoming.

"Let's go inside and see Gran. She's been looking forward to seeing you for weeks." I walked up the back steps and into the house, putting my bags down on the checkered green linoleum floor of the kitchen. I ran over to the rocking chair in the living room to hug my Gran.

"Now, then." My mother glanced at me and then walked away, as if attempting to downplay the importance of whatever she was about to tell me. Not one for confrontation, she chose an upbeat, clipped voice and delivered her message in a tone that enabled me to choose whether to dismiss it or take it seriously.

"What's all this silly business with being skinny? Stop all this silly rot, all this carrying on and eat normally like everyone else, girl!"

A surge of anger bitter like acid flooded my empty body.

Silly? She calls your hard work "silly?" She doesn't care about you. She thinks you did it for attention. You're exhausting to her. You're pathetic for trying to get sympathy. She's not concerned about you, she's sick of you.

"I'm going for a run."

And with that I exploded out the door. I ran down the busy main street of Camberwell, narrowly avoiding cars as they were pulling out of their driveways. I picked up my pace and charged up the hill, past the old people's home and the church and held my stomach tight and twisted from side to side as I ran down the hill toward the shops at Camberwell junction. If my Pilates instructor likened this movement to wringing water out of a towel, then I was wringing out all the acidic anger from my organs that became flooded with it when my mother dismissively called my hard work silly. I waited for the walk signal at the busy intersection and jogged in place to keep my muscles warm, to keep my brain from thinking I was done with my workout or done with the anger that fueled it, since I could use the anger to propel me forward. I sprinted up the busy shopping street, past people walking in and out of the bakery, past the sidewalk café, dodging dogs tied to outdoor tables. I ran past my favorite bookstore, past deathly still people who were standing and reading blurbs of books that promised to help them, entertain them, teach them who they were. It seemed that all the people shopping on that street turned to look at the fool who was sprinting in jeans and platform heels. But I didn't let their obvious disapproval of my running slow me down. I ran fast, right by all of them. I ran until I couldn't run anymore.

I stopped at the train station opposite the doctor's office where my mother used to work. I stood at the corner of Stanhope Grove and watched the trains as they exploded into the station and heaved their way back out once they'd stopped to deliver people and receive people. I watched a green tram putter up the hill. I watched teenagers walk in and out of McDonald's. I was watching my memories. I sat down on the wooden bench next to the taxicab rank and imagined myself in a navy blue school uniform with permed hair, walking out of the train station and across the street to my mother's work, where I would wait for her to take me home. I smiled at that thought. Why I would wait for an hour for my mother to take me home when home was only one more train stop away was something my adult brain couldn't fathom. Maybe it was because I could use the time to sneak off to McDonald's and eat fries and a vanilla milk shake, pretending I was waiting for someone to disguise my embarrassment of being in there alone when all the other tables were full of kids from other schools. I was a model and so I could never go to McDonald's with my friends. I couldn't go with anyone, not only because I thought models shouldn't eat McDonald's but also because I constantly complained about being overweight.

I could never eat in front of anyone because it would be evidence. It would confirm suspicions that I wasn't helping myself and was unworthy of their sympathy. Only a crazy person would console someone for being distressed about her weight and then take her out for McDonald's fries to cheer her up.

As I sat on the wooden bench I became aware of how much pain I was feeling. I pushed down onto the palms of my hands that had been limply resting on either side of my seated legs, elevating my seat bones away from the bench. That immediately alleviated the pain that was caused by my full weight resting on the hard wooden bench. I briefly wondered if it hurt because I was too heavy, that my seat bones couldn't support the weight of my upper body, but quickly dismissed the thought as crazy. Fat people sit on hard things all the time. The pain of being seated and the exhaustion it took to keep me slightly off the bench made me stand. I needed to stand anyway. Standing burns more calories than sitting, and I had forgotten that rule while I had temporarily lost my mind to nostalgia. But standing there, I found myself stuck. I had run quite far and was a long way from home. If I'd had money I could have taken the train or the tram, but since I left the house without any, walking was my only option. After the long flight with no food at all, running back home was out of the question. I should never have stopped. I was not angry anymore and without any motivation I could now only walk. Losing weight really wasn't enough motivation either. My mother's reaction was confusing and it made me wonder whether I had taken this whole thing too far. As I started the long journey home, I wished I could just walk across the street to find my mother behind the desk in the doctor's waiting room, waiting for me. Then she could take me home.

By the time I arrived back at the house, I had completely forgiven Mom. I had thought about her dismissive attitude toward my weight loss and understood it from many different angles. She grew up in the Marilyn Monroe era and liked women to have curves, so she simply didn't appreciate how I looked. She called my efforts "skinny business and rot" because she no doubt realized that she'd completely over-reacted. But even if she incorrectly thought that I was emaciated and sick, I understood why she downplayed her feelings about it, because it was her worry that she was dismissing, not the supposed sickness. My mother often tried to make light of heavy things. When I was a little girl with a gash on my knee, she'd tell me it was just a scratch. If I felt too sick to go to school, she'd tell me that it was in my head, that I just needed a change of scenery. She'd tell me to go to school and if I still felt sick, I could come home. She was usually right; once I got to school I forgot about being sick. She was usually right to ignore it because ignoring it often did make it go away.

When I returned, my gran told me that Mom had gone to the supermarket to get groceries. She yelled this information out to me as she was quite deaf and since she had to yell to hear herself, she assumed she needed to yell to be heard.

"Marg said you could meet her there if you wanted anything!"

"Thanks, Gran!" I yelled back at her.

I grabbed a knitted shrug and headed out to the supermarket to find my mother. The sleeves covered up my skinny arms, and with them the evidence that achieving a nice all-over body was an effort. My arms were the only giveaway that my weight should have been something other than it was. If you just saw my waist and my legs, you'd have thought I was in terrific shape. You'd have thought that I was just naturally thin. Besides, my legs weren't even skinny. They were very average in size. I had to be extreme just to achieve average-size thighs.

I wore the knitted sleeves in an effort retreat from the front line, to surrender from the battle, to silently apologize to her for exploding out of the house in anger. I wanted her to feel proud of me as we shopped together, and she wouldn't have been proud if the other grocery shoppers and shopkeepers had seen my arms. I didn't have to hear that from her, I just knew it. She had bragged about me to everyone in the neighborhood and now I had to live up to the image of me she'd been presenting. Everyone wants to see effortless beauty, ease, and confidence. Every script I read described the female leads as "beautiful yet doesn't know it" or "naturally thin and muscular and doesn't have to work at it." Effortlessness is an attractive thing. And it takes a lot of effort to achieve it. "Never let 'em see you sweat" was a principle I'd adopted, and so actual effort was yet another thing for me to hide from the people I was trying to impress. The list of unacceptable things about me that I had to cover up was getting longer. My arms had just made that list.

When I saw my mother she was taking a jar of peanut butter off a shelf in the condiment aisle. She looked so small from where I was standing that I suddenly didn't want her to see me. I felt like a giant. I felt like I was taller and wider than all the people in there and the grocery aisles themselves. I was a big, fat, gluttonous American in comparison to the petite Australians. The shopping carts were small. The boxes of food on the shelves looked like they belonged to a children's tea set. The jam jars were the size of shot glasses, the "family-sized" bags of chips looked like they contained a single serving. When she saw me standing at the end of the aisle, she smiled and waved me over. She had forgotten about her worry, my reaction, her reaction, and my thinness. It's amazing what sleeves can do.

"Hi, Bubbles! I thought we could get some food for you. I don't know what you like to eat now."

As we walked up and down the aisles, she made food suggestions like, "How about I make you a Ki Si Ming? You used to love that." Or, "Should I get some Tim Tams? You always loved Tim Tams." Tim Tams were the chocolate-covered cookies that she'd had to hide from me if she wanted any for the rest of the family.

"Ma. Just let me do my own thing, okay? I eat differently now."

I had finally understood that I couldn't eat normally like everyone else if I wanted to be an actress. Couldn't she see that? Couldn't she see that I'd finally figured out that I had to sacrifice Tim Tams and casseroles and happy family dinners so I could give her something to brag about? As a child model I learned that success and money came when I refused the casseroles and the Tim Tams, and as an adult actress, the rules were still the same. Why would she suggest I eat all the foods that would make me fat?

I did briefly think about eating the Ki Si Ming because I loved it. But I quickly dismissed the thought. I wouldn't deviate from my regular routine. I wouldn't dare. If I ate the curried rice and stir-fry vegetable dish, I worried that I would gain weight. More than gaining a pound I worried that I would keep gaining pound after pound after that; that if I stopped for a moment, got off the train, maybe I couldn't get back on. If I suspended the belief that dieting was the only way for me to be a success in all aspects of life, then in that small window of time it took to eat Ki Si Ming, my desire not to diet would overtake me again. If I ate the Ki Si Ming, I would have to start over, and I knew how much harder it was to start something than to maintain it. Maybe I just had enough willpower to start it one time and if I stopped I would become very fat? I worried that this time the bingeing to make up for all the things I denied myself would never end.

All I ever thought about was the food that I couldn't eat. Sometimes I even dreamt about it. Dieting is hard. That's why everyone admires someone who is successful at it. I had thought my mother would be proud of my precision and my calculations, my self-control, but I had the sense that she thought I was out of control. As I sat down to a tablespoon of dry turkey and watched my mother and grandmother eat the dish they had always made to welcome me home, I wondered if her thoughts were correct. I wondered if I was out of control. If I couldn't eat a scoop of stir-fry because I was terrified of getting fat, then who was in control?

23

What did you eat last night?

WOKE UP at 5:00 a.m. to a quiet, dark house and rummaged through my suitcase for my gym shorts and sneakers. It was time to go running. I wanted to get my workout out of the way so I could see Sacha and my old friend Bill and spend some time with my brother, who was coming home later that morning. I ran down the same roads as I did the day before and thought about how proud Sacha would be when she saw me. The last time we'd seen each other was in St. Barths when I was fat and struggling—at first with her rejection of my advances toward her, but my struggle with my weight closely followed. Of the two issues, my weight problem was the more painful. Her rejection of me didn't hurt my feelings; rather, it clarified my feelings toward her. I was never in love with her. I was merely in love with the idea of being in a relationship with a woman. Over piña coladas, she'd helped me arrive at the conclusion that my future girlfriend would have to be a gay woman, not a straight one. I knew that once I had made enough money where I no longer had to worry about losing my career, I would find a girlfriend. I needed a lot of money, however, because I had an apartment to renovate. But after that, I would find someone to love.

I ran with money in my shoe this time. I wasn't going to be caught again. Besides, I thought it would be nice to eat breakfast at my favorite outdoor café. As well as money, I brought cigarettes so I could run and

look forward to ending my workout with a cup of hot coffee and a cigarette. The workout gear I wore for the run made me invisible. It worked
as a kind of disguise. No one looked at a girl running in spandex shorts
and tennis shoes even if she was running up and down a busy shopping street. Unlike the day before, I could run past the bookstore and
McDonald's without turning a head. It is strange that clothes can make
that much of a difference.

I stood at the counter of the café and waited to get the attention of
the owner. When he finally saw me, I didn't know whether to acknowledge him with a warm smile that suggested we knew each other or just
skip the smile and get my coffee. I decided on the latter as it's always
very embarrassing when people don't smile back because they are too
busy wondering who you are. I used to go there a lot, and although
we'd never officially met, he seemed to recognize me when I was with
my mother. She's the friendly one in the family.

"Black coffee, please."

"Coming right up." He turned his back to me to pour the coffee,
but when he turned around again with a big smile on his face it was
clear that he had remembered me.

"Back from America, are ya?"

"Yep. Back home for Christmas."

"Geez!" He blatantly looked me up and down. "Don't they feed ya
in Hollywood?"

I couldn't think of a joke. I didn't know what to say.

"How much is that?"

"For you, love, it's free."

I thanked him and took my coffee outside. I found a spot in a clus-
ter of iron tables and chairs separated from the parking lot by a potted
boxwood hedge. A couple was sitting at the next table very close to
mine, and as I took out the cigarette to light it, I wondered if I should
be polite and ask for their approval or just do it and hope I could get
a few drags in before they complained. Doing what I wanted without

permission and then dealing with the fallout was the method I'd always used with my brother. If I wanted to wear his favorite sweater, the one that he'd never let me borrow in a million years, I'd just take it and deal with the consequences. I liked to think I had grown up a lot since then, but it occurred to me my lighting that cigarette was the same principle. As it turned out, the couple next to me didn't mind the smoke and so I sat there, inhaling smoke and nicotine and feeling quite elated that I was home in Australia with its easygoing people and its trees and its birds with their raucous singing. I would see Sacha later in the day and . . .

"I thought you might like a good Aussie breakfast! Here's some eggs, love. Put a little meat on your bones!"

The owner of the café shoved a white porcelain plate on the metal table in front of me, interrupting my thoughts. Then he dropped a knife and fork wrapped in a napkin next to the plate. On the plate were two eggs, two big orange eyeballs of yolk staring up at me confrontationally, as if looking for a fight. I was too shocked and speechless to send them back immediately and so I was left looking at the eggs as they looked back at me, challenging me to make them disappear. I looked at the planter box filled with the boxwood hedge and wondered if eggs would somehow dissolve into the soil, or if the dirt was loose enough that I could cover up the evidence, but upon feeling the soil I found that it was too tightly packed and almost to the top of the planter. Besides, even if I could cut them up into millions of pieces, how could I get them in there without people seeing me? The café owner came back out to the patio again to deliver food to another table. He winked at me. "On the house," he said quietly so the other customers couldn't hear. For a brief moment I considered eating them just to save him from hurt feelings as he clearly liked his self-appointed role of a nurturing café owner who derived pleasure from seeing people enjoy his food. But that thought was ridiculous. I wasn't going to break my diet for a man who, only moments before, I'd been scared to acknowledge with a nod for fear he wouldn't remember me. I wasn't going to break my diet for that guy.

Disposing of the eggs into the planter wasn't an option and there was no trash can on the patio, so I was left with either cutting the eggs up into tiny pieces and moving the pieces around on the plate to make it look like I'd eaten some or leaving them whole and coming up with a reason for not wanting them, other than the obvious one, which was that I didn't order them. The longer I was confronted with this unsolicited situation, his so-called generosity, the angrier I became. It was quite disrespectful of him, actually, to feed me like this, as if I were a child. I was an adult capable of making my own decisions about what went into my body. I decided that I wasn't even going to attempt to please him. I was going to leave the eggs exactly as they were delivered to me. Now he could deal with not knowing what to do with the two monstrous, confrontational eyelike yolks. My only dilemma was how to appear normal, and as normal people are greedy and love receiving free things, how would I spin this? Who wouldn't want free food? Who wouldn't want free deliciously fresh eggs with their coffee? I found the perfect answer to this riddle just as he came out to check on me.

"Thank you so much for the eggs, but I'm vegan. I don't eat any animal products."

"Vegan." He said the word like he was hearing it for the first time, repeating it as if to get it right. He shook his head. "God, you Hollywood people are a bunch of weirdos."

I laughed at what I assumed was a joke and got up from the table to end this awkward interaction where I was force-fed and called a skinny weirdo. All I had wanted was to sit peacefully and bask in the joy of being home and instead I was ambushed by this Australian weirdo who thought he knew better than I did about what I needed. I jogged home and arrived just as a cab delivered my brother from the airport to the house where we had spent our teenage years ignoring each other.

"Hey!" I hugged my brother as he was collecting his luggage. "God, you stink."

"So do you."

No I don't. I don't stink anymore. I don't get my period. My hair hardly ever gets greasy and I don't sweat, either.

He looked me up and down. "You look awful, Porshe."

"Yeah, well, so do you."

"I'm not joking. You look like a skeleton."

Usually any comment about my thinness made me happy, but being called a skeleton hurt my feelings. My brother and I were always so jokingly sarcastic with each other, sometimes we took it too far. Usually I would've told him that he was being rude, but I didn't want to bring attention to it. I needed to make the conversation casual so that he would let it go. I had to appease everyone lately.

"It's just 'cause I'm in my running clothes."

"You've been running already? It's so early. Why don't you take a break from it? I think you're thin enough, if that's what you're worried about."

It was strange that all of a sudden it seemed like I had to lie constantly just to be left alone.

"I know I'm too thin. I'm gaining weight. And I wouldn't have gone running if I weren't this jet-lagged. I was going crazy lying there—although your bed is really comfortable."

"What?"

"First come, first served, Brother."

I walked into the house through the back door and found my mother in the kitchen.

"Good morning, Bubbles. Do you want some breakfast?"

Jesus.

"No. That man at the café we go to all the time gave me eggs this morning."

That wasn't a lie.

"Michael's here."

My mother ran to the kitchen door and hugged him.

"Mike's home! Look, Gran," she yelled, "it's Mike!"

"Hi, Ma."

As I slipped through the kitchen and down the hall I heard him say, "Hey, you didn't give her my room, did you?"

My brother's arrival diverted mom's attention away from my breakfast, thank God, and I escaped into my bedroom where I had lived my teenage years listening to records loudly and smoking cigarettes, believing that neither noise nor smoke could penetrate my bedroom door. It continued to act as a magic shield from the demands of my family, for when I emerged from my room, dressed in long sleeves and a full, long skirt, breakfast was over and I was greeted with easy smiles. No one seemed to care if I was running or eating. I was wearing a lot of makeup, too, and I think that helped.

"Porshe, you wanna go shopping?"

"Seriously?" I said incredulously. "Again?"

My brother had an enviable ability to dismiss any thoughts of Christmas gifts for the family until Christmas Eve, and I was always dragged along to help shop for them. Strangely enough, though, he never needed my help. He had an uncanny knack for finding the perfect thing, the most thoughtful gift at the last possible second. I loathed him for it and admired him for it. Most times, I secretly enjoyed the ritual, too, because it ended with a trip to our favorite pub. The ritual had a rhythm to it: I had to start out with being pissed off and pretend to have my own plans. He'd beg me to help him although he didn't need it, and I'd grudgingly agree, telling him he owed me a beer. Then it'd end with him asking me to wrap the gifts, which really did piss me off. That was the way it always went. But to my surprise, today I actually was agitated. I was anxiously wondering how and when I was going to eat. I had been waiting for the moment my mother left the house to weigh and eat my turkey, as I wanted to avoid any possible comments that weighing out a portion of turkey might elicit. Then, after that, I thought I could cook and eat egg whites before going to the Hyatt hotel. I had decided to book the presidential suite of the Hyatt and spend Christmas Eve there with my brother to decorate the Christmas tree and to ready the room for our family Christmas dinner the following day. Getting the hotel suite was a gift that I was giving my family, since cooking Christmas dinner in the small kitchen of my mother's house always seemed to be challenging. But leaving my mother's house for the hotel earlier than I'd planned was worrying. Traveling and dieting was hard enough, but without access to my mother's kitchen all day, I began to fret, wondering when I would next eat.

"Why can't you get your shit together like everyone else? I have plans, too, you know. I wanted to see Sacha today."

"I'm not going to carry a whole bunch of crap from LA in a suitcase. Come on, it'll take an hour."

"No it won't." I grabbed my bag, got in the car, and shrugged off my irritation enough to continue the banter. "You owe me a beer." It sounded fun to say it, but I had no intention of holding him to it. I would never drink my entire day's calories in a beer, even if it is Victoria Bitter.

"Hey, what do you think of this?"

Michael was standing in front of a full-length mirror in Myer, Melbourne's largest department store, wearing a purse.

"Who for?" I barely even looked at it. I really didn't care at that point. I hated shopping—especially department store shopping, and I'd been with him in that store for hours. He'd bought about ten gifts so I'd thought we were done.

"It's for me. I need something to carry my work stuff in."

That made me look. My brother, as serious as I'd ever seen him, was checking himself out in the mirror, a thin strap over his right shoulder that connected to a shiny black leather rectangular pouch that was at waist height due to the shortness of the strap. I stared at him, expressionless.

"Guys have bags now! I saw it in *In Flight* magazine on the plane." He turned to me and modeled it a little and by his swagger it was obvious that he thought he looked pretty good.

The ground floor of this department store where we were standing sold shoes and accessories. There was a side that sold men's accessories and a side that sold women's. The two departments were separated with an aisle. While he was certainly standing near a couple of large satchel-type man-bags, he had picked up a bag from the wrong side of the aisle. I waited for him to realize his mistake. After staring at my expressionless face for many moments, he gestured for me to hurry up with my opinion.

"It's a purse."

A look of panic flooded his face as he spun back to face the mirror. He looked at himself and regained his composure, the purse still over his shoulder. He calmly read the tag attached to it.

"Yes," he said simply. "Yes, it is."

We cracked up. We laughed so hard we were snorting. Nearby Christmas shoppers saw us laughing and couldn't help but laugh, too. We left the store and were cracking up all the way to the parking garage, dropping shopping bags as we doubled over. Even after we'd recovered for several minutes, I'd burst out laughing again on our drive to the pub, thinking about my macho helicopter pilot brother wearing a purse. That would set him off again, too, and as I laughed with my brother and drove past red brick Victorian terrace houses and through the eucalyptus-lined streets of my hometown, I felt that I was truly home.

When we arrived at the Great Britain, GB for short, Michael went to the bar and I settled in at a high-top table. I looked around my favorite pub. There was a goldfish above the bar in an old black-and-white TV set and tableaus of mini living rooms, with vintage floor lamps lighting worn sofas and mismatched coffee tables. I never felt more myself as I did in that grungy pub. Bill, an old school friend whom I rarely went anywhere at night without, used to drive me to the GB where we'd meet Sacha and friends from law school. Occasionally I was introduced to girls. Although I was too shy to really do much about it, I loved feeling that excitement of getting dressed to go out thinking that perhaps that night I could meet someone and fall in love. The hope of falling in love was a lot to sacrifice for the sake of my career. Apart from that feeling, I missed being able to relax in public without fear of being noticed, and talking to whomever I chose without worrying about people finding out my big secret.

There was no real reason why I hadn't told my brother that I was gay. Then again, I just didn't really have a reason to tell him. I wasn't dating anyone, and because none of his friends had any idea that I was gay, I wasn't worried that he'd find out from someone other than me. I knew Mom wouldn't tell him. She didn't want anyone to know.

I could hear my brother talking to the bartender about how he just arrived from LA and the old-fashioned cash register make the *ding* sound as it popped open its drawer to swallow up the gold two-dollar coins. I took a drag of my cigarette and found it hard to breathe the smoke back out of my mouth. My throat had constricted with anxiety, trapping the smoke in my lungs. It was time to reveal myself to my brother. I was sure he'd be confused and have a lot of questions, but I had to tell him how alone and misunderstood I've felt. I could no longer keep this secret from him and I just had to hope that he would understand.

He returned with the beers. He put them down on the table. He sat down. He took a sip.

"Brother. There's something I've been meaning to tell you for a long time. Something I've known since I was a kid, really. Well, teenager, I guess. Umm . . ." I took a deep breath and looked at him in his eyes. "I'm gay."

There was an eruption of laughter at the pool table. One man had apparently scratched by sinking the white ball in behind the black to lose the game. The man who won was yelling and walking backward with his arms spread wide, a pool cue in his right hand. He was coming dangerously close to our table. To my surprise, my brother didn't seem to notice and to my even bigger surprise he looked angry. He'd been staring at the table for what seemed like an eternity and for a brief moment I wondered if he'd even heard what I'd said.

"What did you think I would say, Porshe? Why would you think that I'd care about something like that? I'm not some narrow-minded bigot that you'd have to hide this from. I mean, who do you think I am?"

Of all the feelings I thought he would have, betrayal had never crossed my mind. I had betrayed him by hiding the person I really was from him for fear that he would reject me. I had insulted him by insinuating that he harbored thoughts of discrimination and bigotry. His reaction was so surprising to me and it left me feeling ashamed for judging him. And yet I couldn't remember feeling happier. I could tell by his expression that once he got over his anger at me for keeping this secret from him, there was nothing left to talk about. He wasn't confused. He didn't need questions answered. He didn't ask why or how or with whom or whether I thought maybe it might just be a phase. He didn't ask who knew and who didn't know or whether I thought it might ruin my career. I was his sister and he didn't care whether I was straight or gay; it simply didn't matter to him. I'd been worried that he wouldn't believe me, but he didn't even question me. All that mattered to him was that I had been struggling with this tortuous secret without his help.

His phone rang. It was a work call from LA; it wasn't yet Christmas Eve over there—it was just the twenty-third of the month, a day like any other. He took the call and spoke in a tone that was all business. In his voice there was no evidence of anger or betrayal—it was light and friendly without a hint of emotion. He spoke and chugged down his beer.

"You ready?" He didn't even look at my untouched beer.

"Let's go."

As we walked side by side down the Melbourne street in the late-afternoon heat of summer, he put his arm around my shoulder. He understood. He still loved me. We sauntered down the city street listening to the magpies that squarked so loudly we couldn't have heard each other even if we had needed to talk. But we didn't. We just needed to silently acknowledge that we were home, that we were where we came from, that for that moment we didn't need to live in another country just to feel accomplished. We were okay just as we were. Our silence was broken by the remote unlocking the rental car. He uncharacteristically opened my side first, like a gentleman, and just as I was about to thank him for his valor he said:

"You're good at wrapping gifts, aren't you?"

24

CHRISTMAS MORNING, like every other morning since I'd arrived in Melbourne, began in the dark, as jet lag, the discomfort of an unfamiliar bed, and hunger prevented me from sleeping past 4:00 or 5:00 a.m. I lay in the darkness of the master bedroom of my two-bedroom hotel suite and ran through my calorie consumption and calorie burn of the day before. This mental calculation had become a ritual, and it was done with precision and some urgency. Only when I could solve the equation of calories in and calories out could I feel relief and begin my day. There was a scale in the bathroom. I saw it when I arrived the night before. It was digital and measured weight in pounds, unlike other Australian scales, which measured in kilograms. Could I possibly stand on it? Could I weigh myself? I'd been too scared to check my weight since arriving in Australia because of the water retention that can occur during plane travel, and I didn't want to upset myself. But lying in bed Christmas morning, I felt thin. I could feel my hip bones and my ribs. I lay on my side with my legs slightly bent with one knee on top of the other for the ultimate test of weight loss: if the fat on my top thigh didn't touch my bottom thigh, if there was a gap between my thighs even when I was lying down, then my thighs had to be thin. There was a wide gap and I made a mental note to measure that gap with one of those stiff metal tape measures when I got back home. I felt as though I could get on that digital scale and give myself the Christmas present of a good number, a number that would show my hard work; a number that would congratulate me for dieting successfully for eight months.

For eight months, I hadn't gained a pound. I'd stayed the same for a few days at a time, but I hadn't gained. My initial goal weight was 115 pounds. My mistake was that I set a goal weight thinking that 115 pounds would feel different from how it really felt. I thought I would look thinner than I did at that weight. At 115 pounds, although my stomach was flatter and my arms looked good, my thighs were still too big. At 110 pounds, I was happy. I really liked how I looked. I only went under that weight because I needed a cushion in case that uncontrollable urge to binge happened again and it wasn't chewing gum, but ice cream, candy, or potato chips that abducted me.

The only thing I cared about now was not gaining. As long as I never gained, weight loss was no longer that important. But seeing a new low on the scale did give me a high. And the lower the number, the bigger the high.

I walked into the bathroom and used the toilet. I then held my breath as I eased onto the scale, my arms holding me up on the bathroom counter, holding my weight off the scale for as long as it took to gently add weight pound by pound until I could let go of the counter and stand with my arms by my side. In this hotel bathroom, naked and vulnerable, I closed my eyes and prayed. The red digital number in between and just in front of my feet would determine whether I had a happy Christmas or a miserable one. To no one in particular I said out loud, "Please let me be in the nineties. I'll take ninety-five, I'm not greedy, just don't let it be in the hundreds. I'd rather die than be in the hundreds. Please, please, please, please." I started to cry with anxiety, but I quickly calmed myself down as I was worried the jerkiness my body makes when I cry might have caused the number on the scale to shoot up and not come down again. In fact, the more I thought about it, the more I realized that I needed to start over, to ease back on the scale again just to make sure that the number I saw would be the accurate one. As I got off the scale looking straight ahead at my reflection in the mirror, I felt as though I needed to use the bathroom again and I did so hoping that I'd gotten all the excess water out of my body. I eased myself back onto the scale feeling fortunate that I hadn't read the first number, that God had whispered in my ear and told me to get off the scale and use the bathroom so I could avoid the pain that the false read would've given me. I stood now with my hands by my side. I was empty. I was no longer crying. I was ready to receive my Christmas present, the gift of health and self-love that I'd given myself this year. With complete calmness and acceptance, I looked down at my feet.

89

"Merry Christmas, Portia."

"Merry Christmas, Portia." My aunt Gwen and Uncle Len walked through the door of the hotel suite bearing gifts and my uncle's famous Christmas fruit cake. Frank Sinatra was crooning carols in the background, a giant, fully trimmed Christmas tree was the centerpiece of the spacious living room, and my grandmother and mother were sitting on chairs together in front of it, talking. Moments later, my cousins wandered in and the tableau was complete. I silently congratulated myself for providing this lovely experience for my family. This was what I could do with the money that was given to me in exchange for my freedom. I could create a Christmas where they could all relax and enjoy one another without having to worry about anything. I could create the perfect holiday.

The day started out perfect for me, too. I did sit-ups and leg lifts with renewed energy and vigor. I was eighty-nine pounds. It sounded so mysterious and magical I could barely say it out loud. It was special. Who weighed eighty-nine pounds? It was an accomplishment that felt uniquely mine, uniquely special. I went to the gym at 5:30 and ran up and down the hall for thirty minutes, waiting for it to open at six. I was the only one in the gym on Christmas morning, as I was the only one who took health and fitness seriously. In a way, working hard in the gym Christmas morning was the answer to the question I had asked of myself when I began this journey six months prior. This wasn't a passing phase. This was my new way of life. On the day when everyone else slacked off, I worked because being thin was what I liked more than anything else. But something else happened in there, too. I felt lonely. For a brief moment, as I pressed the up arrow on the treadmill until the speed climbed to 7.0, I felt very alone. I heard the thud of my feet as they found the rhythm of the belt and wondered why I had a demanding taskmaster of a voice in my head that could be silenced only if I ran instead of slept, when everyone else in this hotel was waking up gently to a quiet voice that was telling them to stay in bed, that it's only six, it's not time to think just yet.

"Have some champagne, Porshe."

"I don't drink anymore, Ma. You know that."

"Oh, come on. It won't hurt you."

My mother likes tradition and the idea that the family clan will pass on all the same habits and morals and ideas, generation after generation. A tradition in our family was to drink champagne with a pureed strawberry liqueur concoction my cousin made especially for Christmas morning. I felt that I couldn't refuse.

I drank the champagne and my mother instantly looked relieved. I'm not sure if it was the alcohol from the champagne that loosened my tight grip on my diet, but the simple act of drinking a glass of champagne with my family was exhilarating. I was happier in that moment than I had been in eight months. For just that one day, I was going to put the "cushion" theory in play. Seeing my family relax as I drank the champagne encouraged me to continue to drink and eat and be merry.

Next I ate turkey meat and my mother smiled. Then, at my family's urging, I ate potatoes. They relaxed. They laughed. It seemed that my eating potatoes gave them more pleasure than opening gifts, not having to cook, and Christmas Day itself. So I ate some more. I felt invincible at eighty-nine pounds. And I loved that for the first time since I was a small child, I could just be like everyone else. I wasn't a model or an actress who had to eat special food, nor was I an overweight girl who complained about her weight, making everyone else bored and uncomfortable. I was just one of the family at that dining table, partaking in their rituals, their food.

By the time everyone but my brother and my cousin, Megan, had left, however, I was no longer happy or relaxed. I was in shock. I had drunk a glass of champagne. I had eaten turkey roasted in its own fat. I had eaten beans glazed with oil. But what shocked me the most was that I had eaten potatoes. I had eaten two medium-sized roasted potatoes with oil and rosemary and salt. I started to panic. I clenched and unclenched my fists and started circling my wrists in an attempt to take the horror of what was digesting in my gut away from my mind's eye. My body was shaking. I couldn't control the shaking because the panic that was setting in to make it shake felt like itching. Somehow I had to get relief. I raised my arms above my head and shook out my hands as if to expel the energy. My cousin and my brother were still in the living room, sitting by the Christmas tree, but I no longer cared. In front of my cousin and my brother, I started jumping up and down with my arms above my head and shaking my hands to try to get rid of the calories in the potatoes.

"Porshe, what are you doing?" Megan asked me in a tone that suggested she wasn't waiting for an answer. She had something to say to me. She was quite emotional. I could tell because when Australians are emotional, sometimes they can sound bossy.

"I pigged out at lunch and I'm just trying to work some of it off." To downplay the fact that I was jumping up and down and shaking, I tried to sound nonchalant and used a smiley voice that was on a frequency that sat high above the panic. I smiled and in between bounces shrugged my shoulders in a "you know how it is" way that I was sure all women would understand. But I didn't really care if I was understood. I just had to get rid of all that crap in my stomach. I felt so panicked I couldn't be still.

"Portia. You ate potatoes, just some potatoes. They're not going to make you fat, okay? What's the big deal?"

They will make me fat because it's not just some potatoes that I just ate, it's the potatoes I know I'm going to eat in the future now I've allowed myself to eat those. That by eating those potatoes I could get back on the same old yo-yo dieting pattern and suffer in the way that I'd suffered from age twelve to twenty-five. Eating those potatoes could cost me my career, money, and my ability to make money. Eating those potatoes will make me poor. So eating those potatoes will make me fat. Because without any money or a career, I will definitely end up fat.

"I'm going for a run." I quickly walked past her and my brother to the bedroom, changed into gym clothes, and strode past them again and out the front door. Compared to the earlier laughing and talking and singing, the suite was eerily quiet. I don't think they spoke to each other the whole time I was changing. As I jogged down the hall, I replayed the scene in my mind. I knew I'd end up ruining Christmas no matter how hard I tried to make it perfect. I knew I'd end up upsetting the people I love with my selfishness and my lack of thought for others. I had tried so hard to make everyone happy and yet I just couldn't lie well enough to do it. Lying was too hard. As I ran out of the elevator and through the lobby, I could sense that people were staring.

I wasn't like everyone else. I was an actress. I changed my name, my accent, my nationality. I was gay. It was time to stop even trying to pretend.

25

T GOT quiet at night on the streets of Camberwell. It was always quiet with Bill unless I was prepared to talk. Sitting on the stoop of the fish and chip shop next to 7-Eleven was something that we liked to do after we'd done everything else. After we drove across town to the less gentrified neighborhood, where the architecture was better but where the people who lived in it were generally poorer, had coffee, drank beer, played pool, saw a band, and drove back across town to the middle-class suburban neighborhood where my mother lived, we'd sit on the stoop of the Camberwell fish and chips shop enjoying the balmy weather and the freedom of not having to look at a clock. There were as many hours as we needed in the middle of the night, if in fact, 2:00 a.m. was considered the middle of it. Usually with these free hours I would tell Bill my troubles, my plans, my desires, but tonight I really didn't have any. I was just sitting there, living. Living was in stark contrast to dreaming about living. Usually I would tell him my plan to make Sacha fall in love with me, the directors I had hopes to meet, why being in Los Angeles was better than being in Australia. When I was bored of talking about myself, I would talk about him, challenge him about why he didn't have a girlfriend, a job, an escape plan from his life. But I was still really just talking about me, talking myself into the reasons why I didn't have a girlfriend, a job that I liked, but mostly, I was trying to find a reason for having had to escape from the place that was my home. To convince myself of my choice, I had to make it a place that everyone should want to escape from. But tonight I really had nothing to say. I wasn't excited about anything. I realized that in stark contrast to Christmases past, I had no drive, no reason to propel me forward. I had nothing to say. And because Bill doesn't really like to talk, Camberwell at 2:00 a.m. was pretty quiet.

Although there were several more days before I had to return to LA, it felt like the holiday was over. The excitement of seeing my family after many months and the thrill of showing off my new body was over. My cousins, my uncles, and my aunts all saw my body. They were all seemingly unimpressed. No one mentioned that I had lost weight or that I looked good or that I was thin. It was baffling to me that they didn't say anything. I didn't even try to hide my arms anymore. I took my sleeves off, put my gym clothes on, and called Sacha. She would be impressed. She would understand the work it had taken to achieve this body. I called her and convinced her to take me to her gym. I told her that she and I were going to work off our indulgences over the holidays. I couldn't wait to see her, to make sure I still had my best friend after what I'd put her through in St. Barths.

I walked past my brother in my gym clothes, my bag slung over my shoulder.

"Where are you going?"

"I'm meeting Sacha at her gym in Prahran."

He looked simultaneously disappointed and determined as he said, "I'll drive you."

I knew I couldn't argue with him. Not when his face looked like that.

My brother pulled into the parking lot at the gym but instead of leaving to go do whatever he'd come into town to do, he parked and shut the engine down.

"Aren't you going to run errands or something?"

"No. I thought I might come in with you."

"To the gym?"

"Yeah."

Shit. I'd told Sacha to meet me at noon. It was only ten. I wanted to give myself a good solid two-hour workout before she arrived.

"Why do you want to go to the gym? I thought you were just dropping me off. You know what me and Sacha are like, we'll be goofing around for hours." Goofing around? Geez.

Now it looked like it was his turn scan his brain for a reason in the form of a rational-sounding lie. But why? What was he doing?

"I thought I might like to see Sacha. I haven't seen her in ages."

Bullshit. Jesus. I wished I'd taken the tram. I didn't know how to get around the fact that Sacha wasn't going to be at the gym for two more hours. As I walked into the almost empty gym with my brother trailing behind me, I decided to cover the lie by acting annoyed at Sacha's lateness. That would do.

"What are you going to do in here? Stand around like a pervert?" He was wearing jeans and boots. He looked like a total weirdo.

"I'm just gonna check it out. Don't worry about me. Do your thing."

I took his direction and stopped worrying about him. I didn't care about the whole Sacha lie either. Once I checked in to the gym I got to work. I did what I came to do. I got on the treadmill and started sprinting for twenty minutes. Then I got on the elliptical. I did twenty minutes and burned 137 calories on that, which I counted as 100. In my mind, twenty minutes on any cardio machine gave me a 100-calorie burn even if the red digital digits said otherwise. I couldn't trust machines. They were all different. By the time I was done with cardio (I felt okay about only doing forty minutes because I'd run for over an hour that morning) and moved to the mats on the floor to begin the glorified sit-ups they call Pilates, I noticed my brother still standing in the corner. I had forgotten him completely.

"Why are you still here?" I had to speak loudly over the whirr of the machines and the yelling of the sports commentators on the TVs.

"Oh. Ahh . . . I dunno. Just do your thing. I'll wait for you." He was acting strangely. He had his head down and was avoiding eye contact, which was so unlike him. He was a helicopter pilot. He loved eye contact. He'd have laughed if he could have seen himself like I did. He really looked creepy standing around in the darkest corner of the gym in jeans and boots. I hoped all the women in there didn't know he was with me.

I did my thing. I finished my forty-minute mat workout (so many reps to be effective!) and moved to the weights. I occasionally did weights to tone my arms and back, and I figured that since I wasn't doing a photo shoot or appearing on camera for a couple of weeks, the muscles would have time to deflate if by accident I somehow pumped them up. I would've hated to look fat because I'd worked out too hard and my muscles added the inches I'd painstakingly taken away.

After I'd worked my bi's, tri's and deltoids, I saw that my brother had found a friend. It was Sacha. My desire to run to her was curbed by the seriousness of the conversation she was having with my policeman of a brother, creepily brooding in the dark corner. I wondered what the hell they could be talking about. Could they be talking about my having come out to him? It seemed unlikely, as I doubted that either of them would betray my confidence. Surely it couldn't be my weight. I knew I was a little thin in places, but not enough to have a serious conversation about it. I started to worry, like perhaps their somber mood had nothing to do with me, and so I went over to them in a hurry. As I approached, I realized they were talking about me because Sacha's mood immediately changed when she realized I was within earshot.

"Peeeee!" She squealed my name and hugged me all at once, leaving me deaf in my right ear. But my brother didn't smile. He stayed the same. He looked at me, this time in the eyes.

"Porshe, can I see you outside?" He turned away from me and walked out of the gym.

The seriousness of his tone made me follow him, leaving Sacha alone, but I got the feeling that she was fine with me following him, too. It was exciting almost. It was so different. My brother had never pulled me away to talk to me seriously about anything before. I couldn't help but be excited because it was so different. I could tell that he wasn't angry, but I couldn't quite figure out what he was feeling and why his feelings were so important that he would pull me away from my best friend whom I hadn't seen for months.

We got all the way to the car before we stopped. The longer we walked, the more concerned I became. By the time he spoke, my stomach was in knots. He leaned on the hood of the car with both hands, his broad back to me, blocking his face from mine. I couldn't see where this was going. I started to get really scared.

"Porshe." When he turned around, I could see that he was crying. I was shocked. He bent over now, his hands on his bent knees, his elbows locked. He was looking at the ground. I was shocked and I couldn't speak. I just had to wait.

He started talking and standing upright at the same time, deliberately but with difficulty.

"I'm just really worried about you. I just can't believe how thin you are."

I couldn't believe what I was hearing. I knew I was thin but not nearly thin enough for this reaction. If I'd worked out in a sweater so he didn't see my arms he wouldn't be reacting like this, but I felt that now wasn't the time to explain that to him. Besides, I'd never been so upset, seeing him cry. I'd never been so upset.

He got himself together a little, enough to look at my face. I was speechless, still, but I could see he wasn't asking me to speak.

I watched as his face started breaking again. His face crumbled into creases. It went red. Tears were falling down his cheeks. He looked at me imploringly although he still wasn't asking anything of me. It confused me.

"Porshe . . ." He cried harder. As he inhaled to say what he was leading up to say, his breath caught, making short staccato sounds. "You're gonna die."

My brother had left shortly after I'd pleaded my case. I told him that I knew what I was doing. When that didn't work, I told him that I would eat, that I would gain weight and stop obsessively working out. He seemed pleased to hear all that so he left me to hang out with Sacha, who, after pointing out a very thin girl in the gym, dropped me home. She didn't say anything about my weight, she just pointed to that girl on the treadmill, exclaiming that she was anorexic and how sad it was, and then she dropped me home.

I had cried a lot with my brother. The tears weren't for me. They came because of him, because I hated seeing him cry like that. The only other time I'd seen him cry was when our dad died and to be honest, I didn't know why my weight made him so sad. And I didn't know why Sacha pointed out the so-called anorexic girl. I knew that I was thinner than usual. I knew that I was underweight, but anorexia was never something that I thought I could have. The girl at the gym didn't have it. Not just anyone could have anorexia. It was a disorder of the highly accomplished, cultured, beautiful. It belonged to models, singers, and Princess Diana.

I had always been secretly in awe of anorexics with their superhuman self-restraint. There is a neatness to it, a perfection. Apart from the fact that I could never be thin enough to be anorexic, I didn't want to be anorexic anyway. I just wanted to excel at dieting.

. . .

When I arrived home, my mother intercepted me on my way to take a shower and asked me to come to her room. At a glance it was clear to me that my brother had been talking to her about the episode at the gym and it was clear that her nonchalant attitude had been replaced by a very serious one.

"Come in here for a minute, okay? I would really like to talk to you."

I followed her through the living room and into her bedroom. I passed by Gran, who for twenty years had sat in the chair in the corner of the living room, alternating her attention between the TV and her family's lives, all played out in front of her as a source of entertainment. But my grandmother didn't appear disconnected or uncaring, she just seemed like she already knew the end to all the stories. She'd seen all the reruns on TV and in life. She'd seen it all before. We were an episode of *The Golden Girls* in a rerun. Blanche, whose self-worth is based on her looks, has something on her mind but can't communicate it in any way other than by acting out and has been called in to talk to problem-solving Dorothy, who had been given a tip by Rose as she stumbled across the truth, but it was something that Sophia had known all along. Gran gave me a look as I passed her that said, "Oh, yeah! I remember this one. This is the one where you confront your mother about her lack of acceptance of you for being gay and she finally accepts you for who you are. Oh yeah! This is a good one . . ." She couldn't really have known that, of course. My mother and I had decided not to tell her about my sexuality. We had decided that she was too old and knowing that truth about me would be a terrible shock. Something like that could kill her. That the words "I'm gay" might just stop her heart, and she'd topple onto the floor, dead from shock.

My mother stood backlit against the window of her dark bedroom. I could just make out her pink scalp underneath her wisps of gray-blond hair and I wondered for how long gray hair could be dyed. Maybe it became so porous that color would just not take to it anymore. Maybe that's why really old people have gray hair. Until this point I had thought it was because people in their eighties and nineties couldn't be bothered because superficial things like looks didn't matter anymore, but what if the desire to hold on to blond or brown hair was still there but the ability to do it was gone? I wondered if that's what aging felt like. That desire and reality were dueling until the day you die, that nobody ever got to a place of peace. I had always wanted to get old so I didn't have to care anymore, but I began to think that it would be best just to skip the getting older part and just die.

"You're so thin, darling. It's awful."

Yes. I'm thin. I'm exactly what you wanted me to be.

"Well, I guess I can get my Swatch watch now."

The Swatch watch was a carrot my mother used to dangle when I was a teenager if I reached 119 pounds, the magical eight and a half stone. As I had always fluctuated between nine and nine and a half, that number was always just a fantasy, a magical land where perfection lived and all the people who were special enough to get there were covered in Swatch watches. As I struggled to get to that number on the scale, the Swatch watches I wanted were going out of style one by one. First it was the clear one I wanted but was too fat to have, then a yellow one with blue hands, then the black one that passed me by without my earning the right to own it. I really did want my plastic Swatch watch. Even though they didn't make them anymore.

"If you don't eat something, you're going to die!"

My mother squatted down with her hand on the corner of the bed. Her other hand was covering her face as she quietly sobbed. I stood over her, looking down. To my surprise I stood there waiting for something to happen. Where was the rush of emotion that had overtaken me when I saw my brother similarly bent over, sobbing and in pain? Where was that panic I felt that made me search for something soothing to say? Where was the deep regret for making my mother so upset?

To my horror, a smirk involuntarily stretched over my face. My mother was crying and I was smiling. I loved my mother very much. Why was I being so cold?

The answer came to me with certainty and clarity.

I can be gay now. I can be who I am without pretending anymore. I'm forcing her to accept me just the way I am.

I bent down and picked my mother up off the floor. I put my arm around her shoulders and we sat like that on the edge of her bed until she stopped crying. I was waiting for her to stop so I could start in on her. As my mother quietly cried, I planned my attack. I would tell her that I was angry that she didn't accept me for being gay, I was angry that she seemed to care more about how I looked than how I felt or who I was. I was going to tell her to change or she would risk losing me. My comments would hurt her, but it was better for her in the long run. I was going to show her the same tough love she'd shown me.

But I didn't do that. Instead, I burst into tears.

"I'm so sorry that I'm gay, Mama. I'm sorry I'm not what you wanted."

I cried for her disappointment, and for mine. I wasn't the daughter she was proud of, I was the daughter that made her ashamed. And no amount of fame could take take shame away.

"Why are you sorry, darling? You are who you are."

"I know! But you're ashamed of me! You won't even tell our family and they're the people who love me!"

"I just thought that your being gay was nobody's business. It was private."

"Michael's relationships weren't private? You had no problem talking about those! You tell everyone the private things you're proud of!"

My mother swiveled toward me, put her hands on my shoulders, and turned me to face her.

"Listen. I'm a stupid old fool. Alright?" She was looking directly at me. It was like she was seeing me for the first time. "I was scared, okay?

I didn't want you to lose everything you'd worked so hard for. But I was wrong. And I was stupid." She folded me into her arms. "I love you so much."

"I love you, too, Mama."

I felt the weight fall away from me. I lost the weight that I'd been carrying around since I was a teenager. Shame weighs a lot more than flesh and bone.

Within moments we were laughing, talking about how crazy I was to take the weight loss too far. We were saying that all of it was really unnecessary, that I was great just the way I was. We decided that it was time to start dating and "to hell with it." Happiness was everything. "And health," she chimed in. "Without them, what's the point?" We laughed and hugged and agreed that the most important things in life are health and happiness and that they were the only things I had to worry about now. That's all she cared about.

My health and happiness were the only things my mom cared about.

We walked directly to the kitchen arm in arm and we made lunch together. We made fried rice with peas and a teaspoon of oil. We were laughing and talking, we ate it together, and my grandmother watched from the corner of the room in her chair, smiling as the credits rolled. The End.

26

WAS STILL 89 pounds. I liked being 89 pounds. Although the image of my brother crying and my mother breaking down was burned into my memory and I had made promises to them that I would gain weight, January was not a good time to gain weight. I had agreed to shoot the cover of *Angeleno* magazine, a big, glossy fashion/lifestyle rag. I had committed to attending the Australia Day Ball, an annual event held in LA that honored Australians in the film and TV industry. I just couldn't gain any weight until all that was done. What would be the point in sliding backward to the middle of the pack when it was just as easy to take the pictures of me at the finish line, alone in my triumph? My ego wouldn't let me gain any weight. I didn't see the point to it until after the cameras were no longer pointed at me.

As the maintenance took up a lot of time, I barely had time for anything else. Even with Carolyn doing the supermarket rounds to find the brands with the least amount of sodium or the lowest fat content, working out took up most of my day. I decided, however, that I needed a social outlet and I joined that ballet class with the yelling Russian and the fat women in makeup and tights. I figured at 89 pounds I was thin enough to wear a leotard and *développé* my leg into the air. Besides, ballet was a kind of workout, too, if you weren't lazy about it. I met a girl there who liked to count calories and to work out. Melody was thinner than me with a better turnout and a higher extension. She was called

on by the yelling Russian to demonstrate good *développés*. I tried to be-
friend her as we had a lot in common, but what we shared in common
made it difficult to be friends. We were both recluses with rituals. Besides, being gay I didn't feel comfortable making new friends. It didn't
seem fair after months of presenting myself as a relatable heterosexual
to suddenly surprise them with the news that a lesbian had been lurking underneath the whole time, had been in their homes, talking about
their sex lives, hugging them and telling them they had good leg exten-
sions in ballet class. I stopped going to ballet class anyway. I didn't
have the thinnest thighs nor was I the best dancer in the class. It didn't
remind me of a time when I was good at something, it made me aware
of the sad reality that if I was good as an eight-year-old, then I had gotten worse. I had peaked at age eight. What was the point in continuing?
The old yelling Russian told me that I was too thin and that I needed
to gain weight. What was the point?

The *Angeleno* cover shoot was a reward for my hard work. I had trained
hard for the event and knowing that I had done the work, all I had
to do was relax and enjoy the ride. The ride was a gentle downhill
slope with smooth pavement beneath me. The ride was my feet off the
pedals, feeling the wind through my hair, smelling the wildflowers as
they rushed past me firmly rooted in place. No panic. No doubts. No
disgrace. The interview was different. It took place at my favorite restaurant, The Ivy, which was my favorite because they blanched all their
vegetables and never brushed them with oil. I ate my vegetables (with
no lip gloss or lip balm—one can never be too careful) and attempted
to maneuver gracefully around personal questions as fundamental and
important to a person's character as their desires to marry and have children. Being secretive was exhausting. But the interviewer had a secret,
too. She secretly didn't like me while pretending to find me delightful.
She suckered me into being a little looser, a little more truthful. What

added to my uncharacteristically easy mood was that the interview took place on my birthday, and when the manager at The Ivy presented me with a large slice of birthday cake, I looked at my new journalist friend and said with a wink in my voice, "Like I'm gonna eat that!"

An Australian tabloid picked up the story and on the cover it printed, "Out to Lunch with Portia."

A cover is still a cover.

"Good news!" I stood in my kitchen looking out onto the Sahara desert that was the yellow wall of the Sunset 5 shopping mall and tried to rally excitement for my impending movie. My mother loved to hear of my accomplishments and because of the hell I had put her through over Christmas, I felt that the "good news" of an exciting role in a big studio movie was what she deserved to hear. As I began to describe the film, "It's called *Cletis Tout*," who was cast to star in it, "Richard Dreyfuss plays my father!" and where it would shoot, "In Toronto—you'll have to come visit," my excited, energetic voice was in stark contrast to the exhaustion I was feeling. Landing the role wasn't exciting to me, it was merely the end of the long uphill climb of auditions, callbacks, and negotiations. Getting the role was a relief, like the moment of collapse at the top of a mountain before you begin worrying about how to get down. Like a tourist who travels not to experience foreign places but rather to tell people that she's well traveled—this was how I viewed this excursion to Toronto with its film set and its respected actors. "I'm doing a movie this summer." That was the reason I wanted the movie. As my *Ally McBeal* cast mates had seemingly all succeeded in landing movie roles, I too must do something extraordinary to fit in.

I hung up the phone and felt empty, vacant, directionless. I knew I should celebrate, but I didn't know who to call. I didn't know who would care. I couldn't call my brother because he would want to take me out for Mexican food and margaritas and I couldn't think of an excuse not to go. I couldn't let him see me in person because I didn't want to upset him again. He could think that I was eating more and loosening up on my strict diet from the picture on his TV screen, as everyone looks ten pounds fatter on TV. He could check in with me as Nelle Porter once a week and be pleased with my progress as the wardrobe department had cleverly quilted a disguise of flattering clothing to cover all my flaws: a patch to cover my thin arms, a patch to cover the gap between my thighs. I thought about a glass of wine—heck, champagne!—but knew I couldn't enjoy it without feeling guilty. I was the leading lady in a movie, after all, and Christian Slater was my man. We had chemistry, apparently. A shape-shifting, sexless androgynous girl could have chemistry with anything. My life was just a fantasy with its fantasy lovers and its make-believe conversations with make-believe people in my head. So I was a perfect candidate to fall in love with a make-believe man and consummate our pretend love in a make-believe house. Reality was the difficult part. And the reality at that moment was that it was Friday at 5:00 and I didn't know what to do. So I went to the Pilates studio.

Santa Monica Boulevard, the gay part of town, had an exciting energy. It was the beginning of the weekend, and the restaurant workers were placing candles on the outdoor tables, setting a welcoming scene for their patrons to drink, talk, and unwind from the week of work. As I drove down the boulevard, past the lesbian coffee shop I'd gone to the day I got *Ally McBeal,* hoping no one could see me through my tinted car window, I was once again aware of the emptiness. Losing weight was no longer exciting to me, and maintaining it was hard. I was exhausted most of the time and the ante on exercise seemed to keep going up. Unexpectedly, a voice would sound in my head at the point of my workout where I would usually have quit, telling me to march on, to keep going, that it wasn't enough. It told me I wasn't good enough, I didn't do it long enough, that there was still a long way to go before I could rest.

The drill sergeant voice accompanied me everywhere, recorded all the missed moments when I was sitting but should've been standing, moving around, doing something. It was hard for me to drive anywhere, even to the Pilates studio. I had figured out several different blocks in LA where I could get out of my car and stretch my legs. I wouldn't always run around the block, sometimes I would just walk with a deliberate stride. Sometimes I didn't have the energy to run. I had the urge to get up from being immobile, but I didn't have the energy to make it a useful excursion. The voice that made me get out of my car, that called me a lazy pig for walking instead of running around the block, would get back in the car with me and accompany me all the way to the studio, where it laughed at me for being late to work with no burned calories to show for it.

I pulled into the valet parking lot of the Pilates studio. The parking lot was shared with a restaurant and if you liked to work out when other people were going to dinner, then a valet would take your car. The voice told me to get out of the car as fast as I could and go burn calories. I got out of the car in a hurry and left my keys in the ignition for the valet.

How are you going to pull it off? How could you ever be pretty enough to be a leading lady? You're not even thin. You don't have long, lean limbs. You have ordinary looks and an ordinary body. You can't play a leading lady in a movie. You're gay. What a joke! What happens when people find out you're gay and you've fooled them into thinking you were Christian Slater's love interest? How is that going to work? Give it up, you stupid dyke. How long are you going to pretend you're something you're not? How long do you think people are going to fall for it?

As I reached the top stair and looked down at where I'd left my car, I saw it moving. My car was moving!

"Help!" I screamed. "Somebody's stealing my car!"

I ran down the stairs, my heart beating in my throat. Jesus! Where's my dog? Is she in the car?

"Help! Help me! Somebody's stealing my car!" I got to the bottom step, flung my body around the railing, and ran to my car feeling like there were weights tied to my ankles, like I was running with someone holding me back. Evil was holding me back, allowing my car to be stolen in front of my eyes. And my dog! Oh my God! Bean! I screamed out her name, "BEAN!!!"

The car stopped and a man got out. He was wearing black pants and a blue vest. He held the keys up to me, silently. He looked frightened. We stood there, facing each other, him in his blue vest and me in my platform off-camera shoes and spandex shorts with the elastic waistband that was too loose for my hips. We stared at each other, and now it was my turn to be frightened. I gently took the keys from him and quietly sat down on the warm leather seat. I checked for Bean and she wasn't there. I drove away in silence. No metronome. No marching orders. I drove back down Santa Monica Boulevard and past the lesbian café. Staring into the café, I drove through a red light. I knew that because a man crossing the street at the crosswalk slapped the hood of my car as he narrowly avoided getting hit and then by the time the noise registered, I saw that I was in the middle of an intersection, all alone except for a car rushing at my side. I drove home to my cold, empty apartment and vowed never to go out again.

The number 82 on the scale should've meant something other than what it did to me. All it meant to me was that I was seven pounds lighter than the last time I weighed myself. The number 82 was the reward for my hard work, a nod to my dedication, a flashing red digital recognition of my self-control. It was a way to silence the drill sergeant in my head, and in this subjective world full of conflicting opinions, it was a way to objectively measure my success. Another way to measure my success was to use a tape measure. I had begun measuring the objects and the space surrounding the objects. Like a study of semiotics,

I measured the white and black surrounding the white, the vacuous space that held its object and gave it substance. I measured my big legs with their thighs and the space between my thighs. I measured my footballer's calves and watched as the chunky fat withered away to become a dancer's calves and then a little child's calves, too new and underdeveloped to be labeled anything other than just legs. I measured myself daily after weighing for a more accurate understanding of my progress. Occasionally, I would measure myself visually. I would stand naked in front of a mirror and look at myself. Sometimes I even loved what I saw. Sometimes I saw a boy, maybe twelve years of age, with a straight skinny body and no ugly penis that he would forever be measuring, wondering if he measured up. I sometimes saw a teenage girl with no breasts and no curves that would turn her into a woman with desires and complicate her perfect, sterile life. Sometimes I didn't see a person at all, I just saw the inch of fat on a stomach and thighs that encouraged me to continue to lose weight. I knew I wasn't attractive, and I was very happy about that. I didn't want to be attractive. I didn't want to attract. As long as no one wanted to be let in, I didn't have to shut anyone out. If I could keep people from being interested enough to ask me questions, I didn't have to lie. As long as I could be alone with my secrets, I didn't have to worry about being found out.

At 82 pounds, I wanted to photograph myself. I wanted to document my success. But first I had to silence the drill sergeant that reminded me of that extra inch of fat. First I had to get rid of that.

27

"HECK THE gate." There was a suspended moment as the cameraman shone a flashlight at the film in the camera.

"Good gate."

"That's lunch. One hour." The scene of the crew and cast broke apart, first at its edges, with the actors strutting off the set and directly to their trailers, then the lights were shut down, the camera track taken apart, and finally the director on a chair on the far edge of the scene, with his script supervisor and ADs in tow, collected his notes and headed toward catering. It was my first day on the set of *Cletis Tout*. I hadn't done any acting yet; my scene was coming up after lunch, but I had been at the set all morning. I had been asked to go to wardrobe for a final fitting and to work with the props guy as my character was a smart-ass, wisecracking potter who was tough on the outside, cold, hard, and glazed over yet fragile and needing to be handled delicately— like her pots.

I went to wardrobe feeling a little insecure, as I had gained weight since my first fitting. I wasn't sure how much weight I'd gained because I'd stopped weighing myself after seeing the number 82 on the scale. I'd given up on the idea of losing that stubborn inch of fat because of what happened to the rest of my body. At 82 pounds, the veins on my arms looked like thick strands of rope attaching my hands to my forearms and my elbows. The unsightliness of it forced me to put ice on my wrists to try to make them disappear, as the hotter it was, the more they protruded. I knew I couldn't show up to a big-budget movie set needing to ice-down my veins in between takes, so I decided to slowly gain some weight. Although I knew I had to look better at a heavier weight, seeing the number on the scale climb back up through the nineties and head toward a hundred pounds was something I couldn't bear.

It was sheer agony, walking into a fitting, not knowing my weight. It was exactly this kind of anxiety—this fear of not knowing if I could fit into clothes—that I had tried to eradicate. I had told the costume designer that my measurements were thirty-four, twenty-four, thirty-five and, ironically, the ideal measurements as told to me by my modeling agency still didn't apply to me. At the time the costumer asked for them, I was 29½, 22¾, 31⅜. And that was a lot more difficult to say over the phone. As I was playing a tough, bohemian artist, my wardrobe started out dark and layered, gradually shedding layers of clothes and softening the color palette as I gradually shed my tough exterior and dulled my witty barbs. It was a typical storyline for a "good" female leading lady character: she starts out hard and ends up soft and the metamorphosis from undesirable insect to awe-inspiring butterfly is reflected in the wardrobe.

My insecurity about my weight gain was unnecessary, as both the black studded leather and the cream silk organza fit me perfectly. I had gained weight before my first fitting, but thankfully, I had maintained since then. I felt enormous relief. I was still in control after all. Standing in front of the mirror, a leading lady in a movie, I made the decision that when I returned to *Ally* for the next season, instead of trying to fit into the off-the-rack sizes, Vera would have to make the wardrobe to fit me. After all, it was actresses taking over the models' jobs of posing on magazine covers that required that actresses fit into the sample size that designers made for models. I wasn't a nameless model expected to fit into any dress. I was an actress. And because I was a very skinny one, like a model, I just happened to be able to fit into any dress.

The hotel where I was staying during filming in Toronto, the Windsor Arms, was a chic boutique hotel with tasteful decor. It was home to all the transients, the U.S. actors who blow through Canada to work a job. The suite was a little dark because there was only one window and that was in the bedroom of the one-bedroom suite. A wall with a door separated the bedroom from the rest of the suite with its dark carpet and mahogany walls, and its black desk, gray sofa, and mahogany coffee table. The bedroom was all white and light because of the window. The light in there compelled me to spend all my time in the bedroom, which really just consisted of a bed, so I spent all my time in bed. I brought my life in two suitcases from Los Angeles to make my long stay comfortable during the five-week movie schedule. In one suitcase was my kitchen scale, ten I Can't Believe It's Not Butter sprays, a large box of Splenda sachets, twenty cans of tuna, forty packets of oatmeal, Mrs. Dash, Extra chewing gum, a carton of Parliament Lights, and my digital bathroom scale. Although I hadn't weighed myself recently and it was very heavy, I had to bring it because if I had the urge to check in with my weight, I couldn't trust that the hotel would have an accurate scale. I also brought chopsticks, a can opener for the tuna, and my blue Chinese footed bowl with the fake pottery rings. I wasn't sure if I would be able to make my frozen yogurt, so I brought my white and green bowl with the hairline crack in case I had access to a freezer and could find the sugar-free, low-calorie yogurt I ate back home. In the other suitcase were my workout clothes, jeans, and T-shirts and a dress for the mandatory "above the line" dinner. I'd always hated the mandatory dinner for a film production, whose guests ran from the top down to where the line was drawn (from the executive producers to the lowest-paid core cast) even when I wasn't watching my weight. I hated having to talk to the producers because, as I was nearly always on the line, I felt like I could lose the job if I wasn't as funny as the other cast members or if the light at the restaurant showed all my imperfections. I hated having to make the attempt to impress just to keep them from changing their minds and sending me home, replacing me with the prettier actress/girlfriend of the leading man, whose relaxed confidence was appealing and whose torso looked great from across the table. On location, I hated ever having to leave the hotel room. Alone in my hotel room was the only place I could relax. And I somehow always felt less lonely when I was completely alone.

I was scheduled to work only one day a week for five weeks, with the rest of my time for myself. So I decided to take up drinking. Apart from the glass of champagne on Christmas Day, I hadn't drunk alcohol for a long time, and I missed it. Instead of eating dinner, I decided to use up my calories with a glass of wine. I felt like I deserved it. I earned it. I worked out hard and ate little, and so a glass of wine at night was a fitting reward. Apart from the wine, I really didn't ingest calories. Because wine didn't contain calorie information on the labels and not all wine had the same amount of calories, I limited myself to one glass a day. But because the calories were unquantifiable I didn't really trust eating anything. Occasionally, if I were working that day, I would start my day with 30 calories of oatmeal with Splenda and butter spray, and maybe have a bite of tuna for lunch, but mostly, I would order pickles from the hotel kitchen and just have pickles and mustard for the day. It wasn't terrific, but having wine was, so it was worth it just for the duration of filming.

"Cut. Back to one." I stood on top of a rooftop building in downtown Toronto gasping for air. "One," my starting position, was all the way down at the other end of the rooftop, and "action" was the cue to sprint from the other end to the front of the building, dive down on my knees, whip out a machine gun, and start shooting. As it was a comedy, the kickback from the machine gun knocked me over onto my back, where I had to wait a beat as the realization that I was in trouble set in, then in a panic hurl myself and my heavy machine gun off my back using my stomach muscles and struggle back onto my feet to make my escape. The rain made it harder. A fine and constant drizzle, not heavy enough to read through a camera lens, made the rooftop slick and dangerous and froze my fingers, destroyed my makeup and hair, and saturated my wardrobe.

Hour after hour of wide shots from the street, aerial shots from a crane, and coverage from the rooftop exhausted me, making it hard for me to keep running. But I had a bigger problem. My joints ached. My joints had occasionally hurt when I was back in LA, after exercise and at night when I lay in bed. But on that rooftop my wrists, knees, and elbows hurt so much it was hard to move them without feeling intense pain, and so I limited their movement to the action that took place within the space of time between "action" and "cut." Any other time I would stand still, not even able to smoke because the motion of lifting the cigarette to my mouth was excruciating for my elbow. Even if I held the cigarette very close to my lips and turned my head to exhale the smoke, the pain in my elbow seemed to localize to the slightest movement. It seemed to scan my body anticipating where the next movement could be and settle there, ready and waiting to strike. The longer the wait between takes, the worse it got. As we started the action sequence in close-up coverage and gradually widened to include the whole building, making my body look like a black ant scurrying on a rooftop, my movements had to be bigger, more exaggerated. And as the camera was on a crane, by the end of the day, I was alone up there on the rooftop, wildly flailing about, without a PA or an umbrella, since there was nowhere for either assistant or umbrella to hide when the camera rolled. Every moment was agony.

I knew I was in trouble when I couldn't make it down a single step of the staircase after wrap had been called. My knees wouldn't bend. They were stiff. The joke that I kept using to the concerned crew, who rushed onto the rooftop when it was clear for them to do so, was that it was so bloody cold I was frozen stiff. It wasn't a funny joke, but I was in too much pain to care. I was taken to the elevator by two men who held me up, the weapons specialist on my left arm and the medic on my right, all the while I was telling them that their help wasn't necessary, that I just needed to get into a warm bath. I don't know why I refused to let the medic examine me. Maybe it was because his viselike grip on my elbow was more painful than walking on my own would've been. I just knew I didn't want him to touch me, I didn't want him to ask me questions, I just wanted to be alone. I knew that if I told him about my elbows and my wrists that he'd send me to a doctor, and I just wanted to finish the movie without any drama. I was already on the verge of making a scene and I didn't want to do that, I just wanted to act out the scenes already scripted.

When I closed the door to my hotel room after the PA had walked me down the long corridor holding my arm (this time by the biceps), I cried. I cried out in pain and then I just quietly cried as a means to console myself. My gentle sobs seemed to say, "It hurts" and a silent tear falling replied, "I know, old thing. I know." I turned the hot water faucet on to fill the tub and crawled into the bedroom to pour a glass of wine. Now that wine was my dinner, I bought my own bottles and hid them under the bed for fear that the mini-bar Nazis would take the corked bottle away even though I asked them to clear the mini-bar and didn't allow them access to my room. I didn't allow the housekeeping team into my room either. I was too afraid they would take away my chopsticks and my dishes by accident, or steal them. When I was on location shooting the movie *Sirens,* a toy mouse that I'd had since before my dad died was lost. I didn't tell anyone that it was lost when the sheets were changed because I was too ashamed to admit to the concierge that I slept with stuffed toys. The housekeepers at this hotel weren't allowed into my room unless I was there watching them. I couldn't bear to lose my white and green dish with the flowers and the hairline crack. I'd already lost my mouse.

By the time I crawled back to the bathtub on three limbs, one hand holding the wineglass, the tub was full. I made another trip to get cigarettes and an ashtray and attempted to slowly remove my clothes. The joints in my fingers joined the cast of painful joints acting out in my body, needing attention and recognition for the important role they had thanklessly performed prior to this moment, and just unbuttoning my jeans was difficult. By the time I slid into the bathtub, the pain ravaged my body. It was like the hot water boiled the acidic fluid that lubricated my joints and the fluid seeped into my bloodstream, attacking the muscles and organs in its path. Everything hurt. I wept and wept. I was aware, however, that being in the bathtub in excruciating pain was the first time I hadn't felt hungry all day. At least the whining, complaining pain in my gut that was like a five-year-old tugging at my shirtsleeve repeating, "I'm hungry," had given over to the real pain in my body. At least I shut that little girl up.

I threw up the wine before I got into bed. I'd always been a bad bulimic but throwing up wine was the only thing that I found easy. Food was really difficult for me to throw up. I tended to give up after a certain point, never knowing if I got it all out. I felt bad about the whole process; the binge made me feel pathetic and out of control and the purging was the punishment. With every heave I hated myself more. I felt the blood vessels in my eyes burst and I knew that for days they would show everyone who cared to look at me that I was a pathetic loser, that I couldn't control myself. But throwing up wine was different. For one, wine wasn't a particularly nourishing thing to drink, and throwing it up is often better for your body than keeping it in. Also, throwing up alcohol is something that almost everyone has done at some point in their life; it wasn't reserved for sick bulimic girls who didn't have enough self-control over something as pathetic as food. Unlike food, at least alcohol is addictive. I threw up the wine because it was easy and because I was aware that asking my liver to break down alcohol when my body was obviously sick enough to cause me so much pain was destructive. I threw up the wine because I'd put my body through enough.

Throughout the night, as I lay in bed rereading Sylvia Plath's *The Bell Jar*, I drank wine and threw it up. I worried that there would be traces of sugar from the wine that would cause me to ingest incidental, unaccounted-for calories, but I just said, "To hell with it!" I'd gotten so loose with the wine anyway. I felt completely out of control and crazy—but in a good way. My loosening up of calories was a healthy, good thing that would enable me to go out for a beer with the director, who I really liked. I could be social again. I just worked out a little harder in the hotel gym and stopped brushing my teeth with toothpaste. It wasn't that I was crazy thinking that I could get fat from accidentally swallowing toothpaste; I was just ensuring that I cut out those incidental calories wherever I could. I ate less chewing gum and I didn't use toothpaste. It was a compromise that worked for me. I really liked wine.

Five days later, we went on location overnight to an out-of-the-way part of town for the next day of filming. I felt a little better, was well rested, and even ate a little more as I realized food worked like Advil, and the more food I had, the less my joints ached. I went back up to 300 calories but kept my wine ritual. I had to finish eating food by 2:00 p.m. so I wouldn't accidentally throw up tuna when I threw up my wine. The place where we went was so remote we had no choice but to stay at a spiritual retreat that didn't serve wine or allow smoking. As I was given a tour of the log cabin they called a facility, I felt nervous and anxious like I was in rehab. I wondered briefly if the production company had sent me to rehab under the pretense of it being the only place close to the location. (Could they know about the wine?) The woman in a turban showed me the spa, which consisted of saunas and a coffin.

"Please let us know if you'd like to use the hyperthermic chamber."

"It looks like a coffin. How does it work?"

"You lie down in the chamber for forty-five minutes and it removes the toxins in your body."

The thought of being in a capsule for forty-five minutes was bad enough, but the fact that it removed all the toxins in your body gave me pause. My body was made up of toxins. I imagined the inside of my body covered in a spider web of toxins that held it all together. Toxins were the thread that bound my stomach to my intestines and the skin to the muscles. The webs in my body were the unabsorbable chemicals, the residue particles strung together from the artificial sweeteners, chemicals from the butter spray, and chemicals from the Jell-O, the alcohol, and the nicotine.

"If I removed all the toxins in my body, there'd be nothing left!" I knew the turban thought that was a joke, even though she didn't think it funny enough to laugh.

I stared at the chamber that would in fact have become my coffin. I imagined a turbaned woman opening the lid and screaming as she looked at my remains. My body would be dehydrated and my blood extracted as the toxin-fighting machine, on a mission to remove every last toxin, couldn't target the invasive toxins without removing all the fluid and the blood. My organs would be eaten up by the machine as it tore apart every last bit of tissue leaving behind a deflated sack of skin—and maybe my eyeballs.

28

WOKE UP with my eyes closed as the dream I awoke from was so disturbing I tried to finish it for several minutes even after I was aware of being fully conscious. In the dream I had found myself standing naked in front of Tom Cruise, who was lying on a bed wearing a raincoat. I was naked and yet the reason for my being naked wasn't completely obvious; the mood wasn't sexual, it was friendly with nothing sinister implied. This bizarre scene took place in a big loft with concrete floors and a high ceiling, which I assumed to be one of his houses. It was the middle of the night, two or three o'clock maybe. The room was brightly lit like a department store or a supermarket, and the bed was in the middle of this enormous room. As I stood naked in front of him, I talked about being gay. I bared my soul in the same manner that I bared my body. I showed him all of me, inside and out. As I did so, instead of becoming lighter by unburdening myself from the secret that weighed me down, instead of losing weight, I became heavier. I felt burdened, heavy and dark, panicked that something dreadful was about to happen despite the kindness and acceptance he was showing me. After I talked for what seemed like hours, I began to make out shadowy figures in the walls that I thought were painted black. As the sun started to rise I could see that the walls behind his bed and to the side were not painted black. The "walls" were floor-to-ceiling windows. To my horror, I could see the silhouettes of what seemed like hundreds of people looking in, and I could see that I was in a street-level glass building in Times Square. I was on *Good Morning America*, and Tom Cruise was conducting an interview.

As I lay awake trying to trick my brain into thinking that I was asleep so I could make it end differently and take away the nervous, sick feeling that carried over from the dream into my reality, I realized that the sick feeling wasn't only from dreaming about being tricked into exposing myself. The sick feeling was also from drinking and throwing up the bottle of wine I'd snuck into the no-alcohol retreat. (I'd stolen a corkscrew from the mini-bar in the hotel in Toronto and added it to my traveling case of tools and utensils.) I'd had a rough night. The pain in my joints increased to the point that I couldn't find a position to sit or lie in to make myself comfortable, even briefly. I alternated between sitting, lying down, and walking in an attempt to relieve the pain, but the only thing that seemed to work at all was wine. So I kept drinking it. I had to keep drinking it, as its numbing effect seemed to wear off when I threw it up. But since forcing myself to throw it up gave me a splitting headache, I began to feel nauseous, and so the throwing-up part of the ritual became involuntary by the time I'd drunk my way down to the middle of the label. In between drinking and throwing up, I ran my wrists under the hot water in the bathroom sink, as the room didn't have a bathtub and hot water seemed to help a little. I felt sorry for myself. I cried a lot. I thought about calling my mother, but I didn't know what to say. I was in the middle of shooting my first big Hollywood movie. I was doing exactly what I was supposed to do. I knew that if I complained to her at all, she would respond in the same way she did when I cried to her about not being able to eat ordinary food with my family. If I were selfish enough to tell her how sad I was and how much pain I was in, I knew she would respond angrily because being angry was easier than being worried, and so she'd say, "Well, I don't know what to tell you. You wanted to be an actress."

And I would say, "Yes, Mama. I wanted to be an actress. I wanted to be a model, and I wanted to be an actress. I wanted to be special, and I wanted people to think I was pretty. What I didn't know was how hard it was going to be to be thin, to be considered pretty, and to be worthy of attention. I've had to work a little bit harder than I first thought, Mama. My journey was a little longer than most girls'. I was born with big legs and small eyes and a round face that's only pretty from one angle." Then I would tell her what I've always wanted to say to her but because we tend not to talk about heavy and emotional things, I've never been able to. "I don't blame you, Mama. I blame Dad."

I blame you, Dad. I blame you for telling me that I was pretty. I blame you for dying before you had time to change your mind. Because of you I make up stories, have fantasy lives, fill in the missing words. You're the blank. You're the "Dear Mum and . . ." letter I had to make up because all the other children at camp had a dad and not a blank where a dad was missing. Being forced to write that letter was the first time I really knew you were missing. And it was a year after you died.

April Fool's Day is a bad day to die for a practical joker. I thought that because you winked only at me, I was the only one that got the joke. Remember when the Easter Bunny came and how you winked at me as you ate the carrot with his bunny teeth marks? We got the jokes, you and I. We were smart and we got the joke.

I didn't sleep at all until morning. I'd seen the shadowy dawn become the light of day, which no doubt set the scene for my horrific dream that was hard to shake even after I opened my eyes.

As I carefully applied concealer to achieve the perfect no-makeup look before going to makeup, I thought about my subconscious and its lack of imagination. It seemed to me that as I became thinner, I became dumber, as even my subconscious failed to conjure up a decent metaphor. One part of the dream stuck with me, however, and that was my casting of Tom Cruise in the role of sneaky interrogator. My mother had always wanted me to marry Tom Cruise. Not just any famous actor, Tom Cruise in particular. He was the living image of the perfect movie star who seemed to separate his private life from his public life—a man of mystery, a private man. Choosing Tom Cruise as an example was perhaps another way of my mother reinforcing that there was a payoff to being private. "There's a reason they call it a private life," I'd often say to interviewers. But there's a fine line between being private and being ashamed.

The day wasn't just any day. It was DAY ELEVEN of filming. Day Eleven was a long bike ride to where the only known photograph of my character's mother was buried in a box under a tree along with the money my character's father had buried after he robbed the bank and before he was incarcerated. The bike ride began with a race for the treasure between a sweet, caring guy and an emotionally bankrupt girl, climaxed when she told him through her tears that she only wanted the picture of her mother, not the money, and ended with the two of them in love. It was a big day. And although I was prepared—I'd learned my lines and could comfortably fit into my wardrobe—I was not ready. I was in agony. And the day hadn't even begun.

"Ride as fast as you can past camera. And go as close to camera as you can, too." The director had to literally cut to the chase to make his day, a term used in movie making that meant that all the shots for all the scenes for that day had to be completed. Today he didn't have a smile in his eyes; he wasn't as full of jokes as usual. Directors can get very stressed about making their days.

"Yes, boss. No problem."

I called the director "boss" because I liked Chris, but I also had no problem lying to him. Because riding the bike fast was a big problem. Nothing hurt my knees more than pushing down on the pedals, especially if I had to lift myself off the seat to get speed. After two takes of riding as fast as I could, I wondered whether or not I would make my day. My ankles, wrists, and elbows hurt almost as much as my knees. My lungs ached with every deep breath. I couldn't believe how unfit I was considering how much I worked out. I'd continued my regular workout routine while in Toronto—an hour on the treadmill at 7.0, 105 sit-ups followed by 105 leg lifts—the only difference being that it wasn't as fun. I no longer had to lose weight and so there was no motivation, no lower number on the scale to look forward to, only a higher number to dread. I had weighed myself that morning. I was 96 pounds and I was never going beneath it. I didn't want to. But what scared me the most was how little I had to eat to avoid gaining the weight back. I ate 300 calories a day and I was just maintaining. I felt trapped, knowing that I would have to continue to be this extreme just to maintain the body I'd starved myself to achieve. It was a realization that was hard to digest.

The next scene was the crying scene. Ironically, I need to be in a happy mood in order to cry; I need to feel pretty self-confident and strong before I can pretend to be insecure and fragile. Usually, crying in a scene makes me feel good, as I get to show off my acting skills. But there was no joy in crying about the death of my father. It was too real, too close to me. I shut down with pain, both physical and emotional. Despite my condition, I managed to cry a little for the scene, but by the end of the day I was crying a lot. I didn't even need to cry anymore, the scene was over; my character was completely over her father's death and on to falling in love with Christian Slater. But I wasn't. I wasn't over my dad leaving me and I wasn't falling in love with anyone. I couldn't stop crying. It was like a flash flood. Its onset and its end were unpredictable and uncontrollable. It just happened, and like a flood, it was devastating.

I was in pain, so I cried. I couldn't move my legs, my wrists, and my fingers, so I cried. I had to be carried into the makeup trailer, so I cried. I was embarrassed, so I cried. I had ruined my career, so I cried. I had ruined my enjoyment of life and wanted to die, so I cried.

I wanted to escape just like my dad had escaped, to fly away, to fade gently into black.

I sat stiffly in the makeup chair to have my makeup removed. It was the first time I'd ever allowed that to happen because I didn't like the makeup artist to see all the flaws I'd concealed before she began her work concealing my flaws—before she made my skin color more even, my eyes bigger, my lips fuller. It was ironic to me that I allowed this end-of-day pampering ritual for the first time on the last day of my career. It was over. I was over.

The lights around the mirror began to bleed into my face. I couldn't quite see my face for the white light around it. I saw two ugly black dots that were my pupils until I couldn't see them anymore either. I felt myself floating away, fading into black. I knew I was passing out, but I could no longer hold on. The last thing I remembered was a hot towel being pressed onto my face. Then I let go.

Out of the blackness came a vision of myself as a little girl spinning around in a tiara and a pinkish-red tutu with a rhinestone-sequined bodice. I'm spinning around and around, doing pirouettes in a church hall. My mother is in the center of the first row. I use her as a spot by focusing only on her, turning my body first before whipping my head around and back to the spot that is my mother's smiling face. With each piroutte, however, instead of being more impressed, she is less impressed. With each spot she is smiling less. The smile turns into a frown and the little girl is no longer wearing a tiara and a tutu but jeans and a black tank top. The little girl has spun into an adult and my mother is no longer there. I search for her in the front row, but she isn't there. Instead I see myself. I realize that the person in the front row, disapproving of me, unhappy with me is not my mother. It's me. I look disgusted by the image of myself. It is clear by the way my head is partially turned away, my face contorted in a grimace, that I hate myself. I pirouette again fast, to spin away from the image, too disturbing to look at any longer. But I keep spinning and gathering momentum, the centrifugal force won't allow me to stop. I can't stop. Now I can't see anything. I am tumbling now. I have fallen off my axis. I'm spinning into the blackness. The spinning suddenly stops.

I have escaped.

29

ISS DE Rossi? I have Dr. Andrews on the line."

I sat in my dressing room on the set of *Ally McBeal*, lit a cigarette, and breathlessly awaited my test results. I had to get off the treadmill to answer the phone and both the treadmill and the fan I'd rigged to blow air onto my face were straining and noisily whirring. It was quite an effort to get to the phone quickly because sharp movements caused me to feel a lot of pain, sometimes to the point of almost blacking out. I could barely work out anymore, not only because of the pain but because I was too tired. I was tired because I was often too hungry to sleep. When I did sleep I dreamt about food. Last night I had a dream that I took a sip of regular Coke thinking it was diet and the shock of accidentally ingesting real sugar catapulted me back into consciousness. Most times, though, I dreamt about willingly stuffing my face. I dreamt about eating a whole pizza or plate full of French fries. I tended to feel so bad about it when I woke up, I cried. I sobbed as if I'd really done it—it just felt so jarring, so frightening. I thought that I had a problem because I was scared to eat. I was actually scared of food. I no longer trusted myself. I figured I'd lost my willpower.

I felt nervous. Not that I didn't feel anxious all the time, but I felt even worse knowing that what came next was going to change everything.

I can't stay thin. I just wasn't built for it. I wasn't born with thin legs and I can't keep them. For over a year I've managed to maintain my weight, but if I keep up that maintenance to the exclusion of everything else, then I'll have anorexia.

As I sat at the desk and held for the doctor (didn't he call me?), I felt a roll of fat on my stomach. I pinched it with my thumb and forefinger. There was about an inch of fat that went right around to the sides, and yet at 98 pounds, I knew I was grossly underweight. I almost laughed out loud at the irony of it. My rib cage and my hip bones were jutting out, yet there was a roll of fat on my stomach taunting me, letting me know that it had outsmarted me, that it had won. It was ironic also that in order to get rid of that fat, I'd have to have had the energy to do crunches, but without putting caloric energy in my body I didn't have the strength to do them, so now it would just stay there on my stomach in triumph, never to be challenged again. As I sat and waited to hear my results, I felt a little relief knowing that everything was about to change. I couldn't imagine living year after year constantly battling in a fight you could never win. Anorexia is exhausting.

I will listen to what the doctor says and do what he tells me to do.

After collapsing in Toronto, I had no choice but to get help. I blacked out in the makeup chair and my private medical information seemed to be passed around and shared with anyone who cared to ask. My body was no longer under my control. I woke up to the medic taking my blood pressure and ordering blood tests. He called my physician, who called specialists and within days I had undergone a battery of tests. Blood tests, bone density tests; I had to show up with my body to whatever test it was he thought might contribute a puzzle piece to his diagnosis. I couldn't argue. I was under contract and I could barely finish the movie.

But the movie ended two weeks ago and I was still being compliant with the doctors. One doctor turned into four, and so there always seemed to be someone to answer to. They had me cornered. I couldn't escape them even if I wanted to.

But I don't want to. I'm tired. I'm sad all the time, and I'm in pain. I want to give up.

"Hi, Portia?"

"Hi, Dr. Andrews." I waited for some pleasantries to be exchanged but none were forthcoming.

"There are quite a few things I'm seeing from the test results." He took a beat as if to ready himself before delivering a blow. It scared me. I knew there would be something wrong, but his hesitation sent a wave of fear through my body. The wave of adrenaline connected the pain from my ankles to my wrists, and my head began to spin. My head had been feeling like half of its regular weight even when it wasn't spinning. Because of that, I often felt unbalanced. I took a drag of my cigarette. Maybe my head is spinning from the nicotine? I calmed myself.

There is no point in being nervous because I can't affect the outcome. What's done is done.

"Okay. Let's start with your bone density. Uh . . . according to these results it shows that you have osteoporosis."

"Ah . . . how long has it been since you've had your period?"

"A year or more."

"Okay. Your liver enzymes were extremely elevated, which are actually at the levels of cirrhosis."

"Okay. Your electrolyte and potassium levels are pretty dangerous. At this rate, they could effect how your organs are functioning."

"Okay. I guess the most important thing that the tests showed is that you have an autoimmune disease called lupus."

I exhaled the smoke in my lungs and extinguished my cigarette in one motion. I limply held the phone and sat staring into the full-length mirror opposite my desk. I saw a round face, thin arms, a bony rib cage, a thick waist, and big, thick legs. It was the same body I had always seen, only smaller. The proportions were the same. If y is exactly half of x, then 2:1 is the ratio of my body parts. My thighs would always be the same in relation to my waist and my arms—it was all the same, but in a smaller version.

Game over. I lose.

The whirring of the treadmill sounded like a vinyl record stuck on a track.

Get on the treadmill.

The bars either side of the belt looked like a cage.

Get on the treadmill.

I don't know what to say to the voice that will shut it up. I'm dying and it still won't be quiet.

"I have lupus! I'm sick!"

You're fat.

"No I'm not!"

The voice was echoing, reverberating. The word *fat* was swirling through my head, sounding the alarms. But above the din of the drill sergeant and the alarms and the ticks of missed beats, a sense of peace overcome me.

I'm sick. I've successfully lowered the bar. I don't have to be a straight-A student or be a movie star to be proud of myself. I just have to live.

I accept myself just as I am. I accept myself.

The voice stops. Apart from laughter coming from the hallway I can't hear anything. It is deathly quiet in my head. And then I said something to the voice I have always wanted to say:

"Go to hell."

EPILOGUE

CAN'T EXPLAIN THE birds to you even if I tried. In the early morning, when the sun's rays peek over the mountain and subtly light up the landscape in a glow that, if audible, would sound like a hum, the birds sing. They sing in a layered symphony, hundreds deep. You really can't believe how beautiful it is. You hear bass notes from across the farm and soprano notes from the tree in front of you all at once, at varying volumes, like a massive choir that stretches across fifty acres of land. I love birds. But not as much as my wife loves them. My wife thinks about them whereas I only notice them once they call for attention. But she looks for them, builds fountains for them, and saves them after they crash into windows. I've seen her save many birds. She holds them gently in the palm of her hand, and she takes them to one of the fountains she's built especially for them and holds their beaks up to the gentle trickle of water to let them drink, to wake them up from their dazed stupor. No matter how much time it takes, she doesn't leave them until they recover. And they mostly always do.

The sound of the big barn doors opening prompts me to begin walking toward the stables. I clutch my coffee mug and walk in bare feet, wearing only my pajama pants and tank to say good morning to my horses.

As I arrive at the barn, Julio, who helps with the horses, is mucking out the stalls, an activity that I would help with were I wearing shoes. I love to muck out stalls.

"Hi, Julio."

"Morning, Portia. Riding today?"

"Yep. A little later."

I love riding horses. I love bathing them and grooming them. I love their strong, muscular bodies, their athleticism, and their kindness. I love the companionship and the trust a rider builds with her horse. I love everything about horses. Horses saved my life.

"Good morning, Mae." The regal head of my big, beautiful Hanoverian horse pokes out from her stall. I wrap my arms around her neck and kiss her muzzle. I bought Mae in 2002 when I was recovering from my eating disorder. Learning how to ride her, learning her language, and being passionate about something other than my weight or looks shifted my focus away from my obsession with being thin long enough to let the doctors and the therapists do their work. I had found love in Mae. I had found a reason to get up in the morning.

"Ellen not up yet?" Ellen usually accompanies me in the mornings to the stables.

"Nah. I'm letting her sleep in."

I crept out of the bedroom this morning and out of the cottage not even grabbing shoes or a sweatshirt as I was trying desperately not to wake her. Ellen works really hard and needs to rest when we're at our farm on the weekends. She especially needed to sleep this morning as she was awake most of the night reading long after I fell asleep. She was awake most of the night reading this book.

After petting Mae, Archie, Femi, Monty, and Diego Garcia, I went back up to the cottage. As I opened the door to the porch I heard the voice that makes my heart the happiest to hear.

"Coff-ee!" Ellen calls out for coffee like a dying man calling out for water as he perishes in the desert. It always makes me laugh.

I walked into the bedroom, plop onto the bed, and wrap my arms around her.

"Baby," she says sleepily, "you were crazy."

"I know."

"So sad. I feel like I was reading about a completely different person."

"I feel like I was writing about a different person."

"You were so sick. What happened to the lupus?"

"It was a misdiagnosis. I just needed to eat. And the cirrhosis and osteoporosis—all of it went away. I was lucky that I didn't do serious damage."

"You poor thing. I wish I could've been there to save you."

"You did save me. You save me every single day."

I kiss her and get up off the bed to make her coffee.

"I'm so proud of you, baby. It'll help a lot of people." As I pour the coffee, she suddenly appears at the doorway of the kitchen, her blond head poking around the door. "Just be sure and tell the people that you're not crazy anymore."

I didn't decide to become anorexic. It snuck up on me disguised as a healthy diet, a professional attitude. Being as thin as possible was a way to make the job of being an actress easier by fitting into a sample size dress, by never worrying that I couldn't zip up my wardrobe from episode to episode, day after day. Just as I didn't decide to become anorexic, I didn't decide to not be anorexic. I didn't decide to become healthy. I decided not to die. I didn't even care to live better than I'd been living, necessarily. I just knew at the moment of hearing my test results that I didn't want to live as a sickly person who would slowly suffer and end up dead. The news that I had seemingly irreversible illnesses punctured my obsessive mind and rendered my weight-loss goals meaningless. I lost anorexia. It was too hard to hold on to. By the end I felt as though I was clinging on to anorexia in the same way you would cling to the rooftop of a building, your body dangling precariously over the other side, begging for release. Because it was more exhausting to hang on, and because I had a real reason for the first time in the form of lupus, I let go of dieting. I watched as my biggest accomplishment, my greatest source of self-worth, plummeted to the ground. I had climbed slowly, methodically, all the way to the top only to fall too fast to even see where I had been.

Anorexia was my first love. We met and were instantly attracted to each other. We spent every moment of the day together. Through its eyes, I saw the world differently. It taught me how to feel good about myself, how to improve myself, and how to think. Through it all, it never left my side. It was always there when everyone else had left, and as long as I didn't ignore it, it never left me alone. Losing anorexia was painful—like losing your sense of purpose. I no longer knew what to do without it to consider. Whether the drill sergeant approved or disapproved was no longer a concern because he was no longer there. I let him go with the overwhelming feeling that continuing to fight for him was futile because he was too good for me; he was too perfect, too strict and demanding. Slowly, over several months, maybe even years, the feeling that I wasn't good enough for him dissipated, and I gradually came to feel as though we were just a mismatch, he and I. We never should've been together in the first place. We were too different for each other, and we wanted different things from life. Knowing that, however, didn't make it less painful. Without anorexia, I had nothing. Without it, I was nothing. I wasn't even a failure; I simply felt like I didn't exist.

I was diagnosed with lupus. I had osteoporosis and was showing signs of cirrhosis of the liver. My potassium and electrolyte balance were at critical levels, threatening the function of my organs. I no longer felt lazy, like I was giving up because it was too hard, I felt defeated. I felt as though I simply didn't have a choice. I had to accept that the road I had chosen was the wrong road. It led to sickness and death. I had to allow the voices of the professionals into my closed mind. I had to try to take their road.

As I began the long journey on the road to recovery, there were a couple of detours that I wasn't prepared for. Initially I had thought that once I began to gain back the weight, I would have the strong support base that I'd felt in Australia. I thought I would have loving, concerned people around me to ensure that I was getting healthy. But after I had gained an acceptable amount of weight and looked like a regular person, mostly everyone in my life assumed that the problem was solved. Almost instantly, I felt like no one was listening anymore, no one cared. It felt like caring was only necessary when my life was on the line. As I gained weight I was no longer something to worry about. I truly felt like a pubescent thirteen-year-old, ugly, voiceless; my cute days of being delightful were in the past, and my future accomplishments were too distant to elicit any kind of hope or joy. At that point, if I had still had the axe to grind, if I hadn't got what I wanted from the disorder, some sense of acceptance of my sexuality, I would have relapsed. It would have been very easy for me to start losing weight again to get the attention and the concern that felt like love. It would have felt like a great accomplishment to not just do it once, but twice, proving to myself that I had the willpower I had always suspected was only fleeting.

Gaining weight is a critical time. The anorexic mind doesn't just magically go away when weight is gained—it gets more active. Anorexia becomes bigger and stronger as it struggles to hold on, as it fights for its life. If I hadn't seen my mother break down and accept me for being gay, I would've gotten right back on the path that made me rebel in the first place, because being anorexic did feel a little like rebellion. It felt like a passive-aggressive way of renouncing my mother's control over me. It was definitely a statement that demanded "accept my sexuality or accept my death!" Being sick allows you to check out of life. Getting well again means you have to check back in. It is absolutely crucial that you are ready to check back into life because you feel as though something has changed from the time before you were sick. Whatever it was that made you feel insecure, less than, or pressured to live in a way that was uncomfortable to you has to change before you want to go back there and start life over. And with all the time it takes to have an eating disorder—literally the whole day is consumed by it, both mentally and physically—it's important to find something other than your body image to be passionate about. You have to create a whole new life to check into, and the life I knew was waiting for me was a future relationship and the acceptance of it from my family. I had the key ingredient to want to check back in: I had hope.

For a straight-A student, a model, an actress on a hit TV show, the bar was set very high. I'm the one who set it. I thought that by accomplishing things that were exciting to people, I would receive their admiration and love. I thought that if I accomplished enough, that somehow I would be let off the hook in the future. Like I didn't have to keep striving and achieving because I had done that already, and it would add up to being enough. Anorexia lowered the bar. Instead of having to be a high achiever to receive love, all I had to do was be alive. All I had to do for the caring, nurturing kind of love was lose another pound. All I had to do for acceptance of my sexuality was not eat. Of course, I didn't think I was doing that at the time. I thought I was just trying to stay thin.

Recovery feels like shit. It didn't feel like I was doing something good; it felt like I was giving up. It feels like having to learn how to walk all over again. I felt pathetic. I remember having so little self-esteem that I couldn't talk loudly; I literally couldn't make myself heard because I wanted to disappear. I didn't want to be spoken to or looked at or acknowledged. When someone paid attention to me, I thought they were doing it out of sympathy, kindness, and so it felt condescending. All recovery meant to me was being fat. Unlike the case of an alcoholic or a drug addict, there are no immediate benefits to getting well. My joints might have stopped aching pretty quickly, but after that, I didn't feel better, I felt worse. I experienced all kinds of physical changes that made me feel gross: my period returned, I had gas and was constipated. And then there was the fat that came back. It was truly awful for me. One week I felt lean and perfect, and the next week I was fat. Again. I felt like a failure. I hated every moment of it. I missed my bones so much. I cried at night because I couldn't feel my hip bones and not having them to physically hold onto was like losing a dear friend.

Being anorexic was incredibly difficult. Eating, once I allowed myself to do it, was easy. Being diagnosed with lupus was like a pardon; it granted me the freedom to give up. It felt like an excuse to let go of starvation, and it allowed me to eat again. I could no longer starve or I'd die. Therefore, it was essential to eat. So I did. I ate everything in sight. I ate everything I had wanted to eat for a year but hadn't allowed myself. I started by eating the healthy foods I'd missed: bran muffins, protein bars, granola, and smoothies. But very quickly the list began to include candy, cake, chocolate, and fried food. I felt that if I were going to give up, I might as well give up all the way. The floodgate had opened.

Just because I'd stopped starving didn't mean I didn't still have an eating disorder. My eating disorder felt the same to me. It took up the same space in my head, and driving around the city to find the perfect comfort foods took up as much time as driving around the city to find the tuna with the lowest sodium content. It was still there. It was the other side of the same coin. As it turned out, I wasn't quite ready to rejoin life. I still wanted to disappear, and I chose to disappear behind layers of fat. I still felt unattractive to both sexes, still not really living, merely existing. I was still testing the theory of whether I would be loved and accepted for my mind, my kindness, for everything about me other than what I looked like. I went from one extreme to the other. I went from 82 pounds to 168 pounds in ten months.

At first, after starving for so long, it was difficult to begin eating again even though I knew I had to in order to regain my health. A component in breaking the cycle of starvation was medicine. When the bone-density results showed that I was osteoporotic, I was put on hormone replacement therapy in an attempt to strengthen my bones. I had also quit smoking after hearing the diagnosis and started on a psychotropic medication after having brain scans by a renowned neuro-pharmacologist, Dr. Hamlin Emory. The chemical changes in my body, and I think most importantly, the psychotropic drug quelling the obses-sive behavior, helped me to eat again and gain weight.

At the time I walked through the doors of the Monte Nido Eating Disorder Treatment Center, I had gained 27 pounds. It was only four weeks after my diagnosis. I had gone from 98 pounds to 125 pounds in four weeks. Toward the end of my starving phase of my eating disorder, I knew that hovering under 100 pounds didn't feel like my real weight. I was almost certain that the second I began to binge I would immediately catapult back to the weight I'd been before I started starving myself. I knew I would be 130 pounds within weeks. And I was.

I have never felt so ashamed as I did walking into an eating dis-order clinic to be treated for anorexia at 125 pounds. I didn't belong there. Even though my treatment was private due to the fact I was ter-rified that my shameful secret would become public, I was fearful that I might run into people who really had anorexia, who really deserved to be there. I struggled with the feeling of unworthiness throughout my entire treatment. Even though I was paying for it and driving almost daily to Malibu to seek treatment with Carolyn Costin, one of the most well respected and successful counselors in the country, I felt com-pelled to lie. Every single session I lied to her about my feelings, my eating habits, and my progress. I lied to her because I was embarrassed. I felt like I wasn't worthy of her time when she had girls in her program who were fatally ill when I was so average in size.

I was being treated for anorexia, but due to the fact I was 125 pounds and at a healthy weight for my height, I thought there was no reason for me to be there. I thought that the psychological healing and my relationship to food were not worth talking about. Bulimia and overeating, abuse of laxatives and excessive exercising were not life-or-death illnesses in my mind, and I really didn't share with Carolyn as much as I should have about my dalliances in all of those practices. Despite the fact I thought anything other than anorexia was a second-class eating disorder not worthy of attention, when I was being treated by Carolyn I was severely bulimic. I was grossly overeating. The pendulum had swung the other way, and I was sicker than I had ever been in my life.

Since ending my bout with starvation, I had become addicted to low-calorie, low-carb, weight-loss food. I especially liked low-calorie frozen yogurt and would drive around town all day to different yogurt stores in search of peanut butter–flavored yogurt as all the stores rotated their flavors almost daily. I would drive from east Hollywood to Santa Monica in a day on the search for peanut butter, eating the less tasty flavors along the way. I figured that if I drove all that way, I might as well sample the flavors they offered. I could've called ahead, but then that would leave me with unfilled hours in the day, and as my work on *Ally McBeal* only occupied two or three half days a week, I really didn't know how to fill them.

There was a yogurt store at the Malibu mall and every day before my session with Carolyn, I would stop there. I would order the 12-ounce yogurt regardless of the flavor they were serving and eat it on the floor of the backseat of my car. I was terrified of being photographed eating in my car by paparazzi. Nothing seemed more piggish and gross to me than eating in your car, with the exception of being seen doing it. I had gained so much weight and was so worried that it was noticeable. I figured that all the press would need to do was to get a photograph of me eating to confirm that I had in fact gained a lot of weight. I couldn't think of anything more shameful than my weight gain being obvious enough to talk about. And because the tabloids seemed very interested in my weight loss, I thought for sure they would be just as interested in my weight gain. In fact, during the months when I was at my highest weight, there was a lot of talk about my weight gain. A morning radio show, *Kevin and Bean* on KROQ, commented on the fact that I had "a face like a pie." I distinctly remember this because I listened to them every morning. I remember this because it's not something that you forget.

After eating the yogurt on the floor of the backseat of my car, I took the plastic bag I had asked for in order to carry the yogurt and I threw up into it. At 9 calories an ounce, it was 108 calories that could easily be eradicated. I would then throw the plastic bag into the trash can that I'd strategically parked very close to, and head to my session with Carolyn, feeling very worried that the whole scenario could have been captured on film as Malibu was a hot spot for paparazzi. Without hesitation, when Carolyn asked me if I had binged or purged since my last session, I would reply that no, I hadn't. I hadn't binged or purged or even thought about bingeing or purging. I would tell her how healthy I was and how great I was doing. I don't know why, but it was very important to me to not appear sick to the only person that could help me get better. However, Carolyn had herself recovered from an eating disorder, and combined with her expertise and knowledge gained from treating hundreds of cases, she could see straight through the lies. There is a great deal of shame surrounding an eating disorder, with its abnormal practices and bizarre rituals, and so lying in treatment is common. My stories were only some of many she has had to decode.

My weight gain was horrific to me. I was bulimic again because I didn't want to be fat. I didn't want to be fat, but I couldn't stop eating. I knew that I should work out again to combat the amount of food I put into my body, but because being fat caused me to be depressed, I didn't have the energy. That's the feeling of pulling away from anorexia. The anxiety of feeling fat turns into depression about being fat, and the lethargy and apathy that depression brings make it impossible to get off the sofa. I had found a passion in being thin. It nearly killed me. And while I hated being fat, my new passion was eating.

Carolyn encouraged me to write down the amount of food I ate, and while I mostly lied to her, copying entries from the journals I used to keep for Suzanne, my nutritionist, I decided to send her this email. I had written this entry in November 2000 but only sent it to her in February 2001. It was one of the rare times I wrote down all that I ate in one day. It read:

Apple
Coffee x 2
Half wheat bagel
Whole sesame bagel
Banana
Bowl of pasta with sauce and cheese
Ritz crackers
4 mini-muffins
1 slice bread with tuna
Chocolate—4 mini
2 slices bread with peanut butter
2 cups dried fruit and nuts
bread—2 slices
bowl tortilla soup
half barbeque chicken sandwich
French fries
THREW UP
3 prunes (out of trash can)
mini-muffin
biscotti
coffee bean coffee (vanilla)
rice and beans
chicken taco
quesadilla
crepe and butter

large sugar cookie

ice-blended mocha

baby ruth

white choc crunch bar

pkt famous amos cookies

French vanilla coffee

THREW UP

4 boxes of (cal free) ricola

1 cup of tea with milk

YUP–THAT'LL ABOUT DO IT!!

Pxx (this was back in November)

Carolyn, knowing what I was doing to my body, went to work on my mind. Her therapy included not only discussions about my past, my sexuality, and the feelings I had surrounding food and weight, but we also talked about body image in the larger social sense. We talked about the image of the ideal woman in the form of models who were mostly unhealthy teenage girls. We talked about the idea that women in the postfeminist era, while supposedly strong and commanding and equal to men in every sense, looked weaker and smaller than ever before. We talked about how most women's sense of self-esteem still largely rests on what they look like and how much they weigh despite their other accomplishments. Carolyn photocopied passages of Naomi Wolf's *The Beauty Myth,* and I read them. I remember lying on my bed, reading the badly photocopied text on the pages and saying out loud to no one but my dog, Bean, "Oh my God. I fell for it." I remember feeling ashamed for calling myself a feminist when I had blatantly succumbed to the oppression of the mass media telling me what was beautiful, how to look, and what to weigh. It was a turning point. I had always prided myself on the fact that I was smart, analytical, and someone who didn't "fall for it." By starving myself into society's beauty ideal, I had compromised my success, my independence, and my quality of life. Being overweight was really no different. It was just the "f– you" response to the same pressure. I was still responding to the pressure to comply to the fashion industry's standards of beauty, just in the negative sense. I was still answering to their demands when really I shouldn't have been listening to them at all. The images of stick-thin prepubescent girls never should have had power over me. I should've had my sights set on successful businesswomen and successful female artists, authors, and politicians to emulate. Instead I stupidly and pointlessly just wanted to be considered pretty. I squandered my brain and my talent to squeeze into a size 2 dress while my male counterparts went to work on making money, making policy, making a difference.

I was told that recovering from an eating disorder is hard and not very fun. But apart from honesty, the gift that Carolyn gave me was the knowledge that I would be recovered. Carolyn had herself recovered, and she told me that I wasn't just going to have to learn to manage anorexia and bulimia like an alcoholic managing her drinking. Managing the disorder—thinking about food to any degree other than something nutritious and enjoyable—is, to me, the very definition of disordered eating. I didn't just want to maintain my weight, suppress the urge to purge, and still have a list of foods that were "safe" to eat. I never wanted to think about food and weight ever again. For me, that's the definition of recovered.

After only a few months, and despite Carolyn's urging, I stopped treatment. I didn't stop because I thought I no longer needed her counsel, but because I no longer wanted it. As I was learning that there were no "good" or "bad" foods, just bad eating practices, I listened not to Carolyn but to my eating disorder as it told me that it felt exposed and unsafe. If I stopped weighing my food and myself, like she suggested, its existence was threatened. My eating disorder and I had been to-gether for my entire life, and at that moment, it was easier to continue down the unhealthy path than to pave a new one. In retrospect, had I continued my treatment at this critical point of recovery, I would've discovered that wellness and happiness were closer than I could've imagined. Instead, I resumed the cycle of starving, bingeing, purging, and grossly overeating. And I gained weight.

My weight, the thing that I was convinced was paramount to my success as an actress, wildly fluctuated as I played the character of Nelle Porter. I whittled down to a size 2 from a size 6 and then I be-came almost like a spectator, watching passively as my clothing size went back up from a 2 to a 4, a 4 to a 6. I watched as my biggest fear came to fruition. I was a size 8. I was the size the stylist for the L'Oréal TV commercial had announced to the executives; the size that told them they'd made a mistake in thinking that I was special enough to sell their hair products. I didn't want to be a size 8. It was seeing that number sewn into the labels of my Theory skirts that made me resort to bulimia. But because I was afraid of lupus, mainly I just overate and cried. After reaching the dreaded size 8, I alternated be-tween extreme anxiety about my weight and just giving up caring. Like a binge, I felt if I was going to do a bad thing, I might as well just keep doing it. Size 8 turned into size 10, then a size 12, and in one instance, a size 14. I was so upset and confused that I could ever be a size 14 that I unfairly accused my costume designer of buying a size 14 just to make me feel badly about myself. I lifted my jacket up to expose my bare midriff to a producer to make my case. I told the producer that I wasn't as fat as my costume designer was making me out to be and it simply wasn't fair that she was playing this psychological game with me. I will never forget the look on the producer's face as I cornered her and showed her my stomach, passionately wailing about the size of my skirt and how the costume designer had brought it to me to make me feel insecure.

. . .

Within a very short time I weighed 168 pounds. More than hating myself, I simply had no sense of myself. It was like I was completely without ego for those months of being at my heaviest. I had reentered life, but it didn't seem like my own life. It seemed like I was passively observing other people's lives. I didn't talk about myself. I was only interested in talking about other people. I had decided that I would very carefully make it known that I was gay to a few gay people around me. I figured that I had completely ruined my career by being fat, so I might as well be gay also. I figured that if I ever worked again, it would be as a "character" actress or playing the best friend to the lead female, so if my homosexuality was rumored around town, it wouldn't really do any further damage to the image I'd already created for myself by being fat. On one very brave occasion I accompanied an acquaintance to a lesbian bar. I stood in the corner at a table facing away from the patrons. I was terrified of being recognized. With a push from my friend I went out onto the dance floor and asked an attractive girl for her phone number. She was attractive not only physically, but there was a sense of freedom about her. The complete opposite of me at the time, she appeared to be both carefree and grounded. We dated for about four months. While I was enjoying being in my first relationship with a woman, my bulimia intensified. I remember after a binge/purge session that lasted hours, she surprised me by dropping over. When she saw the red dots above my eyes and how ill I looked and sounded, she ran to the store to buy ingredients to make chicken soup. As I ate the soup she lovingly made, I felt ashamed. I hated that I had to lie and hide my secrets from my work and from my girlfriend. My paranoia and fear of being exposed—for having an eating disorder and for my sexuality—were excruciating.

There was good reason for my paranoia. A paparazzo had found out that I was gay and made it her mission to out me. She stalked me.

She waited for me every day in front of my building and followed me everywhere, occasionally making eye contact with me and signing to me that she was watching me; that she knew who I was. I had been photographed by paparazzi before, even followed, but this felt like being a deer in a hunter's scope. She and her driver were very aggressive and quite scary. The fear and paranoia led to my relationship's demise as it was impossible for me to leave the house with my girlfriend without feeling intensely anxious and uncomfortable. Not only was I terrified of being exposed as gay, I was scared of being photographed because of what I looked like. I had gained 70 pounds since my last encounter with paparazzi when they were covering stories about anorexic actresses. I didn't want to be in a magazine for being a fat actress.

I met Ellen in 2001 when I weighed 168 pounds. I don't know if I was that weight exactly, but I was heavy enough that the thought that she might have found me attractive or that we could have been a couple never entered my mind. I remember being so excited and overjoyed to be around her that I can still recall the feeling of running after her backstage at a concert we were both attending for Rock the Vote. I caught up to her, sat next to her at a table, and bought her a drink. I remember what she wore: an orange knit sweater, white T-shirt, blue jeans, and white tennis shoes. I remember what we talked about and a joke she made as we were looking down at the mosh pit. I embarrassed myself by laughing too much and too loudly at that joke, but I simply couldn't stop. I thought she was the most amazing person I'd ever met. She was highly intelligent, sharply observant, and funny. She was so beautiful it seemed that light emanated from her bright blue eyes. I had the best night of my life. I felt good about myself around her. I was excited and yet comfortable. At the end of the night, she invited me to come over to her house with the group of friends she'd met up with at the concert. I didn't go. As we'd just met, I thought she was just inviting me to be polite, and I was too shy, too fat, and too insecure to go to her house with her friends. I felt that I had created the perfect memory of being around her that night and I didn't want to ruin it. As it turns out, she had invited those people over only so she would have the excuse of a party to invite me to so she could get to know me better. She was attracted to me. She was attracted to me as a 168-pound woman with a face like a pie. The fact that she got stuck entertaining a whole bunch of people at her house that night because of me is still something we laugh about.

Despite the obvious chemistry at that show in March 2001, Ellen and I didn't reconnect and become a couple until December 2004. Other than the fact that I was overweight, I was also closeted and private about my homosexuality, and so the thought of being with the most famous lesbian in the world didn't cross my mind at that point. I continued working on *Ally McBeal* and taking small steps toward living my life as a gay woman. I had met some lesbians through the girl I'd briefly dated, and I spent time with them, observing them and trying to figure out what it meant to be gay. I soon discovered that I had to figure out what kind of lesbian I was going to be. It was obvious to me almost immediately that I was very different from most other girls. I didn't really fit into either role of "butch" or "femme." I liked wearing makeup and dresses and heels, but I also liked to wear engineer's boots and black tank tops. In the first few months of my coming out to other lesbians, I realized that I was as much a misfit in the gay world as I was in society at large. I was half butch, half femme, neither here nor there. At that point in my life, I didn't understand that playing roles in any relationship is false and will inevitably lead to the relationship's collapse. No one can be any one thing all the time. There is a great deal of lying done while a role is being played in any relationship, homosexual or heterosexual. As I had tried to fit into the sample size clothing, I also tried to fit into a preconceived idea of what it meant to be gay. And any time I try to fit into a mold made by someone else, whether that means sample size clothing or a strict label of "butch" or "femme," I lose myself.

I was a misfit in the lesbian world, I was closeted and scared that I would be outed in the media, so I reverted to being alone. I was still heavy, probably around 150, when 9/11 happened. 9/11 changed my life. I was so deeply disturbed by the realization that I could die without living my life openly and happily that I reached out to a friend who'd wanted me to meet a girl she knew and went on my first date with Francesca. We instantly began a serious and happy relationship that lasted three years. As 9/11 had jolted me into living my life more honestly and fully, my life improved greatly. Although I still struggled with self-acceptance, Francesca was loving and patient and taught me how to be in a relationship. I sold my apartment, and Francesca and I bought a beautiful house in Los Feliz.

When *Ally McBeal* ended, I landed a role in an innovative and exciting new show, *Arrested Development*. I decided to tell my producers and co-stars on *Arrested Development* that I was gay, as I felt that I couldn't be in a serious relationship and hide it from the people I worked with. I felt that trying to do so was very disrespectful to Francesca, even though I was mostly terrified to introduce her as my girlfriend, especially to the show's executive producers, Ron Howard and Brian Grazer. I was truly afraid I could lose my job. But it suddenly seemed pointless to have a girlfriend if I was going to hide her from the rest of my life. Hiding her from the rest of the world was a different story, however.

The paparazzo who had begun stalking me around the time I was beginning to date accomplished her mission to out me when she got photographs of Francesca and me making up after an argument in an alley off Melrose. I had pulled Francesca into the alley after our conversation got a little heated because I didn't want to make a scene and inadvertently out myself to the people walking by on the sidewalk who would surely recognize a couple having an argument. Instead, the photographs went around the world and outed me to everyone who stood in a supermarket checkout line. Because of these photos, I was forced to come out to my aunts and uncles and cousins in Australia before the tabloid hit the stands and hit them over the head with shock. The shock for me was the amount of love and acceptance I received from my extended family, especially my aunt Joan and uncle Stan.

I will be eternally grateful to that paparazzo who I had feared would ruin my life, since she forced me to be honest with my family about being gay. She freed me from a prison in which I had held myself captive my whole life. At my mother's urging, however, I agreed to continue to keep the truth of my sexuality from my grandmother and so began a practice of removing all articles about me from my grandmother's favorite tabloids, something that we continued doing for years. When I finally told my grandmother that I was gay, her reaction was truly amazing. I was back home in Australia to celebrate her hundredth birthday, about a year after Ellen and I had become a couple. My mother and I decided it would be my mother's responsibility to tell Gran that I was gay, since she was going to have to deal with the aftermath if Gran was unhappy about it, which we were almost certain she would be. After Ellen came out on her television show in 1997, Gran stopped watching it, saying that Ellen was "disgusting." My mother, having come to LA for a visit with Ellen and me, was supposed to show Gran pictures of the two of us together: our house and our animals—our life. My mother told me that Gran took the news calmly. But to everyone's surprise, when I sat in front of Gran to yell my hello, she asked me in a yell if I was dating. I yelled at her, "Gran, I'm with Ellen."

"Alan?"

"El-len."

She looked horrified.

"Oh, Porshe. You're not one of those!"

I turned to my mother, panicked. "I thought you showed her pictures and explained everything to her!" My mother swiveled on the sofa to face Gran and yelled, "Gran! I told you Portia was living with Ellen."

"Yes," she yelled back. "As roommates!" She looked perplexed and shook her head. "And all this time I was worried that that lesbian was hitting on my granddaughter!"

Gran closed her eyes for about twenty seconds. There was complete silence. I was holding my breath. It was the longest, quietest twenty seconds of my life.

"Well," she said opening her eyes and holding her arms out for a hug, "I love you just the same." We never talked about my sexuality again, only about how happy my life was with Ellen. From changing the channel in disgust to being Ellen's biggest fan and watching her talk show every day, Gran showed me that people can change, including me, as I was certain that a woman born in 1907 in a small town in rural Australia would never be able to accept me. I had judged her and assumed that she would feel as though I had shamed the family. But I was wrong. In the nursing home where she spent her final few months before passing away at the age of 102, she kept a framed photo of our wedding for all the staff to see on the nightstand next to her bed. She was proud to call Ellen her granddaughter.

By the time I entered into my relationship with Ellen, I had recovered from my eating disorder. Living with Francesca forced me to deal with issues surrounding acceptance of my sexuality, and it also forced me to deal with my relationship to food. I shared a kitchen—and a bathroom. I couldn't binge and purge without a lengthy and embarrassing discussion. I slowly stopped purging and just binged in my car or at work while she wasn't there to see it. The rest of the time I would eat salads with no dressing. I was still fighting a heavier weight over the next two years, but what really became obvious to me was that I was doing something very wrong. I began to understand that every time I restricted my calorie intake, I would binge immediately after. Sometimes I could diet for a week or two without the bingeing and I would lose a few pounds, but then the binge would inevitably follow and I would gain all the weight back, and sometimes a couple of pounds more. I was always on a diet. I was either being "good" or being "bad," but I was always on a diet—even when I was bingeing. I lived my life from day to day by weighing myself and measuring my success or failure solely on weight lost or gained—just as I had done from the time I was twelve. I'd measured my accomplishments and my self-worth on that scale for my entire life, with the same intensity and emotion, from 82 pounds all the way to 168. While I had begun to examine my behavior in treatment, I was forced to continue the self-examination when I was living with Francesca, because simply having to explain my actions to another person made me question them. I finally understood that by being on a perpetual diet, I had practiced a "disordered" form of eating my whole life. I restricted when I was hungry and in need of nutrition and binged when I was so grotesquely full I couldn't be comfortable in any position but lying down. Diets that tell people what to eat or when to eat are the practices in between. And dieting, I discovered, was another form of disordered eating, just as anorexia and bulimia similarly disrupt the natural order of eating. "Ordered" eating is the practice of eating when you are hungry and ceasing to eat when your brain sends the signal that your stomach is full. "Ordered" eating is about eating for enjoyment, for health, and to sustain life. "Ordered" eating is not restricting certain kinds of foods because they are "bad." Obsessing about what and when to eat is not normal, natural, and orderly. Thinking about food to the point of obsession and ignoring your body's signals is a disorder.

Although I had learned about this from Carolyn, my understanding of how it worked was suspended due to my resistance to treatment. At the time of leaving Monte Nido, living without dieting sounded like a utopian philosophical ideal. That is, until I witnessed it at work with Francesca. A naturally thin woman who ate whatever she wanted and never gained or lost a pound was the most fascinating case study for this woman who had spent her life gaining and losing weight. I watched her eat pasta, candy, ice cream, and cheese. I watched her dip her bread in olive oil and wash it down with Coke—real Coke, not diet—while I ate dry salads with no dressing and sipped iced tea. I was dumbfounded that I was eating boring, dry, diet food and maintaining or gaining weight during the course of any given month when she never even thought about what she ate or how her body looked. I was equally amazed as I watched her order food at restaurants and only eat a small portion of her order because she was too full to finish it or skip breakfast or lunch because she got a little too busy and simply forgot to eat. After initially dismissing her eating habits as a result of her just being one of those lucky people who can eat whatever they want and stay thin, it suddenly occurred to me that maybe people who stay thin are the people who eat whatever they want.

I put this theory into practice after an incident between Francesca and me that was fraught with emotion and very revealing. I was sitting in the closet in our master suite crying because I couldn't fit into a pair of pants that I had bought only a month before. They were size 6. I was in despair and when Francesca came to comfort me, I almost accused her of causing my weight gain, saying that she'd let me get fat again and that she didn't care how I felt about myself or that my career depended on my ability to control my weight. After patiently hearing my wailing, she said something that I'll never forget. She said:

"Fine. I'll help you diet. But you'll only gain it back."

It was a simple statement, but the truth of it overwhelmed me. All I had done throughout my life was diet and gain the weight back. Therefore, the only conclusion I could make was that diets don't work. Sitting on the floor of the closet with tears running down my face, I decided that my way wasn't working, that it was time to try something else. From that day on, I decided that I would never diet again.

After that day, instead of watching her eat, I joined in. I ate whatever she ate. We cooked meals together and loaded pasta onto our plates.

We ate ice cream. Because I knew I could eat pasta and ice cream again the very next day if I wanted to, I stopped wanting it in excess. If it were going to be available to me anytime, why eat like it was the last time I'd ever taste it? The fact that I stopped restricting food made it less appealing. The fact that I stopped labeling food as "good" and "bad" made me just see it all as food. Like Carolyn had told me, there was no bad food. There were just bad eating practices. I began eating every single thing I wanted when I wanted it, without guilt, without remorse, without feeling anything other than happy about the taste of the food I had chosen to eat. Initially, I gained a little weight. But over time, I found that I didn't want to eat ice cream every day. Not because of fear of gaining weight, but because it was too cold, or too sweet for my taste buds after a salty pasta. I began tasting food and listening to my internal nutritionist as it told me that I truly wanted to eat a crispy, fresh salad rather than fries. When it told me that fries were what I was craving, it said, "Eat as many as you want knowing that you can always have them again tomorrow." So I'd eat just a few until I was full, or I'd eat the whole damn serving until I couldn't eat anything else on my plate. I stopped overeating. I stopped thinking about food. I ate exactly what I wanted, when I wanted it, without any feelings of guilt or being "good" or "bad."

Within two months of that conversation in the closet, I was maintaining my weight easily at 130 pounds. I was one of those "lucky" people who could eat whatever they wanted and never gain weight. I stopped weighing myself. I simply didn't care about weight anymore because it was always the same, always a comfortable, good weight for my body, and I stopped thinking about food because every single food item was available to me at any moment of the day. There was nothing left to think about.

As I listened to my internal nutritionist, I stopped wanting to eat meat, eggs, and dairy. This was something that carried over from childhood, as I never liked eating chicken breasts or steaks because I was worried about finding veins or fatty tissue. I also didn't like eating processed meat, like chicken nuggets and ground beef, because I was worried that I'd get a mouthful of gristle. I definitely would never eat off a bone because the bones really reminded me of the fact that a living animal that had a heart and a mind and a family had been attached to those bones. I also hated the thought of ingesting the growth hormones that are given to so many animals in recent years to increase their weight and therefore their market value. And it disturbed me that I would drink a cow's milk, which is designed to increase its calf's weight to 400 pounds in as short a time as possible. I have always been a little squeamish at the thought of drinking another mammal's milk. I find it odd that humans are the only species that not only drinks another species's milk, but that we keep doing it as adults.

While I have never felt more healthy and energized, the most important thing that happened to me when I stopped eating animals was a sense of connectedness. When I was suffering with an eating disorder, my life was solely about me. I was living through my ego and didn't care about life around me. I was selfish and angry, and because I didn't care about myself, I also didn't care about littering in the street or polluting the environment. My decision not to eat animals anymore was paramount to my growth as a spiritual person. It made me aware of greed and made me more sensitive to cruelty. It made me feel like I was contributing to making the world better and that I was connected to everything around me. I felt like I was part of the whole by respecting every living thing rather than using it and destroying it by living unconsciously. Healing comes from love. And loving every living thing in turn helps you love yourself.

While I was learning how to eat again (or perhaps for the first time), I cultivated new hobbies that had nothing to do with how I appeared to other people in terms of how I looked or professional accomplishment. My new hobbies required skill, focus, intelligence, and most important, honing and relying upon my own natural instincts. My brother owns a helicopter charter and training business called Los Angeles Helicop ters, and I began taking flying lessons with his instructors. Although I didn't get my private pilot's license, I racked up forty hours of flying in a Robinson R22 and moved my focus from weight loss to learning this new and challenging skill. Driving to Long Beach, studying aeronautical physics and learning autorotations took up the time that driving around town to find yogurt had previously occupied.

My passion for riding horses was reignited after spending time with Francesca's mother in England over the holidays. As a small child, I loved horses but after suffering a dislocated shoulder from slipping off a cantering horse, I stopped riding out of fear. Twenty years later, I found myself with the same enthusiasm and excitement for horses that I'd had when I was a child. Over that Christmas in England I would wake up at 6:00 a.m. and head down to the barn hoping to be able to watch Fran-cesca's mother ride dressage and take a lesson on the Welsh cob she kept for interested visitors. When I returned to Los Angeles, I joined a hunter/jumper barn and within a few months bought a horse of my own.

To say that my first horse, Mae, saved my life isn't an overstatement. Just being outdoors all day and breathing in fresh country air and noticing the beauty of the trees as I rode on meandering deer trails through the woods was enough to alter my consciousness, to respect nature and my place within it. The horse was like an extension of myself, a mirror showing me my underlying emotions that I'd become skilled at ignoring. When Mae was afraid, she was telling me that I was afraid. When she refused to jump a fence, she let me know that I was intimidated by the hurdles in my life. She'd speed up when I thought I was telling her to slow down, as she was responding to my internal anxiety not to my voice weakly saying "whoa." Sometimes I couldn't even get her to go. I'd squeeze her sides and she'd just know that I didn't mean it. She'd know that I just wanted to stay still for a while.

· · ·

Do I love myself just the way I am? Yes. (Well, I'm working on it!) But that doesn't mean I love my body just the way it is. People who recover from eating disorders can't be expected to have higher standards than the rest of society, most of whom would like to alter a body part or two. I'd still like thighs the size of my calves, but the difference is that I'm no longer willing to compromise my health to achieve that. I'm not even willing to compromise my happiness to achieve it, or for the thought of my thighs to take up valuable space in my mind. It's just not that important. And while there are things I don't like about the look of my body, I'm very grateful to it for what it does. I'm grateful that it doesn't restrict me from doing my job the way I restricted it from doing its job. When I sit quietly and silently thank the universe for all the blessings in my life, I start with Ellen and end with my thighs. I thank my thighs for being strong and allowing me to walk my dogs around my neighborhood and ride my horses. I thank my body for not punishing me for what I put it through and for being a healthy vessel in which I get to experience this amazing world and the beautiful life I am living full of love.

I have recovered from anorexia and bulimia. I am immensely grateful that the disorders, although robbing me of living freely and happily for almost twenty years, aren't continuing to rob me of health. Not everyone who has suffered from eating disorders has the same good fortune. The disorders have left me unscathed both physically and mentally. However, having anorexia has left me with an intense resistance to exercise. As well as being resistant to exercise, I have an intense resistance to counting calories. And reading labels on the backs of jars and cans. And weighing myself.

I hate the word *exercise*. I am allergic to gyms. But I don't think that "formal" exercise in a gym is the only way to achieve a healthy, toned body. I have discovered that enjoyable daily activities that are easy, like walking, can be equally beneficial. I have noticed on my daily walk with my dogs that I rarely see an overweight person walking a dog, whereas I see many overweight people walking on treadmills in a gym. I attribute this not only to the frequency of having to walk your dog, but also the good feeling one has when doing something good for another being. Seeing my dogs' excitement as I walk them around my neighborhood every day makes me happy, and when I'm happy I walk a little taller and a little more briskly. I can only imagine the enjoyment parents must experience when seeing the joy on their kids' faces as they play tag football or shoot hoops with them. I also enjoy being outdoors. I like breathing the cold night air deeply into my lungs as I walk up the hills in my neighborhood and smelling the forest air as I walk on hiking trails after a morning rain. Another way for me to stay fit is to do activities where I can learn a skill, like horse riding or tennis or dancing. I find that if I can concentrate on getting better at something, rather than getting fitter or looking better, I accomplish all three things—the latter two being happy by-products of the original goal. Doing an activity to relax is also important for me. I swim to clear my head rather than count laps and burn calories. Swimming slowly is a form of meditation for me.

I have found ways to increase my heart rate, stretch my muscles, and breathe deeply every day in an enjoyable way that I would never label as exercise. I eat every kind of food that I like, moderating the portions using my appetite and not a calorie counter. I love fat and I love carbohydrates. Nothing fills you up and feels more satisfying than a mashed potato or pasta and olive oil. There are days when I eat a large bag of potato chips for lunch and I feel too full and greasy to eat anything else until dinner. It may not be the healthiest, most balanced day in a lifetime of days, but I more than likely won't repeat it the following day.

To say that you can stay at your natural body weight and be healthy by eating what you want and not working out sounds extremely controversial, and yet people have lived this way for hundreds of years. It seems to me that it's only since around 1970 that the concept of diet and exercise has existed in the way it does now, which is based on exertion and restriction being the key to weight loss, and yet since then, we have seen an increase in obesity in countries that have adopted it. (These are also the countries where the fast-food industry boomed during that time.) The diet industry is making a lot of money selling us fad diets, nonfat foods full of chemicals, gym memberships, and pills while we lose a little of our self-esteem every time we fail another diet or neglect to use the gym membership we could barely afford. Restriction generates yearning. You want what you can't have. There are many ways to explain why the pendulum swing occurs and why restriction almost always leads to bingeing. I was forced to understand this in order to recover from a life-threatening disorder. And in a way, I wrote this memoir to help myself understand how I came to have an eating disorder and how I recovered from it. I really hope that my self-exploration can help not only people who are suffering from anorexia and bulimia, but also the perpetual dieters. You don't have to be emaciated or vomiting to be suffering. All people who live their lives on a diet are suffering.

If you can accept your natural body weight—the weight that is easy for you to maintain, or your "set point"—and not force it to beneath your body's natural, healthy weight, then you can live your life free of dieting, of restriction, of feeling guilty every time you eat a slice of your kid's birthday cake. But the key is to accept your body just as it is. Just as I have had to learn to accept that I have thighs that are a little bigger than I'd like, you may have to accept that your arms are naturally a little thicker or your hips are a little wider. In other words, accept yourself. Love your body the way it is and feel grateful toward it. Most important, in order to find real happiness, you must learn to love yourself for the totality of who you are and not just what you look like.

I made the mistake of thinking that what I look like is more important than who I am—that what I weigh is more important than what I think or what I do. I was ashamed of being gay, and so I only heard the voices that said that being gay is shameful. As I changed, I no longer heard the condemning voices. When my relationship with Ellen became public, I was amazed by how well the news was received. I was still very scared, but I was also very much in love, and love outweighed the fear. I wanted to celebrate our love. I was so proud to call myself her girlfriend that whatever people might have thought about my sexuality wasn't important anymore. I simply didn't hear a single negative comment. I began to see myself as someone who can help others understand diversity rather than feeling like a social outcast. Ellen taught me to not care about other people's opinions. She taught me to be truthful. She taught me to be free. I began to live my life in love and complete acceptance. For the first time I had truly accepted myself.

August 16, 2008

I walk out of the bedroom of the guest apartment where Kellen and Jen, Ellen's and my stylists, have just finished tying the bows of my Lanvin pink ballet flats. The act of getting me into my wedding dress, a fairytale wedding dress designed for me by Zac Posen, is performed slowly and meticulously, with the gravity and respect all ancient rituals demand. My mother, dressed beautifully in a teal dress and jacket that we had bought together at Barneys just days before, is waiting excitedly to see her daughter in a wedding dress, a sight that she could have never imagined experiencing after learning that I was gay. When she sees me, she cries. She tells me that she is proud of me. She tells me that she loves me.

"I love you too, Mom. Now stop crying or you'll start me crying. I can't mess up my makeup."

We never hold ourselves back now. We can get very emotional.

As Molly and Mark put their final touches on my makeup and hair, I recite my vows to my mother for a practice run. I can't wait to tell

Ellen how I feel about her in front of the people who are the closest to us and who support and love us, for richer or for poorer, in sickness and in health, in fame or in obscurity. Among our assembled guests are Wayne Dyer, who is officiating the wedding, Sacha and her husband Matt, the partner she chose over me ten years prior in St. Barths, and my brother and his incredible second wife, Casey.

"This ring means that I choose to spend the rest of my life with you. I promise to love you in the nurturing and selfless way that you love me. I've changed so much since I've known you. Your love has given me the strength to be softer. You've taught me kindness and compassion. You make me better."

I stop reciting and look at my mother. She is proud. She is calm. She is smiling at her healthy daughter who has found a deep profound love with another woman. And not just any woman, Ellen DeGeneres, the woman I used to use as an example of why my public outings with previous girlfriends were nothing to worry about. My mother would say to me, "Now you're in a relationship people will find out that you're gay!" And I would reply, "Relax, Ma. At least I'm not dating Ellen DeGeneres." Ellen DeGeneres was the "worst-case scenario." She would expose me as being gay. She would force me to live a truthful, honest life, to be exactly who I am with no pretense. I thank God for her every day.

I highly recommend inviting the worse-case scenario into your life. I met Ellen when I was 168 pounds and she loved me. She didn't see that I was heavy; she only saw the person inside. My two greatest fears, being fat and being gay, when realized, led to my greatest joy. It's ironic, really, when all I've ever wanted is to be loved for my true self, and yet I tried so hard to present myself as anything other than who I am. And I didn't just one day wake up and be true to myself. Ellen saw a glimpse of my inner being from underneath the flesh and bone, reached in, and pulled me out. I continued reciting my vows to my mother although I was a little nervous about her reaction to what I was about to say. Although I was completely recovered before Ellen and I became a couple, I wanted to remind Ellen of my struggle for self-acceptance and to tell her that because she saw something in me that I hadn't previously seen in myself, my perception of myself changed. She didn't see an average girl, a mediocre girl from a middle-class family who had to win the race and change her name in order to be considered special. She saw a unique and special person. She saw a woman who was worthy of care.

"You treat me better than I've ever treated myself . . ."

As I had expected would happen, my mother interrupts. "But you're all better now, aren't you?" She is extremely concerned about the possibility of my relapsing into the dark and lonely world of an eating disorder.

I look at my reflection in the mirror and I like what I see. I'm not looking at a childhood fantasy of what I should look like on my wedding day or a bride in a wedding dress. I am looking at me. I contemplate the idea of being better and it brings to mind my favorite quote from Wayne Dyer, our friend and the man who is about to marry me to the woman of my dreams. "True nobility isn't about being better than anyone else; it's about being better than you used to be."

"Yes, Ma. I am better."

I am better than I used to be.

ACKNOWLEDGMENTS

I am so incredibly grateful to everyone who made *Unbearable Lightness* possible and who encouraged and supported me along the way.

Peter Borland
Alysha Bullock
Ann Catrina-Kligman
Carolyn Costin
Judith Curr
Ellen DeGeneres
Jonathan Safran Foer
Victor Fresco
Kathy Freston
Mike Hathaway
Judy Hoffland
Nancy Josephson
Alex Kohner
Jeanne Lee
Annick Muller
Harley Neuman
Paul Olsewski
Megan Pachon
Donna Pall
Craig Peralta
Gina Phillips

ACKNOWLEDGMENTS

Sacha Plumbridge

Casey Rogers

Margaret Rogers

Michael Rogers

Patty Romanowski

Kali Sanders

Lisa Sciambra

Nick Simonds

Dana Sloan

Randee St. Nicholas

Megan Stone

Jennifer Rudolph Walsh

Oprah Winfrey

Kevin Yorn